DATE			

Magazine Writing: The Inside Angle

Art Spikol

Writer's Digest Books ⟨Writer's Digest Books⟩ Cincinnati, Ohio

Library of Congress Cataloging in Publication Data
Spikol, Art, 1936-
  Magazine writing.
  Includes index.
  1. Authorship.   I. Title.
PN147.S66   808'.025   79-10308
ISBN 0-911654-65-8

Contents

Well . . .

"Think it's worth a shot? Tell me how many words—and I'll send you column number one on spec."

When the column arrived, of course, it was love at first write; in fact, Art Spikol's column—called "Nonfiction"—has appeared in every issue of *Writer's Digest* since. And Art Spikol is an editor's and reader's delight. He brings to his columns—many of them gathered, expanded, updated here—an insider's view of problems that face both writer and editor, with down-to-earth approaches to handling them. His is the voice of experience . . . and of friendship.

The book you are now holding is a hard-driving yet easygoing appraisal of the magazine business and the business of freelancing today. You will find tips here that are available nowhere else. You will find ideas that can bring you sales and success in quick order. Beyond that, you will find what thousands of Art Spikol readers know and delight in each month: You have a friend in the business.

John Brady

Editor, *Writer's Digest*

Foreword

When Art Spikol first suggested that he do a column called "A Friend in the Business" for *Writer's Digest,* I was cool to the idea. "Here I am, a top-notch magazine editor," he wrote, "who gets all kinds of questions, knows most of the answers, and does almost nothing about it."

Between humility lessons, I thought. What a terrible title. And I wonder how this guy pronounces his last name.

"What I'm suggesting," he continued, "is a column in which I could be totally candid about the magazine business and the games editors play. Also the human side: Editors as just people doing jobs, sweating and worrying, getting enthusiastic when something really super comes in over the transom."

Who *is* this guy, I wondered. (His name rhymes with *pickle,* I'd discovered.)

"I started at *Philadelphia Magazine* as art director in 1969," he wrote. "I wrote my first article, at age 35, in 1971. (It received the Philadelphia Chapter of Sigma Delta Chi's 'Best Feature Writing' Award for that year.) Since then I've written and sold dozens of articles, and in 1974 I received the first 'Special Award' ever given by the JC Penney-University of Missouri Journalism Awards Committee for my article, 'Thirty Rapes a Day.' "

All right, he can write. What else?

"I'm now executive editor at *Philadelphia,* and my major function is to make the decisions regarding all freelance queries and manuscripts. If somebody wants to find out how to make a buck writing for the magazine market, I can help. Being an editor, I can tell them things that hardly anybody else will."

Such as?

"I can write about all the components of magazine journalism— from what editors really look for and how they make 'buy' or 'assign' decisions, to what constitutes reasonable limits of editing, to libel, to investigative reporting. I can talk about how to read what's between the lines of a rejection letter. I can compare taping, and its advantages to taking longhand notes. I can make an excellent case for using a camera while writing a story, and I can inform the reader when it's permissible to take photos and when it might create problems."

To Linda

PART III

PART IV

Introduction

In 1976, I started teaching a night class in nonfiction—15 students, all ages, sexes. I had stringers for local papers, emerging middle-aged housewives, young journalism graduates, one or two pros, and people who, as the saying goes, have always wanted to write. God bless Woodward and Bernstein.

Some members of my class were going to write nonfiction for the first time. Others were going to put their stuff in my hands for critiques, knowing full well that I might tell them that they should maybe take up needlepoint. Others—those who thought they were pretty good to start with—were going to take a chance, for the first time, by putting their journalistic product into the hands of a professional.

They had guts. But as strong as they were trying to be, and as confident as they would have liked to appear as they sat around the large circular table, some of them were pretty scared. They were going to have to put themselves, and their beliefs in themselves, on the line.

And I figured that there must be a heck of a lot of people out there who are pretty scared. Maybe it's the nature of the business: Journalism is one of the few enterprises where somebody with *no* credentials can put his talents in front of a representative of a high-paying national market—somebody with *lots* of credentials—for the price of a few stamps. You really need confidence to do that, and most people do it with trepidation. It's like a guy who sings in the shower getting an audition at the Met.

Assuming that many readers of this book bought it in the hopes that someday they'll get off their duffs and actually try to write something for publication, and assuming that many of the same people will use little mental tricks to keep from actually doing that, I think it might be interesting to explore some of the excuses prevalent in the world of the hopeful, but not yet realized, writer—some of the fears, the feelings of inadequacy, the self-defeating and self-perpetuating myths.

"My goal isn't realistic." This is common: You're afraid to jump into writing from your present job because your present job is something that you neither like nor are proud of. In your mind, the transition from file clerk to writer is too big to make; *nobody* is that presumptuous. One person who was about to join my class—let's call him Clark Kent—hedged on it at the last minute. From my conversations with him, I knew that this was because of his present position, which he's uncomfortable about because it doesn't require, in his words, "much in the way of thinking." He's a construction worker. That was the first thing he told me. The second thing he told me was that he didn't think it made much difference what he was; he thought he could write anyway. That wouldn't have surprised me one bit: Eric Hoffer was a merchant seaman; hundreds of other examples abound. I was once a clerk-typist for a paper company, so I was sympathetic.

But Kent didn't believe his own publicity. He pictured himself in the company of some fine writers, people who had been selling articles while he was lugging concrete, and he figured he just couldn't hack it. I read the letter he wrote to me, and I know he could have made it. But not without putting it to the test, and not without being willing to be less than the best in the class.

Conclusion: If you're letting your current position influence what you can be, the problem is with you, not with the publishing industry. It's a self-fulfilling prophecy: As long as you can convince yourself that the air in the world of journalism is too rarefied, it will be. And if you don't try to do what you *are,* you may become what you *do.*

A young woman in my class told me that she lives in the suburbs. "It's a very small suburb," she said, "one of those places with lots of lawns and nothing happening. The people are, for the most part, not in touch with the big city; they live isolated little lives. I'm not very cosmopolitan; I don't know if anything I would write would be very interesting to a large readership." There she was, sitting on at least one story, and she didn't know it.

A terrific writer can make almost *anything* interesting. A boring writer can make almost anything boring. That's the truth. If you hesitate to write, we'll never find out which you are.

Conclusion: If your life is so dull that you have nothing to say and can't find anything of interest to write about, you may not be breathing. Consult your doctor. If alive, remember that how you write is far more important than what you write about.

"I've never done this; therefore, I can't." A surprising number of people believe this—subconsciously, at least. Here is another self-fulfilling prophecy. The logic, of course, is full of holes, unless you really believe that each published writer wrote terrific articles from the time he was old enough to hold a pencil; if you don't believe that, you must believe that at one point he simply *started.* And if he started, no matter who he was, he got rejection slips and wondered about his talents.

Becoming a writer is like running a race: There's a starting point, and every step you take brings you closer to your goal. As long as you keep going, you're closing the gap. As you go along, of course, the goal itself may change—*you'll* change it as the demands you place upon yourself increase—but, having gone part of the way, you'll know that the rest of the way is traversable.

Conclusion: Do it. Get experience. Writing ability doesn't diminish; nobody can take away from you anything you've learned. There's no place to go but up.

"I'm too old to start." A woman in my class complains of being in her forties and wonders if it's too late for her. I ask her what her life expectancy might be. She says that if she's lucky, she might reach 75 or more. So I ask her how many years it will take her to write a publishable article. Thirty? No. Twenty? No. Ten? No, probably a good deal less. Then why is she too old to start?

I point out that I didn't write a magazine article until I was 35, and that many writers started much later than that. Again, I use the proposition mentioned before: Everything you learn is yours to keep. I tell her she could be getting published in a matter of weeks or months; why worry about how old she is? How much time does she need? For each day that she delays, is she gaining or losing?

Publishing is practically a unique business in this respect. If you wanted to be a movie star, for instance, you'd have to worry about your appearance, and age might figure into that. A gymnast would have to worry about physical condition; certainly, age could affect that. Many occupations hinge on age, but not writing. When an editor receives a query, he doesn't know how old the writer is: could be 17, could be 77. Assignments are not given on that basis.

Conclusion: If you can convince yourself that you're too old, you *are* too old.

"The people I see in print are better than I am." That's enough to stop anybody, and sometimes it holds water. Sure, Gail Sheehy is probably better than you—credit where it's due. But look. Say you're a young, hopeful singer listening to a recording by a star. It inspires you to record your own voice (in your bedroom) and listen to the playback. Then you put on a record by your idol and, good grief, there's no comparison. Your idol is terrific. You stink.

But how about the echo chamber? How about a good sound engineer? How about the professional studio with its perfect acoustics? How about the background music enhancing the singer? The point is: There's a difference between work hot off the typewriter and work hot off the press.

What few writers stop to think about is that the stuff they see in magazines *has been edited.* Somebody's put in time and effort to make sure that the grammar, the punctuation, the spelling are right. Some-one has worked to make sure the pacing is on target, that the story un-folds logically, that there's a balance between quotes and narrative and description. *That's what editors do.* When you see the article in print, does it say anywhere how many rewrites have been done, or how much editing has been done, or how many changes it's been through? Of course not—so don't compare your own work with it. Sure, you have to set standards, but you don't have to let yourself become intimidated by them.

Conclusion: Don't rush to judgment regarding your ability, and don't compare your work with a final-edited product. Do the best you can and expect to be guided along the way. Every writer is.

"I don't want to sell until I'm sure I'm good enough." That sounds noble, but there are two problems inherent: One, you're going to learn to be your own toughest critic, and the tougher you are, the better you'll become. But you'll never be 100 percent satisfied. So, two, you might never know when you're good enough to sell.

Some writers think that an editor who has rejected them will remember them and not give much credence to whatever they might write in the future. That's nonsense. For any editor to remember who you are, you'd have to be an absurdly horrible writer, one who might have your work passed around just so everybody could see how bad you are. If that's the case, you're probably a lost cause anyway. And even if an editor does somehow remember your name, it's unlikely that he'll associate you with the article you submitted.

Conclusion: The only way you're going to get good outside judg-ment of your work is to put it up for sale. And *caveat emptor.*

"I don't care if I sell or not. I just do this for my own enjoyment." Well, there may be one person in a thousand who really feels this way, but for the others, it just doesn't hold water. If you write for your own enjoyment, you enjoy writing. If you enjoy writing, you'd like to do more of it. Assuming that you need money to exist, being able to sell your work would buy you time and help you do more writing. What people are usually saying when they make the above statement is this: I think I'm good, but I'm not sure that other people will think I'm good, and I'm not willing to risk rejection. If I get rejected, maybe I'll be discouraged and won't do it anymore. Since I like doing it, and can continue to feel secure as long as I don't subject myself to the scrutiny of a professional, I'm not going to try.

The same people who say they don't care if they sell usually enjoy showing their work to *somebody,* preferably someone who will say "terrific" without knowing what terrific is. If this is you, you're hold-ing onto your amateur standing so that you can disregard professional standards. The fact that you enjoy showing your work, even if it's only to a husband or wife or close friend, reveals a desire to com-municate.

Conclusion: You're not kidding anybody. As long as you hold onto this argument, you *won't* sell—because you won't try—and the enjoyment you profess will never be complete.

The key question is: Do you want to write, or do you want to be a writer? The second answer, which is much more the glamorous one, can't be obtained without the first. There is no easy way.

What this all comes down to is biting the bullet, risking rejection, trying to find out what you're made of. It's not easy, but don't worry about failure—it sometimes takes years to get it all together. The only way you can fail is if you don't try.

I almost didn't try. I know what it's like, putting everything on the line. That's why it took me so long to start: I didn't want to learn that I wasn't good enough. I wanted to learn that I *was.* But of course there were no guarantees.

This was when I was art director for *Philadelphia Magazine*—finally in the right place at the right time, after about five years in advertising—and still paralyzed with fear. I was in my mid-thirties, and I still hadn't done what I'd wanted to do since I was a kid: write and sell a story to a magazine.

One day I told Alan Halpern, the editor there, that I had a story I just had to write. He said, "Look, you're a terrific art director. Why not just stick to that?" And then, sighing, he added, "Everybody wants to write."

I went home and wrote the first 13 pages of an article anyway, my first serious attempt at writing. Halpern took one look, said, "It's terrific. Don't stop," and I was on my way. The kid's dream was finally going to come true. The article won an award, and I learned that the only way you can *really* fail is if you never try.

At about the same time, I learned that people with bylines were just that—people with bylines—and before that they were something else: pet-shop employees, clerk-typists, government workers in anonymous jobs, all of which I was.

But nobody will make it easy for you. When I tried to sell *Writer's Digest* a column, at first John Brady told me that he thought he had enough columns. He said there wasn't room for another. The rest is history. My nonfiction column for *Writer's Digest* contributed largely to this book.

I wish I had known all this ten, 15, even 20 years ago. Or maybe not. Part of what I am now is due to all the things I *wasn't* then; I think meteoric success may rob one of empathy and humility. Nothing should come that easy.

When you read this book, I hope you'll think about that in terms of yourself. Be patient. But also remember how quickly the future becomes the past. Don't let fear make you inert. If you want to do something, do it, and don't let what you *are* determine what you *can* be.

* * *

Before I start, there is a small matter of the English language. It has not managed to keep pace with the requirements of social change in one particular area. It is no longer acceptable to say, "Everyone will hand in his article prior to deadline," because there are a lot of *hers* out there, and there is no reason why a *her* must be lumped into a masculine category. However, the language has not yet created a neuter singular pronoun with which to describe humans; the closest we have come is *it*. But I do not want everyone to hand in *its* article. I could say, and sometimes do in this book, that everyone should hand in *his or her* article, and that I will have his or her mark before his or her next article is due, but that gets a big unwieldy. So most of the time I will probably say *his,* except, where possible, I can say *their,* which really gets me off the hook. I hope that everyone will understand, in his or her heart, that *my* heart is in the right place.

I would, in addition, like to say thanks to all the people who have helped, who fall into two groups thusly:

First, the editors in my life—Alan Halpern for having been such a good friend, editor and mentor, in that order, for so many years; John Brady, a Texas-sized pussycat, for genuinely caring not only about what I wrote but also about who was doing the writing, and handling each with respect; and the editors of this book, Elizabeth MacCallum, who made me feel like a cherished author, and Carol Cartaino for worrying about the book *to herself*—and to them all for the times when they exercised a light touch.

I will describe a second group this way: Those of us who are really fortunate have a certain number of people who think we are genuinely *special.* I am lucky to have had a good number of those people around me, and they are partly responsible for anything that I do. It is through them that I continue to recognize myself, and from there it is only a matter of time until I actually accomplish something. If you are surrounded by people who support you and tell you you can do it, then you are lucky indeed—perhaps as lucky as I am to have had, on my side, my wife, Linda, especially, and my kids, Liz and Vicky—and the following, most of whom probably would never know their effect if I didn't mention it here, since all they did was think well of me and let me know it. In no special order, but with my sincere appreciation: Rose Adkins; Martin Gelman; Shirley Warren; Polly Hurst; Elizabeth Fenn; Loretta Schwartz; Dorothy Cupich; Linda Wark; Harvey Spikol, my brother, and his wife, Pat; Susan Lipkin; George Gendron; Heidi Trombert; Sue Weiss; Allan Kalish; Sue Furman; Carol Saline; Caroline Meline; Lisa Davis; Beverly Brownstein; Bloomie Parent, a terrific mother-in-law; and last but not least, the people without whom this all could not have happened, Yetta and

Manny, my mother and father, for loving me and guiding me; and one predecessor, my grandfather, William Levy, who died many years ago, but who was a carpenter, and whom I watched many Saturday mornings in his basement workshop when I was a child—watched him measure and shape and smooth and fit, tirelessly, with whatever talent he had, until the chair leg or shelf was as lovely as a chair leg or shelf could be; who ended his days making cabinets for Philco television sets, but who left me a legacy: I too measure and shape and smooth and fit, tirelessly.

Part I

Chapter 1

The Way We Are

"Know thyself," said Plato—or Pythagoras or Socrates or Alexander Pope or half a dozen others, all of whom have been credited with the statement—and presumably all of whom were admonishing you to be aware of your capabilities, to not try what is obviously impossible for you, to understand the nature of yourself so as to make the best use of your talents and, by the way, to keep yourself from temptation. It is advice to hold back, not to go forward—a warning. To *not* know yourself is to invite failure. A person with acrophobia, in short, does not attempt to conquer Everest.

But if ever one *did* go forward, although he might not conquer Everest, he just might conquer his acrophobia.

The problem is, you can't tell until you try, and you can't try if you're more afraid of defeat than you are convinced that you might snatch victory from its jaws.

People don't get worse and worse at anything; they can only get better and better. But that's not all I've learned.

I've observed that writers have peculiarities about them that are so consistent as to make them almost a species unto themselves: In the same way we know, for instance, that all reptiles are cold-blooded, we know that all writers are certain things, too. Not necessarily those things that cartoonists would have us believe—not simply sloppy dressers and martini drinkers, for instance—but other things.

Nor are writers people who will remain those things for a lifetime. They do change. Experience changes them. And nothing changes a writer more than does success.

I've been thinking about writing this book for a long time. It is not a how-to. It won't tell you anything that will ever affect how you write a sentence. But it will do something else, perhaps, something more valuable.

It will make you understand that you are not alone—that other writers, almost as a breed, are as screwed up as you are.

Further, it will make you see how this screwed-upness has a positive influence on everything you write, making it less an anomaly and more something to be treasured. And it will also show you how to push yourself in the right direction, through the recognition of your nature, to compensate for its shortcomings.

First, here's what you have to know about yourself—and if you don't quite fit my description, just hang in. You'll find yourself.

First of all, *writers are shy, quiet, vulnerable.* At least, that's how many of them start out. They are hardly ever children who are sports heroes, and they are rarely the class troublemakers. They grow up, often, in private worlds in which they're surrounded by items like books and small animals—the products of their own introspection, the things that provide them company and permit them to escape from the more competitive world outside. They are most often people who do not achieve in the world of high adventure, and most often they are not the more handsome or beautiful of their peers. Therefore, they are not particularly adventurous and they are not particularly competitive—except in their fantasies—because they have been unsuccessful in those areas. They would, in fact, like to be able to better control the outcome of their daily lives.

Understandably, then, and point number two, *writers are much better in print than they are in person.* The typical writer-to-be would hardly be chosen Most Likely To Succeed, would probably not be a good candidate for any sort of school office and would be among the most reluctant to get up and address the class. It takes years for most writers to become good speakers—not because they don't have anything to say, but because if they could have communicated in that manner, they probably never would have written. I remember one occasion where, as a teenager, I had to give a speech to a crowd of adults. I had written the speech, and it was good—because all that expression had to come out *somewhere.* But when I got up before the crowd and mumbled and stumbled my way through it, the audience didn't hear a word I said.

Third, *writers need encouragement as flowers need water.* Maybe more. They rarely get it. Rejection slips are never uplifting; even letters from editors that say pretty much the same thing are rejections. My classes often point out to me that, while they are in need of criticism and want to know what they're doing wrong, they also need to know what they're doing *right*—they need some sense of victory. There's no question that some writers who should be able to find careers in writing stop writing before they do so, and stop only because they haven't received any encouragement. Nobody can run on zero fuel.

Fourth, *writers are generally insecure,* if that isn't obvious by this time. Most of them don't think they'll be permitted to make it—that even though they have the talent, it is likely that some conspiracy of life will keep them from ever proving it. They go through the motions, though, because they say that they are trying to be writers and know that they *must* go through the motions, if only to save face—but most are afraid they'll fail. It is not the *act* of failing that they fear—after all, anybody can fail—but they are afraid of the implications of failing. *Because* they are vulnerable, *because* they are already somewhat certain that their writing won't be bought, they fear that any failure could be the ultimate failure, the one that discourages them from trying any longer.

In other words, they fear that one of the rejections will be the final one, the one that dashes all present and future hope.

And then what?

* * *

Why am I spelling all this out? First of all, just hearing it will enable you to know that there's a little of you in every writer, and a little of every writer in you. There was, at one time or another, a little of this negative life view in every writer who ever became famous, and some had more than their share; not even fame could make most of them happy with their achievements. They did not all start out as sunshiny children who were obviously gifted; in fact, many spent afternoon hours in attics and under porches, alone with their fantasies. And many ended up under those same porches, or worse.

And second of all, because knowing the nature of the beast is tantamount to holding the secret of its taming. To wit:

If writers seem not particularly adventurous, it's likely that they find themselves constantly surrounded with the same types of stimuli. This doesn't apply only to writers, of course, but writers are less likely to do anything about it.

Yet adventure is important to writers. Whenever I've spoken to writers who claimed that they had no ideas for articles, I've found that I was speaking to those who needed a spiritual change of climate. A person who writes in his spare time and spends most of his work time as an engineer, and his off time with *other* engineers, is going to be bored stiff—and certainly won't come up with any exciting ideas for articles. Many times I've told housewives to take themselves out to a nice local pub, sit around for a while, and see what happens. (In all fairness, I doubt that many of them have done it—but I got them thinking about the possibilities of altering their environments.) And I've suggested that people go spend an evening at a hospital emergency room, just to see how the other half lives. One good friend of mine did it purely by accident as the victim of sudden stomach pains; out of it came a story. And another very good writer I know took herself out of her housewifely role, went on an arduous outdoor trip with a group of other women, and ended up selling her adventure to *McCall's,* then (in revised form) to *Philadelphia Magazine,* then to *Reader's Digest,* and now is talking to some people who are interested in turning it into a movie—all because she decided to get out of her rut.

I've seen it happen again and again: Take writers out of their normal environments and they come back with story ideas. Loretta Schwartz, who wrote a number of national prizewinners for us while I was at *Philadelphia Magazine,* would never have brought them home if she hadn't gone out and found them. To do this she went into rat-infested slums, took dark elevators in dangerous housing projects, subjected herself to frisking by police officials in prisons and similar facilities, and generally put herself into more compromising situations within two years than do most people in a lifetime. She would, on occasion, come back to the office in tears—but she came back with stories.

This is what you do—knowing that it is exactly what your nature would keep you from doing. You can't find stories in your kitchen.

I say that writers are better in print than they are orally. There's no question about this as far as I'm concerned. In fact, almost every time I come across a writer who is a good speaker, it's usually either a writer who's not *that* good a writer, or one who has developed the speaking art over a long period of time, necessity's being the mother of invention. I, for example, managed to become the world's least effective public speaker before I reached the age of 35; the very idea of addressing a group—and it could be a group as small as two or three people, assuming that they were strangers—would cause my throat to tighten. But nothing succeeds like success, and knowing that, I pushed myself—made myself agree to speak when the occasion came up. I am still not terrific at it, but I do have a certain spark of humor that I am able to inject, and I do have something to say, and if nothing else, I give people confidence: "Gee," they say, "if *he's* not embarrassed to get up there and speak. . . ."

The last two points aren't as easy to deal with. *Writers need encouragement,* we said, and *writers are insecure.* There's nothing much anyone can do about that. The encouragement may occasionally come from the outside; when it does, it's gravy. When it doesn't, you have to have it inside to keep yourself going. As for the insecurity, the fear of failing, that's not easy to deal with either. But remember the premise of this chapter: Writers are almost a species unto themselves, and it is *characteristic* of them to need encouragement and to feel insecure. Knowing this is like learning that you belong to a group; you can now say, with conviction, "This is what I am, and, knowing that, I have to fight it without entirely losing it." In other words, you don't want to stop being all the things you are that make you able to put things into words that help you to translate feeling into paragraphs that will enable readers to feel those same feelings—but you do want to control those things, want to make them work their maximum *for* you and their minimum *against* you.

People who believe in astrology are engaged in this kind of struggle. They think that their signs give them certain characteristics that make them behave in a particular manner; then along comes their horoscope and it tells them a little daily prediction which they can then combine with their own data and know how to act. There are people who do this every day of their lives and are no better (or worse) off than you or I.

I don't believe in horoscopes, but I do believe that I am impulsive. And, since my impulses are often damned foolish, I have learned to control some of them. I'm the kind of guy, therefore, who will see something he wants and go back three times before he buys it. I do this because sometimes I decide I don't want it the third time around. I save money this way; I also end up with less junk.

The last part of this is, then, up to you. You know what you are, and now you know that you're not alone. You know that you'd be very uncomfortable taking yourself out of your everyday environment; you also should know, by experience, that the discomfort could very well end up in a good story. You know, in fact, that every step forward in this business comes from a certain amount of agony—growing pains, you might say. And that real progress is never easy.

What you don't know—but what I'll tell you—is that real art, cliché or not, cannot come without knowing what suffering and pain are all about, and that some of the best stories I've ever read were written by people who were genuinely afraid to write them.

Chapter 2

Say! I Have an Idea!

When I was a little kid, I used to think that ideas came from light bulbs that went off in the air near people's heads; that was something I learned from comic books. Later, when I became sophisticated and started reading *The New Yorker* and *Writer's Digest,* I learned that ideas actually came from muses who hovered in the air, half naked, near typewriters.

Unfortunately, I never had an idea delivered to me in that fashion.

But one day I did find out where ideas *really* come from. A writer I knew, young and very talented, was always worried about where she would find something to write next; she would constantly ask me where I got *my* ideas. For a while I answered her as best I could—I shrugged my shoulders and mumbled about ideas' just *being* there. Not exactly the stuff of which gurus are made. Then one day I asked her where she got *her* ideas. She told me. They came from other people, maybe from something as small as a passing remark.

That was what worried her; she felt that because she didn't originate those ideas herself, they were somewhat less than legitimate.

But she was wrong. The world, and the people in it, are where ideas come from. You can't find them on the walls of your room, or on a blank sheet of typewriter paper. You have to spend time at unfamiliar places: a local bar, a taxi stand, a political rally. You have to talk to strangers: bums, cops, dentists, elevator operators. Their gripes, their concerns, may be stories, and the more open you are to new experiences, the more likely you are to come away with something worth writing about.

That doesn't mean you should write about things that don't interest you; but neither should you close yourself off from experiences simply because you have to go out of your way to have them. The best stuff comes, and will always come, from your personal experience—not because your life is so fascinating, but because what you learn firsthand is fascinating, and adds insight and analysis to what might otherwise be straight reportage. Venture outside your normal environment and you'll find plenty to write about. That's Rule One.

What is an idea? It depends on what you're talking about. Some ideas for articles may be only listings of the subjects which interest you. And some ideas are *concepts* that can make a subject intriguing. An article about your town's 100th anniversary celebration is a story idea *without* a concept, even though you might sell it. An article based on an evaluation of the best and worst of the promotion and souvenirs surrounding that anniversary celebration is an article *with* an idea. Ideally, you should be looking for the twist, the hook, the concept.

Now that you know what ideas are, where do you get them? You *don't* get them from those idea-a-day calendars that tell you, for instance, that on July 22, 1889, Emily Perry attempted to swim the English Channel, thereby becoming the first woman to drown in public in a coat of grease. Here's why: Let's say that to commemorate the above-mentioned great occasion, you're going to write a July article. But 160 other freelancers have the same calendar and the same idea. All 161 of you will probably get rejection slips, and once the article is rejected, there's no time to sell it elsewhere since its only significance was its timeliness; nobody cares about the topic. To be salable, an idea must be intriguing, not just a piece of information.

A better source of ideas, then, is the newspaper. Naturally, that big Page One article has already been done in some detail, or will be, and unless you have the resources to do more with it than the paper can, you may have to forget that idea—although a top-drawer journalist can find plenty to write about that the paper has missed. There are some stories in the paper—you can usually tell which ones just by noting where they appear—that won't be explored too deeply to begin with, and there's usually a story behind that story that's worth digging out. A small article about a proposed school budget cut, for instance, will probably be treated rather matter-of-factly by the papers; but you might use it as a stepping-off point to visit a local school and talk to some of the teachers and students, or even spend some time in a class, and then tell your readers what might happen in this class if the budget cut goes through—and with that, you'll probably have a salable article. In fact, newspapers often end up buying stories like that simply because they don't have the time or staff to do them on their own. When the local story has larger implications, think big—you might end up selling it to a national market.

Remember that the story behind the story is a story in microcosm. You're not out to present a broad overview; that's what the papers do. You should refer to the far-reaching effects, sure—and maybe statistics, too—but basically you want to use a microscope, not a telescope. The power of Anne Frank's diary is not in the statistics of the people who died in concentration camps, but in the story of one person who helps us understand the tragedy of the deaths of six million. The most moving stories I've ever read have involved life on the smallest scale, not the largest; and this is something most newspapers, by virtue of their production schedules and of the very nature of news reporting, often overlook. Further, writing for magazines buys you time. You don't have to turn out an article every day. You have the luxury of observing what happens in the aftermath of a story—something newspapers don't often do unless the story is a whopper, or unless they're "revisiting," going back on the anniversary of the story for a recap and update. You, on the other hand, can immediately begin to check out the effects of the news happening, whatever it was, on the neighborhood, and on the person most involved, and on the people on the periphery of the story. You can *live* it, and this will bring your story to life in a way that few newspaper articles ever come really alive.

That, in fact, is one of the greatest strengths of magazine nonfiction—the ability of the writers to immerse themselves for a sustained period of time—and it's a good thing, too, because no writer should become totally dependent upon the newspapers for ideas. You can draw from your own experience; writers are constantly selling articles about their involvement with their groups, jobs, hobbies and neighborhoods. If your knowledge of a particular subject is thorough, you might even get a shot at doing a regular column.

Sometimes, however, it's impossible to do a story strictly from your own experience—take, for example, an article about prostitution. Admittedly, turning a few tricks to get the feel of it would bring more realism to your writing, but if you wanted to do that, you wouldn't have to write. But if you can get to know some prostitutes, find out what makes them tick, attempt to understand their underlying motives as well as the obvious ones—in other words, find the common denominator by immersing yourself into their culture—you can come out with a good story, because you've made *their* life a part of *your* experience.

That's where many of your story ideas will come from—from people who seem, on the surface, to have little in common with you, but who will prove to be motivated by many of the same things that motivate you. And that's what will become completely real and recognizable to your readers.

Watch for trends, too. What looks like a lunatic fringe, for instance, often becomes a popular movement (and even if it doesn't, lunatic fringes are often interesting in and of themselves). Look for new organizations and unusual businesses, and try to find out why they've come about: Are there new crusades, new needs?

Whatever you do, try to develop a nose for news. Just because something sounds bizarre and unbelievable doesn't mean it can't be true; Watergate sounded bizarre and unbelievable. Listen to rumors and try to understand that truth *is* stranger than fiction.

Once you have a few workable (and, one hopes, salable) ideas, how do you decide which to follow up? Your best article is probably the one you most want to do. But you have to temper your enthusiasm with the sales potential of the piece; if you're going to write something that has a very limited market, you should face that before you start. It's often worthwhile to query a few ideas at a time, the ones you feel most strongly about—that will improve your chances of working on an idea that has a real chance of selling.

But don't spend your life querying. If you strike out with the queries often enough, and you still feel sufficiently committed to a story to write it, it's better to invest some energy in the writing than to squander it all on querying. At least you'll end up with a story, and you are, after all, a writer. For that matter, there's a lot to be said for simply sitting down and knocking out a story and *then* trying to sell it, provided that (1) you're convinced you have a winner, or (2) you simply *have* to write the story—or forget about sleeping, or (3) you have no track record and are going to have to do at least one story anyway "on speculation"—that is, without a definite assignment— before anybody buys it from you.

What kinds of ideas are most likely to sell? I have compiled, at no great expense and no large amount of consideration, the following list/theory. Like most theories, this one probably has holes in it, but it's better than no theory at all, and it *is* based on having done a lot of buying for a general-interest magazine. Naturally, the list doesn't apply to magazines of specific interest (for instance, while I show sports articles to be among the worst sellers, that wouldn't hold true at *Sports Illustrated*), nor are the individual items within each category in any special order. After all, this isn't a science.

Here we go:

Sure Things: *sex* (the mating habits of average—better still, above-average—people: extramarital sex, si; bondage and discipline, no. In other words, not *too* kinky); *lifestyles; physical and mental health; money; self-improvement; things to do; movements* (unorthodox but not crazy); *relationships; how-to-do-its.*

Good Bets: *personalities; crime* (the kinds that don't harm the reader directly, like gambling and other victimless crimes, and adventures of the Mafia); *institutions; entertainment; sex* (kinky); *psychic phenomena and the supernatural; the home; the law; neighborhoods.*

Chancy: *sports; politics; the arts; the distant past; criticism; crimes to the person* (like mugging and rape); *death.*

If you don't see the pattern, here it is: The most salable stuff usually involves readers directly and entertainingly, and/or tells them things they think they need to know; the subjects of the second category involve readers peripherally and appeal to their voyeurism, telling them things they'd like to know about; and the third category is limited by its specific audiences or by the fact that its subjects make readers uncomfortable.

You think you have a formula here? Then you should understand that time may affect those boundaries; that a good story transcends any boundaries; that certain subjects may move from one category to another simply because of the way they're handled. For instance, each of the above categories can be affected by the way the article is *packaged,* a subject you'll read more about in this book. Suffice it to say that an article entitled "Sexual Mores among the American Aristocracy" would not appeal to as many markets as would "Ten Ways Nobody Knows To Be a Better Lover." And some subjects are so dependent on treatment that they defy categorization, such as those relating to food and dining. Use a little common sense and you can probably figure out just where your story fits in.

And then throw this away and write it anyway.

Chapter 3

Getting the Assignment

Funny thing about query letters. The person who writes them thinks they're terrific. The person who's supposed to think they're terrific—the editor—often doesn't. At least, that's what you assume when you get one back with a little note of no thanks.

Now, you're not stupid, so you know that *all* your ideas can't be bad—but somehow you're being treated as though they are.

You figure that you're just not turning on the various editors involved.

But the fact is, you may be turning them off.

Editors are human beings who are probably more easily bored by your writing than are just about any other members of the species, mainly because they can't read your stuff for diversion. It's their *job*. Diversion is doing something *else*. And that makes editors easy to annoy and tough to interest. Getting an assignment in this kind of arena is no easy matter.

I'm going to tell you a few things that really annoy me. Whether they annoy other editors or not, I can't say—but if I were a writer, I wouldn't take the chance.

The big annoyance is getting material that has no relevance to my market. It's not that I'm unwilling to look at something a little different, and I don't mind breaking the rules occasionally for a particuarly good piece—because that's what keeps a publication unpredictable. However, editors are not dopes, and we know that most writers read *Writer's Market,* and that any good pro will know more than a little about the market he's shooting for, and we know that when we get a query that's totally wrong for us—a query that no writer in his or her right mind would have sent to us except as a last resort—that what we've gotten is just that, a last resort, something that failed to sell in a lot of other places.

We assume that the query went to all the *logical* markets before it started making the rounds of the *illogical* ones. Common sense, right?

So we're turned off. Now, suppose you're the one in a thousand—the exception who's sending us this illogical query for a very legitimate reason. Then point it out in the first paragraph. You'll probably get rejected anyway, but at least you'll get a fair hearing.

Query letters can also bug editors when the writer is following a query-letter-writing formula. The problem with formulas is that they make everything sound alike. Not exactly what editors are looking for.

Let me sidestep for a moment. Formula-type query letters have a function. They give new writers a pattern to follow. But nobody who ever invented a formula-type query format intended for people to follow that format exactly.

Editors have seen just about every formula query, and we recognize them immediately. And what we say is, *no originality here.* That's why writing a formula query is sure death to any writer, just as sure as if the article started, "It was a dark and stormy night."

Can I tell you what a query *should* sound like? No. If I did, you'd just have another formula to follow. My suggestion is to forget "query" and think "letter." That's what you should write. A letter. A good, interesting one, the kind of letter you write to your friends. Forget that it's a query. Write a letter that nobody—editor or no—could put down. A strong opening sentence that tells the editor, up front, what's on your mind—and then build: a fact here and there, a provocative statement, a question when it's warranted, whatever it takes—*but make him care what happens.* Give him a stake in the outcome.

Here's an example. A writer recently sent me a query that was virtually irresistible. She told me that a great number of people in a particular age group—possibly hundreds of thousands throughout the U.S.—were walking around with "time bombs" in their throats. These people, it seemed, had been children in the late '30s and early '40s, during a period when doctors were trying to inhibit the growth of tonsils through X-ray treatments, and that the incidence of throat cancer in these people is much higher today than that of the general public. Trouble is, she said, these people *don't know it.*

If she didn't have me then, she threw in the clincher: Did I care what happened to her when a growth was found in her own throat, a growth thought to have been caused by that kind of X-ray therapy? Sure I did. In fact, I started worrying about my own throat. She got the assignment.

A query letter has to grab me—just as an article would have to. If you can't excite me about an article in a letter, you can't sell me at all—and "me" is virtually every editor out there. Forget that I have hundreds of thousands of readers, forget that I'm a name high up on a masthead, forget that I'm also supposed to conduct myself like a businessperson. Just write me an exciting letter. *Me,* not my readers. Let me hear the kind of enthusiasm you feel for the article. And write your letter to the human being in me, not the editor in me and not the businessperson in me. I'm like anybody else when it comes to reading a good story. If your story concerns you, and if you can get that feeling of concern across to me, and if I'm concerned enough to feel that my readers will be concerned, you've got a sale.

But *how* you do it is important. And that's what's wrong with the formula query. Not long ago I got one of those, a particularly good example (or bad example, if you prefer) of the genre. The writer made the following mistakes:

1. He started his letter with a did-you-know question. Yawn. There's no better way to put an editor to sleep (unless, of course, the rest of the sentence is, "your house is burning?"). This is not because editors know everything, but because they *do* know most of the things they *should* know and aren't likely to be catapulted out of their seats by a fact which reveals, say, a decline in the number of streetcars in their city. Facts revealed can, despite their validity, be boring; much better to start with a statement designed to make the editor *care* in some way. Compare, for instance, the difference between these two openings:

"Did you know that it's possible to retire at age 30?"
and
"I know a guy who, at age 18—and without a cent in the bank—said that he was going to retire by the time he reached 30."

Now, which letter are you going to continue reading? Me too.

2. He told me how all of my readers would really be interested in hearing more about his subject, and how he was sure we could expect to sell a good many more copies if we used his article. The point. Don't tell the editor his business; show him that you know yours. Predictions relating to audience reaction show only naiveté on the part of the writer.

3. Formula queries tend to have their own language, and this writer used every cliché in the book. "I propose to tell your readers . . . etc." Look, when you're writing to us, pretend we're old army buddies. Or sorority sisters. Just talk. Don't tell us what you want to tell our readers: *Tell us the story.*

4. He told me he could write his article in 8000 words. That's fine; I hope he can sell it somewhere. But not here. One look at *Writer's Market,* our magazine, or our Guidelines for Writers, and he would have known that we couldn't possibly use this kind of story at that length. So what to do? Don't talk length at all. Sell me on the story. If I'm interested, then talk length.

5. He told me that he would work within our rate structure and that he would sell us whatever rights we normally buy. I wasn't surprised.

Norman Mailer he wasn't. But the only time to mention that kind of thing is when you intend to depart from the norm.

6. By this time, the effect was cumulative. I knew he was an amateur. I don't mind somebody saying, "I've never been published before." In fact, it's nice to hear somebody be that honest and open. But I *do* mind knowing that without being told.

I can hear the protestations already, so let me clarify a point. When I use the word "amateur," I don't mean novice or beginner. I mean *unprofessional.* Your approach can be professional even if you've never had a letter-to-the-editor published. But you can't get anywhere if your approach is amateurish.

Now that I've told you what *didn't* work—what *will?* What do I—and most editors—want in a query letter? As far as I'm concerned, it might not be a bad idea to tack the following up over your typewriter:

I AM AN EDITOR.

I want an opening sentence that is going to get me to the next sentence and the next, until I've read your whole letter—without trying.

I want to care about your article and the people in it. And I want to feel that I, as a reader, have a definite stake in its outcome.

I want you to tell me enough to get me involved—but not so much that you'll answer all my questions. By the time I'm finished reading your letter, I should be willing to pay to learn more. And then I will.

I want to know just what I'm getting: what kind of article, what kinds of information it will include, what will be your point of view. And don't tell me you intend to be objective; that's not your function and you can't do it anyway.

I want you to tell me why you should get the assignment. Why you? If you have some professional expertise in the subject, mention it. If you've been an interested observer of it for a long time, mention it.

I don't want to have to guess about your abilities, and just because you can write a decent letter doesn't mean that you'll get an assignment. If I don't know who you are, you'd better send samples or clips. If you don't have any, the chances of your getting an assignment other than on spec are small—but you can improve those chances by writing an excellent letter.

I don't want to see anything that isn't right for my market. And I don't want to see any "last resort" types of submissions.

I admire stick-to-itiveness, but I don't want to get a query a week from anybody. There are people who send out 52 queries a year and figure to play the percentages, but all you'll get is a reputation for your lack of discretion.

In addition: I am not impressed by bad grammar, incorrect punctuation, misspellings, etc. I am not impressed by college degrees, friends of mine that you claim to know, sweeping generalizations, or language that makes you sound like you're out to dazzle me. I do not

care what you think of the magazine for which I work, and particularly I don't care to know how you think I could improve it. I probably do not want to meet you now; if I ever do, it will be because I
respect you as a writer or need you as a supplier.

That's it, and by this time you should be fairly well turned off.
What kind of editor is this, you ask; he sounds about as friendly as a
rattlesnake.

Actually, I *am* friendly. But I'm honest, too, and there's no way to
say these things without just saying them. Because if you make one
mistake it could cost you an assignment. Sure, you may get a very nice
letter. After all, we don't want to be unkind. But neither do we have
time to change the world; we don't have time to tell you everything
you did wrong. A nice letter doesn't pay the rent; knowing this kind of
stuff just might.

That's why I'm coming on strong now: so you won't make the
mistakes. If you're going to be a professional, don't behave like an
amateur. Write the editor a letter that's every bit as good, and every
bit as representative of your style, as your article will be. Take it from
me, we're receptive. We're waiting, always, for the blockbuster.
Maybe yours.

* * *

But let's say you're doing everything right—and you're still not getting assignments. And maybe you're beginning to think that you're
just a lousy writer.

Maybe that's true. But maybe—well, here's another trade secret.

Editors have budgets. And no editor can respect his budget and
also assign all the articles he'd like to assign—not unless he assigns
some on spec, which means that he'll tell you to go ahead and if he
likes it, he'll buy it. If you want to work with an editor who does that,
feel free to gamble—but don't expect much in the way of sales.

On the other hand, when most magazines give definite assignments,
they also agree to pay "kill fees," fixed percentages of the original
assigned fee, should they eventually reject the article. This kill fee arrangement represents a loss, pure and simple, to the magazine—a loss
that affects editorial budgets. So most editors, to keep those losses to
a minimum, assign very carefully—and that's why they prefer to
assign writers who have already worked for them, or whose work they
know. For a stranger without credentials to get an assignment based
on one query—well, that's pretty rare.

Some magazines pay on publication. They're easy to sell, because
they don't have to pay you until your article actually appears. It
doesn't hurt such a magazine to buy ten articles a day; it pays only for
what it uses. Before you work on that basis, ask yourself if you're willing to sell your house to people who will have to pay for it only if they

decide to live in it. You'd have to be crazy, right?

So what do you do?

One thing you can do is send along the first four pages of your manuscript. If the editor gets that far and wants to read further, he'll usually be willing to pay for the privilege without worrying too much about the outcome. After all, you'll have shown him that you can write.

The problem with that is that it's often not possible to send the first four pages without first doing most of the research and interviewing that would be necessary for the entire article.

Next best is to send along some previous printed material. I say "next best" because your samples aren't going to be slanted to his particular publication, and while he may recognize that you can write, he still doesn't know that you can write *for him*.

Best of all: the first four pages *plus* the samples.

With a terrific query letter, a fast-moving four pages, and a dossier of your credits and some samples of your work, there are only a few things that can keep you from getting an assignment—like a heavy freelance backlog, or a similar article in the works, or something like that—but the problem will be with the publication, and not with you.

There are, in short, no sure things. But you still want a sure thing, right? Well, if you're really confident that nobody will turn down a particular story once he's seen it, go ahead and write it—and send it in unsolicited. Most magazines read over-the-transom submissions, unless they say otherwise in their printed guidelines or in *Writer's Market,* and I've personally purchased articles that way that I would never have assigned due to the subject matter or the inexperience of the writer. In fact, I once bought three unsolicited manuscripts in *one day.* That's a record, I admit—and it isn't likely to happen again—but it did happen once.

No one will deny that unsolicited manuscripts are the riskiest way for you to try to do business. It means a lot of time invested and possibly wasted. You'll have a story, but if the publication you slanted for doesn't want to buy it, it isn't easy to unload it elsewhere.

Better, I think, to send a letter—and then listen to the reason they won't assign you. If they don't give you a reason, there's not much you can do. But if the editor says, "Gee, that sounds like a good article, but we simply have too much stuff assigned right now to take a chance. . . ." then you can always offer to do it on spec. At least you'll know that you have an *idea* worth pursuing.

One last thing: Some writers think that a phone query saves a lot of time. And it does. You get a faster "no." Buying a story over the phone is like buying a car over the phone; editors are a lot more secure with something they can see. On the other hand, it doesn't hurt to phone an editor—if you're lucky enough to get through—and ask if he'd like to see a *query* on a particular subject. If he says no, chances are he'll tell you why, and that may save you a good bit of time in some other market as well.

Ten Ways to Turn Editors Off

What you say:	What they think:
1. "Have you done a story yet about . . . ."	You should know this before you query. There are ways to find out.
2. "I am writing to give you the opportunity to publish . . . ."	How did we get so lucky?
3. "Would you be interested in the truly hilarious (or tragic) story of . . . ."	I don't know if we can survive it.
4. "This is the kind of story you should be doing . . . ."	Don't hold your breath.
5. "Just tell me which approach you'd like me to take . . . ."	Just tell us which approach is appropriate.
6. "The author can . . . ."	What're you, an agent?
7. "There would obviously be two sides to the story . . . ."	If it's obvious, isn't it a bit patronizing to tell us about it?
8. "I know I can write this better than so-and-so did for you some time back . . . ."	We'll bet your mother told you so.
9. "If you're not interested, please let me know, since I'm sure I can sell this elsewhere . . . ."	Go to it.
10. "I'll be willing to take a little less than your regular fee to get this published . . . ."	Yes, but we're not willing to pay less, assuming it's worth publishing.

Chapter 4

The Way It Works

Once, after a few months of writing my *Writer's Digest* column, I received a letter from a reader who had one complaint: "No matter how much I read," he said, "it all seems unconnected. I don't have any feeling of continuity, of understanding what happens to an idea from the time it first occurs to a writer to the time that it appears in a magazine. I feel like somebody who rides the bus to work every day and knows where to get picked up and dropped off, but one day the bus company gets hit by a strike and it's up to me—and while I know the destination, I don't know the route."

And finally, the point of the letter: "I think I might better be able to sell to a market if I knew more about the process. How do you feel about this?"

Well, frankly—I'm ambivalent. Pursuing the bus-driving metaphor a little, I'm inclined to say, "Leave the driving to us." In other words, come up with a strong idea, develop it, and we'll do the rest. On the other hand, I can remember writers saying things like, "Gee, if only I'd known you'd be looking for photographs, there was a photographer on the spot who seemed to be getting some terrific stuff. . . ." And being a big believer that little things mean a lot, here's the life story of an article in ten never-as-simple-as-they-seem steps, with the understanding that there will be variations on the theme from magazine to magazine.

1. Presenting the idea. We'll gloss over the more obvious points here in order to stick to the specific idea of this chapter. We'll assume that you, in submitting an idea to a magazine, have checked to make sure that the magazine hasn't done it or anything like it recently, and that your slant and subject matter are compatible with those of the magazine. We'll also assume that you've packaged your idea in the most interesting and provocative manner possible; that is, *How Using the Wrong Bank Can Cost You Plenty* instead of *How to Choose a Bank*.

Assuming all this—you'd either phone or write the editor to ask for the assignment, explaining just what your story angle is and why he or she should be interested in it—and then if all goes well, negotiate for money. Those negotiations don't amount to much usually—if you're brand new, you'll probably be asked if you'd like to write it on spec, and if you're the shy type, albeit published, you'll probably be grateful for (although possibly humbled by) the kind of editor who tells you what the going rate is, take it or leave it. On the other hand, if the editor asks you what *you* want for the story, it's a clear indication that: (1) he's unwilling to spend much on your not-so-hot idea, and wants to telegraph this to you so that you'll come in cheap, or (2) he's impressed with you to the degree that he's not at all sure you'll be happy with his chintzy going rate, and wants to feel you out on the subject, or (3) he does business this way all the time. If these don't seem like particularly clear indications, that's because I forgot to mention the other essential: His voice and demeanor will give him away if you're smart enough. Maybe.

In any event, there's always one thing that makes good sense in negotiating: Ask for slightly more than you think you can get. If an editor has already arrived at the stage where he's talking money, that means he wants your article. If you're too high, he won't say goodbye; he'll simply ask you to come down some, which is better than your asking him to come up some.

2. Establishing connections. Now it's time to go out and do the digging, interviews or whatever. Remember that you'll be able to say that you're on assignment from whichever magazine gave you the job. (If you're doing it on speculation—that is, with a definite assignment— you can still mention the magazine's name—but be careful not to mislead anyone with promises of publication. A safe way to say it: "Such-and-Such magazine has expressed an interest in. . . .") Naturally, going out and doing anything in the name of a publication carries with it a responsibility—to conduct yourself professionally and not do anything that would embarrass the publication. It also represents marvelous opportunities for you, since it allows you to walk into situations using the name of a magazine that might have considerable clout. You could, at this time, establish excellent contacts that will either be helpful in the future on other articles or will actually be the inspiration for other articles.

3. Writing the story. This is the part with which you're most familiar. You have the assignment, and you execute it and deliver it on time; it contains approximately the number of words or pages agreed upon. Don't write anything too long for the publication; if you do, cut it unless you either want to see it cut by a stranger or think you can sell the editor on the longer version. I remember once getting an article that was very well-written but prohibitively long. In this case, the writer did get paid for the article—it wasn't rejected—but it's been sitting in a slush pile for years, waiting for a publication date that will probably never come. That's unlucky enough for a writer who needs the byline as much as the money, but it could've been worse—it could've been rejected. And, all things considered, it should have been.

4. Handing it in. The article completed, you now give it to the person who assigned it. This can be done through the mail or in the flesh. Naturally, you keep a good copy—good enough and clear enough to enable you to make a photocopy in the event of loss. To be most popular, use a fresh typewriter ribbon, *don't* use erasable bond (pain-in-the-neck stuff when it comes to making copies or editing), and send the manuscript flat—not folded down to fit a number 10 envelope.

(At this time, we should acknowledge that a good number of the articles that appear in publications are neither on assignment nor on speculation, but magically appear on the editor's desk via the US Post Office. Sometimes that's the best way to get a foot in the door, because it enables an editor to see your work without committing his magazine to any expense. But consult *Writer's Market* to make sure that the magazine you have in mind will consider unsolicited manuscripts.)

5. Editing the article. This process varies from editor to editor; no two editors ever do precisely the same thing. In my years of working with Alan Halpern, the editor of *Philadelphia Magazine,* we often second-guessed each other—and disagreed occasionally on how things should be done—but we also often came up with identical solutions to editing problems or identical reasons why we did not think an article was working. A really good editor knows instinctively what to do, even if no other editor would do it in quite the same way; get a group of really good editors together with a bad manuscript and you'll almost always get unanimity of opinion not only on the poor quality, but also on the probable solutions.

6. Discussing the graphic treatment of the article. This may happen while the editor is editing; sometimes after; sometimes even before you deliver the assigned article. It depends upon the subject. If, for instance, the editor has assigned you to do an article about a football team, it will also occur to him and to the art director that such an article is probably going to be best illustrated with photographs—of the team in action, behind the scenes with team management, in the locker room, etc. Sometimes you, with your expertise in the subject, will work in conjunction with the photographer. But sometimes there will be other considerations and articles that are less easy to illustrate—and that's often when the art director will get heavily involved. Articles about abortion or incest would be extremely difficult to illustrate—no magazine would want to use photographs here, and explicit drawings wouldn't be any better, for that matter—so the art director might come up with some kind of abstract solution. If the story revolves around one or two central characters, that might suggest a possibility for photos. The magazine may depend upon you for this kind of input, as it would for additional art information—the inclusion of a chart, for instance.

Some writers, not so common, take their own photographs to illustrate their articles. It's not easy to do this, particularly during interviews, but a writer who can use a camera is in an enviable position indeed. Watch it, though: Most people are impressed by specialization, and the fact that you both write and take photographs may diminish you in a subject's eyes; they'd rather think of you as a writer who is important enough to rate his own photographer.

7. Copyediting the article. In just about every publication, one or more people are responsible to make sure that you've conformed to the magazine's style (that is, you've capitalized *Street* and you've used *89,* not *eighty-nine*); haven't misspelled anything; didn't say *souffle* when you meant *mousse,* and didn't show the governor living in the governor's mansion where, in fact, he actually hasn't lived for two years. Copyeditors have saved writers from embarrassment more times than anyone can imagine, but don't dump the responsibility on them—essentially, you're the bottom line on the accuracy of every one of your facts.

8. Typesetting the article. You could probably care less about this function—except for the thrill of seeing your words in type for the first time. You'll be far more concerned with the next step.

9. Proofreading the article. The best system is when several people, including the author, copyeditors and other staff members take part in the proofreading. In most publications, the author receives a set of the galleys—the typeset copy—to work from. At that time you'll make any last-minute changes that are necessary to increase accuracy. But it's good to remember that there are two types of changes a typesetter can be asked to make—one of them is an error on the typesetter's part, which is fixed free of charge; the other is a change made by you or the magazine, for which the magazine is usually charged. Further, any extensive changes at this point may change the line count of the article, which makes for difficulty on the paste-up end. In other words, the magazine would rather you make all your factual changes *before* you submit your manuscript.

This may also be the first time you'll see the editor's changes, depending upon how the magazine works (in fact, there are some magazines that will go ahead and edit your manuscript and publish the edited version without giving you any further chance to see what's been done).

10. Pasting up the article. Your article is pasted into a dummy of the book. Now you're almost home free—but what's this? Your article, your wonderful article that is now as perfect as it'll ever be, runs half a column too long. Or too short, depending upon how you look at it. Most magazines will look at it in the former way, since they'll want to conserve space, and there's no such thing as a half column of type in many magazines.

A number of things can be done now. The art director can reduce the size of the art slightly, or crop the bottom or top of a photograph, to get you some extra line spaces. Or the editor may decide to add a copy block—an excerpt, in large type, from the article—to fill an additional half column of space overall. Or, as happens frequently, the editor may decide to cut half a column's worth of words and sentences out of your article. Occasionally there's time to let the author know what's happening; sometimes not. But in all my memory on the subject, I don't recall an author's ever noticing that excision—perhaps because we've always been intelligent enough to pick the right information to eliminate.

That's ten steps, as promised. Sure, there's a little more. You get a check. You get a byline. People come up to you and congratulate you or tell you how good—or bad—your article was. Your mother will drop your name none too subtly at the beauty salon. You'll go out and buy a few copies of the magazine, helping to subsidize your own work.

There is no step number 11. You pass *Go,* collect $200, and start all over again.

Chapter 5

Behind the Masthead

You have to wonder about the people who work at *The New Yorker*. You have to wonder about them because that's as close as you'll ever come to finding out who they are. You won't find their names on the masthead.

Now, if every magazine were like *The New Yorker,* you'd have a perfect excuse to address your submissions To The Editor. Or even To Whom It May Concern.

But that's not the case. Magazines do, for the most part, have mastheads, and every writer's guide you'll ever pick up will tell you that they're there for you to use. It would be appropriate to conclude, then, that mastheads tell you a little bit about how the magazine staff is structured, who's important to you and who isn't, and to whom you should send your queries or articles. In the best of all magazine worlds, that would be the case.

But mainly, mastheads will just confuse hell out of you.

Who reads mastheads anyway? Writers. At least, I don't know of a single writer who doesn't; and I know few other people who do. Beginners do it like voyeurs, vicariously. Those with a few articles under their belts do it through a sense of camaraderie; after all, these are your *colleagues.* And heavyweights do it for old times' sake, to see who's been dropped and who's been added. All of those uses are appropriate. The mistake most writers make is to use the masthead to determine the proper person to whom ideas should be sent.

That's where the confusion comes in. You want to send your stuff to an editor, which would seem logical. But you'll find, at most magazines, that almost *everybody* is an editor of one kind or another. On the masthead of *New York* magazine, for instance, there are well over 100 names, and not one of them is described as a writer. Somewhere along the way, apparently, somebody decided that "editor" was an important-sounding title and that "writer" was sort of pedestrian, noncerebral, and powerless—in other words, just a cut above manual labor. So when people jockey for prestige, magazines being one of the last refuges for egomaniacs, they go for the Big E. Even the *Columbia Journalism Review,* the media bimonthly to which we look for truth and enlightenment, conforms. Editors all over the place, and no writers. Amazing. At *Philadelphia Magazine,* where I worked, they have editors who *do* edit, and editors who *don't* edit. Some of the writers are called editors. But none of the writers are called writers.

It would be fine if all these editors actually *edited.* But a lot of them don't—except for their own writing, of course, which is a qualification generous enough to make every writer in the world, freelance or staff, ad copy or greeting-card verse, an editor.

I tell you this because you should know it if you're going to survive in the magazine business. Not being able to tell the team by the scorecard can be rather confusing to a freelancer or job-seeker who might want to know to whom his stuff should be sent.

Is it important? If you send a manuscript off to a magazine and address it to somebody who's listed as an editor but really isn't, does it matter? Won't it eventually get to the right person anyway?

Sure it will. But it won't get there *as fast.* This is important in the case of any submission that's particularly timely. It's also important in that one of the major complaints of freelancers is that they don't get a response to their submissions as quickly as they think they should. If you pick the wrong name off the masthead and address your query accordingly, what happens if the person—who just *might* be a writer—is out for a few days working on a story? Or worse, on vacation? (Well, you might argue, don't editors—*real* editors—go on vacation too? Sure they do—but because it's their job to handle freelance submissions, they'll put somebody else in charge during that period. A writer won't. The mail will lie there until he or she returns.)

Not that you'll get that fast a response *anyway*—and this is where a lot of freelancers don't understand the staffing mechanics of a magazine. People *aren't* waiting around to pounce on your unopened envelope, and just how fast anybody gets to it will depend on a number of things—how busy it is in the office when your contribution arrives, how sturdy the freelance inventory is, how large a backlog of unread manuscripts and queries already exists. Further, the people whose job it is to read unsolicited mail probably have other responsibilities which have to come first. Expecting a response in less than a couple of weeks, then, might be more unreasonable than it sounds, and you compound the problem and add to the delay if you address your material to the wrong person.

Obviously, editorial titles can lead to some confusion.

I remember one story about a freelancer, just starting out, who used to mail her submissions to a *contributing* editor because she figured that he was one of the editors in charge of freelance *contributions.* Contributing editors are, of course, no more than freelancers themselves—except that they're regular enough to have warranted a spot on the masthead. In this case, the freelancer had picked the contributing editor's name from the masthead based on nothing more than the fact that it represented somebody she thought she would be comfortable working with—opposite sex, same ethnicity—and started bombarding him with article ideas. The contributing editor, who sometimes didn't get into the office for weeks at a stretch, didn't know what to make of her attention. Nor did the *real* editor in charge of freelance submissions.

So what to do? Whom *do* you send your manuscripts to? First of all, forget the mastheads and check *Writer's Market.* It's an appropriate place to look up the appropriate person's name, and even if things do change in the course of a year (which they often do), at least the personnel at the magazine will know just who should get your manuscript, query or whatever, in that particular editor's absence.

But maybe you don't happen to have *Writer's Market* handy. Or maybe you're trying to sell a new, unlisted publication. Can you just read the masthead and send your stuff to *the* editor, the top guy? Sure you can—but that, too, could slow things down. He's *not* the first person who reads unsolicited manuscripts or queries, unless it's a very small magazine. And if he's editor of a biggie, you can imagine how much mail he must get every day.

Okay, how about a senior editor? Not such a good idea in most places. That "senior" may be a matter of seniority—related to how long the person has been there, or how large a contribution he or she makes. It doesn't mean he or she is in charge of submissions. And the same goes for associate editors, assistant editors and the like.

Here's where we break all the rules: There *are* a couple of titles you can use and be fairly certain that your manuscript won't go astray, even though you won't be using a specific name. When in doubt, you can address your mail to the Freelance Editor (even though you'll probably never find one on a masthead), or to the Features Editor or to the Nonfiction Editor. In all cases, it will be routed appropriately and quickly.

Now that you've got it to the right person, will you be able to get it back? Did you enclose a self-addressed, stamped envelope? About one-third of freelancers don't, I find. Some magazines will send the stuff back anyway, of course—but somebody at the magazine, and not you, will be addressing the envelope. That could be trouble.

In fact, somewhere down at the bottom of many mastheads, very tiny, it probably says something like: "Unsolicited manuscripts will not be returned unless accompanied by a stamped, self-addressed envelop." (That's what *Philadelphia Magazine*'s small type says.) Or it might go further, adding, "Publisher assumes no responsibility for care and return of unsolicited materials. In no event shall such material subject this magazine to any claim for holding fees or similar charges." (That's how *Texas Monthly* does it.) And how about this: "Unsolicited manuscripts, photographs, artwork and materials should include ample postage on a self-addressed, stamped envelope (SASE); otherwise, they will not be returned." (That's how *Writer's Digest* does it.)

Well, gee—it sounds like these magazines don't care much about freelancers, right? Wrong. They *do* care. All of them depend heavily upon contributions from outsiders. And it's precisely because they recognize that they'll be getting a lot of submissions from people who haven't learned the ropes, as well as from pros, that they have to cover themselves in order to deal with any unreasonable expectation that a contributor may have. Then why doesn't a magazine like *Esquire,* where the air is rarefied, say anything on its masthead about freelance submissions? Or *New York?* I don't know. Maybe they figure that if you don't already know this stuff, you probably haven't been around long enough to sell them anyway. Which is exactly what you *don't* want anybody to think.

Chapter 6

A Visit With a Friend in the Business

Originally I was going to call this chapter "A Day With an Editor."
I changed my mind. You wouldn't have learned anything in a day,
because this place you've just entered—hey, watch it, you almost
knocked over that pile of papers—this place you've just entered is a
magazine office, not a newspaper office, and things don't happen here
in one day. They happen over a period of *several* days, or even over
many days. Some days, in fact, I spend just sitting at my desk in one or
another basic activities—editing manuscripts, or meeting with
freelancers, or talking on the phone which, needless to say, never
stops ringing. So what you'll have to settle for here is a composite of a
lot of days, with an editor of a magazine that is a composite of a lot of
magazines, keeping in mind that if you give somebody a day to do a
job, it gets done in a day, but that if you have a month, the work will
find a way of expanding to require a month.

Why write this in the first place? It's not my idea. I've had letters
from readers who say that they have no idea what editors do. They
feel funny about that inasmuch as they're going to have to deal with
editors if they ever hope to sell a story. They figure their chances will
be a lot better if they know the enemy, so to speak.

I would first like to say that all editors are nice people who really
appreciate the efforts of freelancers and are always willing to extend a
helping hand. Unfortunately, that would not be true. Editors are no
better and no worse than the rest of the population, which means that
their ranks include good people and bad people, lightweights and
heavyweights, egomaniacs and doormats, people who have too many
martinis and those who have too few, people who are very tall and
people who are very short. So this chapter will have to deal in
generalities. Nevertheless, I am one of the friendlier editors around,
and I therefore hope that you enjoy your visit.

Editors are responsible for the editorial content of magazines. That means they are responsible for everything from determining what will be on the cover to which articles should be *features* (that is, given heavier play in the feature section) and which should be *departments*. It also means—uh, excuse me; there's the phone.

Okay—that was somebody who wanted to know if I'd be interested in an article about the new soccer team that's just getting off the ground in town here. Well, I can see by the calendar on this particular day that the soccer season will be over in one and a half months, and that doesn't give me enough time. It doesn't make any sense to do an article about a ball club and run it at the very end of the season, unless you're fairly sure that the team will be in the playoffs. In this case, I told the writer no—but because it's somebody who I believe can write, I gave him the reasons behind my decision and encouraged him to try again. I spend a good bit of time on the phone with unsolicited callers, but I don't assign a lot of articles that way—and while I won't be unfriendly to new writers who do call, I will be candid: Most often I tell them that the only way to break in is to either send some darned good clips from other magazines, or do the article on spec—or, as a compromise, write a few pages of the proposed article, if possible, and let me decide from that abbreviated submission whether I want to see the rest.

Naturally, most magazines are primarily dependent upon their own staffers and their contributing editors who supply them with monthly specialties—films, dining out, and so on. But even while there's not much room to break in with a regular column, I can recall one fellow who approached me with an idea for one and ended up doing it.

* * *

This guy coming in now is our art director. We'll have to let him know what we think is the best subject for our next cover, which will be on the newsstands in six weeks. It will be his responsibility to ex-ecute that cover—to line up the model or models, to have the cover photographed, to design it—put the type in position, and so on. Naturally, he won't do this entirely alone, since a cover is more than art; many of us in the editorial department will be giving him our in-put and trying to come up with the ideal answer to the cover, right down to the lines of copy which will appear there. Very often that's a group effort, one that we'll sometimes do when we all sit down to come up with titles and subtitles for each article that will appear in the magazine. Rarely, by the way, does a magazine use a title submit-ted by a freelance author, so don't worry about coming up with snap-py titles for your articles.

Not that editors are so terrific at it. For some reason, good titles for magazine articles tend to be more derivative than original. You'd hardly think, for instance, of writing a book and calling it *A Tale of Two Cities* or *How Green Was My Valley,* because there already *are* books by those names, but that won't stop anyone from using one of those names for a magazine article—and the more readily people recognize it, the better. Magazines have used just about every title, from the classics to the best-seller lists, for inspiration, sometimes perverting the titles by a word or two in the process just to make them work. It would surprise no one, for instance, to see a magazine article entitled "A Tree Grows in Brookline."

While our art director is here, we'll talk a little about the general layout and interpretation of some articles. This assumes that art directors may not be particularly literate, or may tend to view articles as backdrops for their art direction—two thoughts which offend me personally inasmuch as I started out in this field as a magazine art director. However, while our art director will ask to read the manuscripts to determine what's appropriate, there are many for whom it is a far, far better thing for the editor to simply explain the thrust of the story and toss out a few suggestions; in most magazines, this is how art director and editor arrive at a conclusion they both can live with. Good art directors have minds of their own and won't let themselves be pushed around too much, but they also know when they're wrong—and admit it.

All the above functions are important, but the editor's most important function, in terms of the end product anyway, is to *edit,* and in that respect we're a little like artists. Ask ten artists to paint an apple and you'll get ten different apples; give a manuscript to ten different editors and, while most of them will touch on the same areas glaringly in need of work, each of them could come up with different solutions. The variation is not only from publication to publication but from editor to editor.

To the writer—that's you, with your feet up on my couch—this means that your story will be affected in one manner or another, depending upon who edits it. And there's not much you can do about it unless you're as tough as nails and willing to withdraw your article from publication. Sure, you have the right to fight about alterations with which you don't agree—after all, it's your byline—but you don't want to be too big a pain for fear of wearing out your welcome. Ultimately, it's anticipated that you'll assume that the editor has been doing his or her job for a long enough time to be able to do it well, and that you'll therefore give the imbecile the benefit of the doubt, but there are, frankly, editors around who teeter on the brink of incompetence. By the same token, there are writers who like to raise hell over any word change just to show they're nobody's fools. Get a fairly open-minded editor and a fairly flexible writer together, and you'll have no problem, but put a dogmatic editor together with an intractable writer, and you'll have a full-scale war. Most writers, I've found, are generally very reasonable because they recognize that their work does not exist in a vacuum: It's in a magazine and most often must accommodate itself to the magazine's style.

While a little of an editor's time is spent making big decisions, like what shuld be featured on the cover, and what particular articles will run in what issue, and how long a special section covering one topic will be, a lot of an editor's time is spent with little things, like captions for photographs, selecting phrases from articles to use as space-filling type boxes, checking continuity, deciding which Letters to the Editor to use, dispatching potentially troublesome manuscripts to the company lawyer and conferring with same. Naturally, the little things merely *seem* little; an incorrect caption can be a dangerous thing, and there have been many libel actions that have hinged on the use of a single, seemingly harmless word. While many of the smaller responsibilities can be delegated, the editor is the bottom line.

This is supposed to be the Decade of the Journalist, and that propaganda has flooded the market not only with journalism grads, most of whom will never get a job in journalism, but crazies as well—people who can't write but think they are sitting on a hot story that somebody else will want to write, or people who are furious over something, real or imagined, and hope to use the press to get even. The problem is that it's hard to tell the difference between a person who is agitated and angered over some injustice that could make a really good story, and a person who is agitated and angered over, say, the doggy-doo on his street, something for which I might not blame him—except that he intends to kill President Carter for not cleaning it up. In other words, it's not always easy to recognize, even with very careful telephone screening, who's nuts and who isn't, and because there's always a chance that one of those calls will be a big story, editors have to have patience and be willing to listen.

In addition, a lot of an editor's time is spent reading manuscripts from freelancers. Of course, the editor wouldn't read them all; somebody else would do the initial screening to determine whether the story might be right for the magazine. If it passes the initial muster, it comes to the decision-maker. Most unsolicited freelance submissions don't get that far, but the ones that do are usually good enough to require some careful reading, whether the magazine is thinking about running one immediately or whether it's simply interested in expanding its freelance inventory. It's easy to reject an obviously tragic piece of writing, or one that's started wrong, but it's very difficult to have to reject something you'd buy if only your budget were healthier.

Hey, I see you're still awake. Good. This job must be more exciting than I thought. But, reading back on this, I can see that this description doesn't seem to have much continuity or logic about it. If it seems that way to you, that's because there are things you can't see, like the constant checking with writers and art directors to make sure that deadlines are being met and that budgets are in line. And the meetings—good grief.

What it comes down to is this: You've been sitting at my desk for a few hours now, and this is as much as you get. You could spend a month here and you wouldn't get much more, although you would get to see more of the same. In that sense, it's like going to an accounting firm; you could watch all day, but unless you understood accounting, you wouldn't know what was going on.

Because of the heavy emphasis placed on heroism through journalism today, I think I just might point out to you that I don't consider it a particularly noble calling. Magazines are important but overrated: after all, they're only magazines, vehicles for profit and entertainment more than anything else, and very few articles—even the best of them—manage to change the world, even in the most insignificant ways, for more than a few minutes. That's something to remember. If you want to change the world, become a doctor—at least maybe you can go home at night knowing you've saved a few lives. And if you want to be an entertainer, be a rock star and you'll reach a lot more people, because a lot more people listen than read. But if you want to be a writer, you will find that it is pretty damned easy to become disillusioned. I think that there are a hell of a lot of magazine editors and writers out there who know that all this is true. The main reason why any magazine exists is to make a profit. The profit comes mostly from advertising.

If you want to be a writer, be one for the right reasons—because you simply love to write, or think you have something to say. Don't think about creating something that will change the world; be happy to change just a little tiny part of a tiny part of it, and hope, but don't expect, that ultimately the residual left by you and all the others like you will have an effect. If you can feel that way, start typing.

Chapter 7

Packaging the Product

I once wrote a column for *Writer's Digest* the point of which was that sometimes the title of an article—such as "Replaceable You," which appeared in *New York* magazine back in 1975—is itself almost justification enough for the article, and that the ability to come up with an attractive title like that one (which pertained to the manufacture of artificial body parts) shows not only a talent for thinking creatively, as editors should, but an appreciation for what makes magazines sell in the first place.

Generally speaking, editors and their staffs decide just what an article ends up being called and, perhaps more important, how it's described on the cover of the magazine. In all the years I've spent on magazines, in fact, it has almost always been the staffers—editors and writers and secretaries and whoever happens to come into the office while the brainstorming session is going on—who come up with the titles. Hardly ever is it the freelancers. That may be because it takes a certain rhythm, a certain meshing of gears over and over again, before this kind of thinking becomes second nature.

For a long time, the name of this game was cleverness—of showing as much flair and imagination in titles as possible. I sense that this is getting a little tired now, and that *relevance* and *communication* are fast becoming more important, and that while the clever title or cover line is still in demand, it's not as often used at the expense of the subject. In fact, a glance at recent issues of *New York* and *Esquire,* which are in many ways industry bellwethers, turns up a preoccupation with directness in terms of description and immediate identification.

Examples: *Esquire*'s cover line on its January 30, 1979, issue, "F. Scott Fitzgerald's Last Unpublished Short Story," is no more than a description of exactly what lies therein. Or take "Decorators . . . and How to Deal With Them" from a February 1979, cover of *New York.* Each magazine has other lines listed on the cover too, but they are not as apt to trip the light fantastic these days. This doesn't mean that imagination and intrigue are out—on the same cover of *Esquire* are, for example, "Phil Donahue: The Man Who Understands Women," and "What Makes a $350 Bowl of Soup and Where to Get It"—but maybe cuteness is.

However, since editors rarely use the titles and cover lines suggested by freelancers anyway, who cares? And why should you?

You should care because the more you think like the editors, the better your chances will be of selling them. If you know exactly what editors are looking for, you can't miss. Those titles, those cover lines, are really condensations of the central ideas of articles. If that article you want to write doesn't suggest one, chances are you don't have any single strong concept behind it—no *focus,* in other words.

So we're going to try to show you how to think a little like an editor. Then all you'll have to do is learn how to write like a writer.

First, say you have a really interesting article you'd like to write. You *know* it's interesting, but your approach to it just isn't making it there in black and white. Exciting subject, dull query. Yours starts, "Are we on the brink of a cancer cure?" You *yourself* are yawning. And yet the story is important. The problem (and you know it) is that you've seen it all before, so you know the editor is probably not going to get past the first sentence. And yet you're convinced that one particular cancer researcher, the guy you want to write about, *is* on the brink of a cure for at least one kind of cancer.

Obviously, what you need to do is rethink the idea, approach it the way an editor would. Right now it's too broad. What's a good cover line for it? What's a good title? What's the *essence* of the piece? What's different about it?

You have this guy, an obscure doctor at some university, who—*maybe*—has a cure. He can't try it on a human. But he's already tried it on some lower forms of life, and it seems to be working. Now he's trying it on a monkey. So you try to work with that: "Harry Smith and His Monkey: On the Trail of a Cancer Cure." Not bad. At least, it's better than it was. But don't stop now; maybe there's a better way to say it, to refine it and individualize it even further.

For instance, what *kind* of monkey? And does it have a name? It's not just an animal with cancer, not any more than Smith is just a researcher who is hopeful that by bombarding the cancer cells with whatever, he can eliminate them. We're dealing with personalities here.

How about the other facts? Let's say that the truth—whatever it turns out to be—will be known by November. If Harry Smith's chimp lives that long, Smith will have discovered—or created—if not a cure, then at least a method of causing remission. And maybe not for many cancers. Maybe for just one. And maybe just in monkeys at this point. Nevertheless, the find would be significant.

Now this is February. You have time to write the article, and time to get it published, and it still won't be resolved. (Maybe the resolution will make another article.)

And maybe you've discovered the first line of your query letter to a potential publisher: "If Martha, a two-year-old champanzee suffering from cancer, lives until the end of 1979, a researcher in a small New England university will have discovered a cure for the nation's most dreaded disease." I'd certainly read the sentence after that one, and I'm sure it's still not being said in the best way, the most provocative way, possible. The point is, you narrow the theme down to a single sentence, and that's what gets you the article's uncommon denominator, the one point of interest that most people will find too unusual or too dramatic to ignore.

Obviously, based on the examples I used previously from *New York* and *Esquire,* you don't have to be tricky to be interesting. Sometimes the mere mention of a particular subject has enough impact to guarantee interest, and certain subjects are loaded with that kind of implicit excitement. For instance, an article about child abuse on the Main Line could simply be called "Child Abuse on the Main Line"; demographically, it would seem to be a contradiction in terms.

* * *

This whole business is called *packaging,* which may indicate why journalists eventually reach the point where they don't have too many illusions. Granted, it is a rather commercial term to be applied to what some consider to be an art form. But magazine covers are what they are, and what they are must sell. Unsold magazines go out of business. It may hurt you to think of your incandescent prose as a box of detergent, but that's not as farfetched as it seems—the current science of packaging owes a lot to supermarket studies, and some of what was learned there has been applied to newsstand magazine sales. In supermarkets, for instance, bright colors sell better than dark colors, all other things being equal; ditto on the newsstands. In supermarkets, items at eye level or slightly below eye level outsell items above eye level; ditto on newsstands. In supermarkets, items that are highly recognizable get greater brand loyalty than those that aren't; the same applies to magazines. This may seem like common sense, but the studies weren't conducted just to keep the researchers off welfare. If you want proof, just visit your supermarket and notice where the expensive items, like meats, are—farthest from the cash registers— while all the cheapies (like paper goods) are up *near* the cash registers. People get nervous around checkout time, something the supermarket scientists learned by counting eye blinks.

It stands to reason that if selling detergent in a supermarket isn't all that different from selling magazines on a newsstand, then selling magazines on a newsstand isn't that much different from selling articles to an editor. With that in mind, it's time to see what you're made of. I'll tell you some cover lines and/or titles that have been used, past and present. You sit down and think about how you'd handle them— what kinds of cover lines and/or titles you'd come up with for the article in question if you had to do it today. Keep in mind the specific medium for each cover; remember that there are no right or wrong answers, but that this is simply an exercise to see how well you can package your ideas and maybe get some untried muscles working. The covers we'll describe here are real—some from national publications, some from regionals. Try to get beneath the surface of each idea, find out what's central to it, then touch a responsive chord in every potential reader.

1. A cover that seems to recur rather often among the city magazines is one that has to do with how much people earn. The cover usually contains pictures of a variety of people—from loan shark to fashion model to politician to janitor and everything in between. Typical cover lines that have been used range from "Who Makes What?" to "Henry Ford Took a $573,000 Cut Last Year. How's Your Salary Doing?" How would you say this, based on the present inflationary economy? Or maybe not based on it at all?

2. Many city magazines have at least one cover a year that talks about the "Best and Worst of (City Name Here)"—from best cheesecake to worst public library. Is there a better way to say that?

3. *House & Garden* has the idea, no doubt bred by success, that a cluttered cover containing lots of hard-to-read type is a good method of attracting their readers; indeed, there's probably something to be said for their chock-full-of-tips look. A typical H&G cover line, however, is somewhat unwieldy, like this one: "How to be so clever with color and fabric no one can tell you're decorating on a budget." That's only one of several on their cover, and while the medium is supposed to be the message, I still think there would be no harm in communicating more effectively. (If clutter is the name of the game, of course, we could always add more stories, reversed out of floral patterns.) Anyway, take that line and run with it—without sacrificing the style in which they prefer to do things.

4. On an early 1979 cover of *Time*, there's an architect holding a model of a building of his own creation; the cover line reads, "U.S. Architects." And then, below that, "Doing Their Own Thing." Kind of stale, right? Okay, improve it.

5. On an issue of *Newsweek:* "Telling All." And under that, "Memoirs of the Stars." And a photo of Lauren Bacall, who'd just written hers. I think that's pretty good. The cutesy way would've been

"Bacall Tells All," and under that, "The Star's Memoirs." I've taken the obvious. Now your turn.

By this time, you should have the idea. Apply this kind of thinking to your own writing whenever you get the feeling that you're not exactly sure what you're writing about. It will help you develop a focus, a single theme. And it will, I believe, help you sell. The first step toward selling like a professional is learning to think like one.

And if this puts you in a position of second-guessing the editors of the country's best magazines, that's probably what you hope to do anyway.

Chapter 8

Two Dozen Mistakes

Looking back over several years' worth of freelance manuscripts that I bought — and a year's worth of rejection letters that I mailed — convinces me that a lot of writers fail to sell because of the *little* things they're doing wrong.

And the problem is, rarely are writers told. Rejection letters or, worse, rejection slips, are usually impersonal and seldom helpful. So if you have enough of them to paper your wall and still don't know why, maybe this chapter is for you.

If they all come out as "don'ts," don't be surprised.

1. Don't preach. Don't tell your readers what to think; let them arrive at the conclusion with your guidance. Thoughts like, "Only if the American public — people like you — complain loudly enough and long enough, will something be done," are sure death. So are phrases like, "It's important to remember that. . . ." Almost every time a sentence begins with *that* kind of propaganda, you'll be better off just eliminating the phrase.

2. Don't be redundant. You like the hero of your story, and you're convinced that the only reason your favorite ball team lost the pennant was that they lost him halfway through the season. Plant the thought, then go on to something else. Don't say it fives times, in five different ways, throughout the article. If you're insecure enough to think that somebody might have missed the thought, consider saying it better — not more often.

3. Don't overestimate the intelligence of your readers. Yes, that's "overestimate." You'd be amazed what readers don't know. For instance, most may have heard of a chromosome, but try getting one of them to describe what a chromosome *does*. That's what *you* have to tell them, and that's why it's okay to say, for instance, "Gambling is illegal in almost every state," even though you might consider that fact to be fairly common knowledge. If you're not certain that at least 95 percent of the readership will know what you're talking about, *make certain.*

4. Don't talk down to your readers. A dilemma. First we tell you not to overestimate their intelligence, and now we're telling you not to talk down to them. Well, there is a way to disseminate basic information without offending. Take the sentence above: "Gambling is illegal in almost every state." If you think that kind of statement is just too condescending for words, try this: "Gambling is, of course, illegal in almost every state." The difference is that now you seem to think that the reader *knows* this; you're simply including it for those who don't, the stupid minority—but never the reader you're writing to. Somehow, breaking that sentence up with a qualifier gets you off the hook, and it's sometimes even better when expressed as part of an opinion: "Gambling is, unfortunately, illegal in almost every state."

5. Don't verbalize assumptions regarding your readers. You don't know who they are, so how can you tell them, "You'll quickly conclude . . ."? This too is one of those sentence starters better left unsaid.

6. Don't use the first person unnecessarily. You must have a compelling reason. I say this even though I've written many first-person articles, and even though the "new journalism" makes liberal use of the first person. The key is: Are you *integral* to the story? If you're writing about your own experiences—not as a reporter, but as a participant—then you are. If you're just a person who started out tracking down a story, like an investigation into some mysterious deaths, you're probably not, and you'll just get in the way. This is a matter of judgment, of course, and sometimes this rule begs to be broken. If it does, break it. But only after you're sure that you're not using yourself gratuitously, because you don't want to end up with sentences like, "I was amazed to find. . . ." After all, nobody knows who you *are,* so they'd hardly be in a position to know just how amazing something would have to be to amaze you.

7. Don't get tricky. Style is nice if you have it—but you can style yourself right out of a sale if you don't recognize your own weaknesses. If you think you're Norman Mailer and you keep getting rejection slips, maybe you're somebody else. If you think you're the funniest writer who ever sat down to type, and you get rejected instead of laughed at, maybe you should face the facts and get serious. Forget style, and maybe, just maybe, you'll develop a recognizable one. Or maybe not. It's not important. Style is not what makes a good writer good.

8. Don't lean too heavily on your loved ones for advice. Take your mother. Please. She loves you. She loves your stuff. She thinks you're terrific. All this because she's your mother. She also happens to be in a vacuum as far as writers are concerned. If she'll buy your articles, fine—listen to her. (On balance, if you have somebody around who reads good writing voraciously, that's different. My wife is one of the best literary critics I've ever met. And she loves my stuff.)

9. Don't use unsupportable generalizations. If you're trying to make a point, don't use information that you can't substantiate. Don't even imply it. You may think that most high-school students have tried drugs, and you may be right—but a byline doesn't make you an expert. Get a quote or some statistics from the *recognized* authorities.

10. Don't depend on material that could be outdated. If you're going to quote studies or statistics, make sure you're quoting the most recent available. And if you're going to write a cover letter to the editor, make sure that you use the name of the current editor. Things can change during a year, even if you consult *Writer's Market,* and there's no point in having an extra strike against you when you could so easily have checked by phone or looked at the latest masthead. If you can't even get the editor's name right, what *can* you do right?

11. Don't tell the editor how terrific your article is. Let him be the judge of that. If you have some really good credentials, however, there's nothing wrong with mentioning them.

12. Don't lean too heavily on narrative. Newspaper readers will settle for the facts and how they unfolded; magazine readers want more depth. Balance your article with quotes, and bring in tangential information that gives the reader a total understanding of what's going on. A description of a child-beating and its aftermath does not a magazine article make—not without lots of fleshing out, tracing trends, interviewing officials, exploring motivations.

13. Don't write of things about which you know little. Say you want to write an article about horse racing, but you know nothing about it. That's okay, provided you educate yourself before you start typing. Nothing is stupider than a writer who doesn't know his subject—unless it's a writer who thinks he can get his stupidity past an editor.

14. Don't burden a story with too many facts. Sometimes you can pack too much information into an article, and that can slow down the action. If that's happening, first eliminate superfluous information, then start thinking in terms of a sidebar—that is, a small story accompanying the main article. Example: an article on vasectomy (male sterilization) was being slowed down by a description of the operation, financial considerations, anticipated side effects, and so on. While the information couldn't be cut out, it looked like it would hold together logically outside the article—meeting the criteria for a solid sidebar. The main article flowed more smoothly, too.

15. Don't just write—edit. The best writers are their own best editors. You shouldn't just sit down and type a first draft, call it a final draft and mail it out. Put it away instead; then go back a few days later and take a fresh look—and pretend you're an editor. Go over every word and phrase and transition to make sure that they simply *can't* be better. Trust your gut: If it doesn't read as well the second time around it isn't what you thought it was.

16. Don't fall in love with your own stuff. Of course, you should have a healthy respect for what you do (Notice how condescending I wasn't when I used "of course"?) but every once in a while you'll come up with a sentence or phrase that is just so damned clever you'll do anything to keep it. That's counterproductive. You have to be heartless. If it's extraneous, if it interrupts the flow, cut it out. (I know a guy who has a drawerful of wonderful lines he had to cut, and he keeps waiting for a chance to use them. He'll probably have a long wait. In another case, a writer gave me a manuscript that opened very poetically, describing the beginning of urban development where he lives. Unfortunately, he was so in love with his metaphors and similes that his introduction ran about five pages. Which explains why editors "butcher" manuscripts.)

17. Don't think that just because it's interesting to you, it'll be interesting to everybody. For the rejection slips to cover this single error alone, we've had to deplete countless forests. Play it safe: *Assume that nobody's interested in what you have to say.* And then give the reader a reason to be, fast, early in the article—something that will keep him guessing about the outcome. That reason, at its best, will be based on a simple human emotion that everybody can share, not a specific interest—not, for example, a love of Bach or a dislike of modern art. (If you must deal with a love of Bach or a dislike of modern art, start with emotions that are further below the surface and more commonly held—like the fact that all human beings respond to some kind of music, and that many resent intellectual art forms.) Think in terms of characterizations that will allow the reader to identify, situations that give him a stake in the action. And do it before you get too far; I remember one article where the murder of a character was described in the first paragraph, and I couldn't have cared less. The writer hadn't given me, personally, a *reason* to care.

18. Don't address the reader directly. It's the sign of an amateur, and it's presumptuous. It tells the reader you *expect* to be read, and who are you to expect that? Further, the relationship between writer and reader is never that personal. Phrases like, "You may not believe this," and salutations like "dear reader" went out with the Remington Noiseless, and so will your manuscript if you include them. On the other hand, an impersonal use of the word "you" is fine—as in, "Those interested in joining the organization may find it easier said than done. You don't simply go in and sign up." Or even, "If you're reading this on a subway . . .," which doesn't imply any knowledge of the reader on your part. Get too personal and you've got trouble.

19. Don't send in a manuscript that's not 100 percent. If there's something wrong *any place* in the manuscript, you know it. But you figure that you might be able to get it past an editor. You won't; those things stick out like sore thumbs, and it's our job to catch them. When something's wrong, we won't even have to wonder about it. We'll know.

20. Don't flirt. There are ways that a writer can make it obvious that he wants the reader to respect him. This is often done by sprinkling in a few strained quotes from famous intellectuals, or dropping a few of the right names as though you know everybody on a first-name basis, or using a vocabulary that is slightly out of kilter considering the target audience, all of which sound terribly unnatural. Flirts are, if nothing else, obvious, and respect is *earned,* not absorbed from other sources and somehow implanted in the reader.

21. Don't be convoluted. Long or complex sentences have their place—and that place is where the thought can't be expressed in any other way without losing something in the translation. Otherwise, be direct.

22. Don't speak one way and write another. Generally, the most effective magazine writers write the way they think, and the best indicator of how you think is how you speak. Keep your writing conversational and informal. If necessary, first concentrate on being a better and more concrete conversationalist. Just think how popular you'll be.

23. Don't ignore English. Many writers figure that small mistakes in punctuation, spelling and grammar aren't really important; that editors will take care of the small stuff, provided the story's a good one. That's true—but a misspelled name, or the wrong use of a word, may jeopardize your credibility with an editor. He may think, "How many *other* facts are wrong?" And he might wonder how much you might have misunderstood while you were conducting your interviews.

24. Don't be bound by these rules. But break them only when necessary.

That's it. Granted, if the article is right for the market and holds the editor's interest, most of these little errors won't have much bearing on whether you sell or not. But why take the chance?

Chapter 9

Neatness Counts

When I was a kid sitting in the office of Irving Stupine, D.D.S., waiting for my numerous cavities to be ground into submission, there was a sign on the wall that fascinated me. It referred, I know now, to the importance of proper dental care—an ounce of prevention's being worth a pound of cure—but it seems particularly relevant for this book as well:

> For want of a nail, the shoe was lost.
> For want of a shoe, the horse was lost.
> For want of a horse, the rider was lost.
> For want of a rider, the message was lost.
> For want of a message, the battle was lost.
> For want of a battle, the war was lost.
> All for the want of a nail.

I used to think it was really sad. And while I didn't know just which war had been lost that way (somehow it seemed to have been ignored by history), it taught me a lesson. For years after that, whenever I got dressed, I always checked my shoes.

The point, of course—which escaped me at age eight—was that little things mean a lot, and that a seemingly insignificant detail can have reverberations many times its size.

This chapter is not about horses or wars, but about the little neatnesses that count. The tendency to think these things unimportant is common among both beginning writers and pros. In the case of the former, it's simply not knowing; and the latter nurture a confidence about the product that seems to make the writer think he can afford slippage elsewhere. In either case, ignoring the small stuff may never cost you a sale—the nail may not cause the loss of the shoe—but I can think of an occasion or two where it has.

Here are some of the things that bug editors:

Queries and manuscripts that don't have phone numbers or ad-

dresses. I mean *right on the query or manuscript,* not just on the envelope or the return envelope. You'd be surprised how many people put their return addresses only on the *envelope* in which they send their submissions, and often that envelope hits the trash before anyone gets a chance to notice the lack of an address inside.

Abbreviated first names. That is, B. J. Smith. Now, is B. J. a man? Or a woman? I don't care about the sex for any personal reason, nor do I discriminate on the basis of sex. But until we're all exactly equal, until women are receiving equal pay for equal work, until women stop writing books about men as enemies and until men stop referring to ambitious women as "aggressive" in a negative sense—until all that and more happens, I want to know the sex of the writer because I feel that it could affect his or her point of view, and I feel that the reader deserves to know that. Naturally, I've received some flak on this point.

Handwritten queries. Rare, and almost a waste of time when I get them. I picture a handwritten final article, and then I wonder who would do that in 1979, and do I want that person writing for us about contemporary society?

Faded typewriter ribbon. Not so bad on queries, but a real pain on finished manuscripts. There are two things wrong with articles typed with a geriatric ribbon: One, they're hard to read, and you don't want to have a distracting element like that working counter to your aims; and two, they're impossible to photocopy on, say, a Xerox machine—and magazines usually make copies of manuscripts for one reason or another.

Erasable bond paper. In case you don't know what this is, it's a highly coated paper, usually quite expensive, from which typing errors can be easily removed with a plain pencil eraser. The typing almost *wipes* off. It makes life easier for the writer, but difficult for the editor, for three reasons: One, the typing itself tends to show up lighter on erasable bond; two, certain kinds of ink bead or smear on this stuff; and three, an editor may do some editing, regret it, and then try to erase the editing—presto, off comes not only the editing, but part of the sentence above it and below it and, of course, the entire typed sentence that was edited. (To avoid the sure death of erasable bond, you don't need any fancy paper with rag content or anything like that. Go out and buy a ream of cheap white bond similar to the kind that's used for Xerox copies. I find it a pleasure to use for typing and editing. If you're typo prone, use a liquid or tape erase method.)

Colored typewriter paper. For some reason—maybe it's a holdover from the old newspaper days—some writers still send in manuscripts typed on newsprint or, just as bad, colored stock. The problem with newsprint, as well as with cheaper colored stocks, is that they're extremely soft and absorbent. Typewriters punch holes through them, pencils tear them, and pencil points sink in and create broader strokes than are preferable. Colored stock has one big problem: Photocopy machines haven't been taught to ignore the color, and even canary yellow paper translates into a dark gray haze on which words are extremely difficult to read and even more difficult to edit. Stick to white; you can't go wrong.

Heavily edited manuscripts. We like 'em clean, but a lot of writers edit heavily in ink *after* they've typed their final versions. The problem with this, in the typical double-spaced typewritten manuscript, is that the writer has already used the space where the editor might want to do some editing.

Cut-and-paste jobs. While cutting and pasting are perfectly acceptable methods of getting a story to flow just right, they can make manuscripts tough to work on, unless they've been neatly done. Best bet: Do a finished typing of the manuscript *after* you've done the revising, not before.

Cellophane or transparent tapes. Often writers, not having heard of rubber cement, will paste two halves of a page together with a strip of tape. Usually that strip of tape will run over some typing. Granted, the typing can still be read, but it can't be edited; a pencil will make no mark at all, or a mark that will smear easily, and most inks won't dry fast enough on tape. It's just another unnecessary annoyance.

Large manuscripts in small envelopes. Common sense: If you have more than three pages, send it flat. Most organizations use letter-opening machines which slice off the top edge of number ten envelopes. If you have half a dozen sheets of paper folded down to a number ten size, chances are that the letter opener will catch one of the folded edges—and there goes your valuable prose, sliced away in a fine strip, after which the magazine's staff has to piece things back together again. It doesn't help the sale any, and forget about sending the same manuscript to another market if it's rejected.

Copies. If you're going to send a carbon copy of anything, you won't sell it. You're lucky if anybody reads it. If you send a photocopy, we're going to wonder if it's part of a multiple submission. If it is, many firms won't read it. If it's not, better say so in your cover letter.

Ancient manuscripts. We'll take the Dead Sea Scrolls, but we don't want anything that just *looks* like it's been around that long. When a manuscript has made the rounds, usually there's a reason, we figure.

Unorthodox spacing. There are typewriters, particularly some European makes, that offer a one-and-one-half line space. This saves paper, but doesn't really give anybody enough room to edit. If you like being different, triple-space. More is more.

And finally, of course, there is:

Punctuation, spelling and grammar. Robert Ripley—he's the guy who used to draw the popular "Believe It or Not"—once told the story of a Russian czar who was one day asked to decide the fate of a thousand captured soldiers. He wrote, "Pardon impossible, to be sent to Siberia."

The messenger, a soft-hearted guy who undoubtedly didn't have much respect for his own life, decided that the sentence was too harsh. He moved the comma. The message now read:

"Pardon, impossible to be sent to Siberia."

That's a perfectly ridiculous story, even if my memory does have some of the details wrong, and the simple moving of a comma won't save a thousand lives when *you* do it—but it may change the meaning of what you're trying to say. To an editor who's used to inspecting words carefully hour after hour, day after day, more than one or two imperfections that leave him or her wondering where a quote ends, or who's saying what, can have you looking like an idiot.

Believe it or not.

Chapter 10

Discipline and the Writer

I am sitting in the bedroom of a small apartment at a seashore resort. My wife and I have moved the kitchen table into this bedroom where it has now been for one week and will remain for another, until we leave. We eat standing or, at best, sitting on the living room sofa, balancing plates on our knees. This is called "art for Art's sake."

On the table are a typewriter, a pile of manila folders, a list of columns to be written for *Writer's Digest;* outside are some powerful temptations for a case of writer's block: The temperature is in the low 90s, the sun high in a cloudless blue sky, the beach is a block away. There is no breeze and the ocean beckons, each wave a caress as it comes in, an invitation to follow as it ebbs.

But I am not so easily seduced.

I have been staring at my IBM Selectric, which I like as much as any concert pianist likes a Steinway Grand, for 20 minutes. Nothing has happened. But ocean or not, I do not abandon the task. *Something* will happen.

In fact, that's one of my secrets for outsmarting writer's block, or whatever you choose to call it: If at first you don't succeed, try, try something else. There is a certain logic which makes you tell yourself that just because you have one particularly tough assignment to do, it is practically the *only* thing you have to do. Most of the time, that isn't so, and you can often choose another task, then come back to the one that's giving you all the trouble. Sometimes you can even find a substitute chore for the original. For instance, that's what I'm doing: I sat down to write a chapter, but it didn't come—so I took the path of least resistance, which has resulted in my writing about the very thing that's hanging me up. Why fight the flow when you can accomplish the same thing by going along with it?

Another technique: Make a list of everything that you hope to get done today, in order of importance. It may be an awful-looking list, but do it anyway. Then just do the top item on the list. That's right: The list may be formidable, but obligate yourself to only the most important item on it, and chances are you'll get that one job done.

Easy for me to talk, you say. Unfortunately, you can't sit down and write a column or a book chapter that will eventually be used. In your case, you simply *can't* get started. Well, try this: Give yourself a time limit. Not for finishing the task—*that* time limit already exists; after all, if you didn't have a deadline—even if it's a self-imposed one—you wouldn't be panicking to such a degree that you can't commit a few words to paper. No, I'm suggesting that you give yourself a time limit for *starting* the task. Say you sit down at nine in the morning to begin to write—but you simply don't feel like writing. You spend half an hour looking at the blank paper, perhaps get off to some bad starts—and then abandon the task, feeling as though you've failed. That is, of course, the worst way to leave a page—having struck out once, the task then looms even larger. The idea here is to have it be *your* decision to abandon the task, and not the decision of a blank piece of paper. Once you've given it the old college try, and can see that the words aren't going to come, go on to something else—and set an alarm clock for a specific time a couple of hours later. When the alarm goes off, you sit down again—and this time you do it.

If you need some extra incentive, you can always bribe yourself. That, in fact, is how I'm getting this chapter done. I figure I can wrap it up in a couple of hours. The sun will still be out. I promise myself that, once I'm finished writing it, I will go to the beach, take a swim, lie in the sun and do some sketching. But I have to stick to the bargain: If I don't finish my writing, I am going to be grown up enough to deprive myself of the beach and the ocean. That being the case, you can bet I'll finish this chapter. It doesn't matter what the reward is. When you don't feel like writing, almost anything else is preferable. If you promise yourself a nap, a beer, a walk in the woods, a bike ride—even a cup of coffee and some uninterrupted minutes watching *As The World Turns*—that's plenty.

Or perhaps you can trick yourself. This takes a little fantasizing, something that should come naturally to you as a writer. Say you have to write a list of 50 items. So change the assignment—you just have to write one. Don't worry that it's not true. The *hardest* item of those 50 is the first, just as the hardest part of an article is the first sentence or paragraph. Even if you're halfway through the article, the next paragraph is always hard unless you're flowing. But if you say, *okay, self, all I need is one paragraph*—you'll get it. And then, of course, you'll get the rest.

Okay, you've tried the imaginary bargain, the time limit, the reward—the mind tricks—and while they work for many, you're too much of a realist to suspend reality. You'll simply have to *alter* it. Read on.

The overwhelming difficulty for freelancers is loneliness. I know several who go to the editorial offices of their favorite magazines not because they have any business there, but because they're tired of sitting at home and staring at the same four walls. The writing life is filled with impersonal, temporary relationships: You interview and collect information from people to whom you're virtually anonymous, then go back to an empty room, silent except for the noise of the striking of the keys. By the time the article's done, you're stir crazy—*if* you were normal when you started. But stir craziness may come before you're finished, and then what?

Then leave the typewriter and get out—go shopping, get among people who know you, even if that means chatting at the corner store or, as I prefer, visiting the pool hall. What you're doing is giving yourself a reward of sorts *before* you earn it, which may just loosen you up—but you must be willing to pay the typewriter when payment becomes due.

You can also change your working environment. This could be something as simple as turning on the radio (or turning it off). If you're turning it on, don't put on your favorite kind of music; you'll find yourself listening instead of working. When I want noise behind me, I usually put on a station that plays music I wouldn't ordinarily listen to, syrupy "beautiful-music" renditions of standards with lots of strings. You couldn't get me to *listen* to that stuff, but it's effective if I just want to fill the air with noise. I know a writer who puts on an all-news station, low, so that he hears the murmurs of the commentator but isn't trapped into listening to the words. With a human voice there, he feels less alone.

Sometimes it's helpful to move your typewriter to another room. Strange as it may seem, that perfect little work environment you've created, despite its superb layout, comfort and seclusion, may be just another place to do a job—along with remembrances of past failures, long hours of sweat and strain, and heartbreak. You may have to leave it on occasion—to get some writing done. My favorite spot, when I want that kind of change, is my backyard. I'll set up the typewriter on a redwood table out there and start typing with only the songs of birds and the water dribbling in the birdbath as background music. That often helps.

One final helpful escape route—do something physical. And I'm not talking about pushing a mop around the kitchen floor. I'm talking about strenuous exercise. Nobody's mental faculties can operate at maximum performance when the body feels punk. I know of one really fine writer, Diane Rubin, who runs whenever her writing won't come. After running, she says, writing becomes simpler, more direct, more pertinent; it is as if she has trimmed away the fat from her thought processes. Some people jump rope; some play tennis. I personally like the idea of doing something that gets you away—*far* away—from the typewriter. For a while I played squash, but I needed something that didn't depend upon a partner, so I started running, too. That's perfect for me and, I think, perfect for anyone who works best alone.

One parting thought on avoiding writer's block: Never take an assignment that you don't feel is right for you. If it doesn't make your heart pound at least a little bit faster, the best thing to do is say right off, "Hey, this isn't my kind of article; I don't think you'd want me to write it." The editor may look a little disappointed, but ultimately you'll get a reputation as someone who can be trusted to be candid, realistic—and one who doesn't disappoint where it really counts.

The bottom line: I don't believe that writer's block actually exists. If you have something worth communicating, nothing can stop you. I have known of stories born in the wee small hours of the morning because the writer could not stay away from the typewriter. And if you don't have anything worth communicating, there's no technique or method that will make you a writer.

In fact, there should be no situation in which a professional writer can't sit down and write. Professionalism alone demands that a job, once accepted, must be finished, delivered—and good. Despite all that's been written about writer's block, and despite all that *hasn't* been written about writer's laziness, the ability to complete the job and do it well is what separates the professionals from the poseurs. Nobody wants to work with a prima donna, and—despite problems we've all had—no editor wants to hear that you just couldn't get started. *If you don't sit down at the typewriter and get moving, genius, you're gonna blow it.*

As for me: Ocean, here I come.

Chapter 11

Bending the Rules

I learned as soon as I started teaching my nonfiction magazine writing course that writers who are otherwise creative and imaginative at solving problems will, when given instructions by a source they respect, follow those instructions out the window and down 30 stories. Instead of interpreting them as recommendations, they hear them as *rules:* Absolute, permanent, inflexible. The same thing happens when they open *Writer's Market.* While it may be the bible of the industry, not everything it says is necessarily gospel.

Consider the following "rules," lifted at random from *Writer's Market.* Each says one thing; each often means something else. We present the real meanings here so that you will know just where you stand and how to translate other similar phrases:

Avoid clichés. Don't do anything we've done.

Our readership is of average income. People who are earning what you'd probably like to earn, but are nowhere near as smart as you. Such figures have nothing to do with the actual (and much lower) national average income which, according to Washington, nobody earns.

Reports promptly. Rejections are handled immediately. Anything else is, of course, held for consideration, traveling through the inevitable chain of command, which must be small if they can promise to report promptly in the first place. After two weeks, though, somebody could *still* decide that they don't want your article. In that case, even rejections can take a little time. Translation: They don't get much mail.

Reports in two to four weeks. Reports in two to eight weeks. Always double the last number and hope for the best.

Rarely uses (a particular type article or subject). Never uses. But they don't want you to think they're closed-minded.

Pays up to $500. Don't hold your breath; that's for one particular contributor with ten years' tenure, lots of talent, and pictures of the editor in a compromising situation.

Pays three to five cents per word. You get three cents.

Pays in copies. Hardly anybody reads this publication, so you might as well.

Sometimes I wish it were otherwise—that there were strict rules associated with magazine writing, and that if you followed those rules you couldn't help but sell. Unfortunately, they don't exist.

Something else does. Call it judgment, rational thinking—common sense, if you will. It's what tells you what to do when there are no set patterns to guide you, and—more important—it tells you when to violate those that might exist.

This brings us to one of the most important things you'll ever read—in *my* book, anyway: If it feels right, *do* it. Trust yourself. You've done it before, and how many times has it been disastrous? Probably never. Some rules are made to be broken. And some, while usually sound, should occasionally be ignored. Appropriateness is the watchword.

Standard behavior for writers might dictate: *Never contact somebody for an interview at home.* And that's fine, unless you've tried unsuccessfully half a dozen times to get somebody at her/his office to ask vital questions for an article you're writing. Common courtesy may dictate one thing, but common sense dictates another. If you've been getting the runaround, here's where you confirm it. On the other hand, a busy person's guilt may just get the best interview you've ever had.

Writer's Market, as well as just about every journalism teacher you'll ever talk to, will load you down with certain conditions that magazines generally prefer you meet. Now, for heaven's sake, *think* about that. These are magazines, not computers. If their editors are worth anything, chances are they break their own "rules" at least once in a while. There's no reason why you shouldn't do the same. Here, for instance, are some of the rules—along with some good reasons for bending them:

1. Never telephone an editor; write a query instead. Sometimes that's good advice; you don't want to make a pest of yourself. *But:* Let's say that you have a hot idea, something you feel pretty confident will sell—and there's a time factor. If you wait for the mails, you're going to be late or unable to offer your idea elsewhere. Call. There are other reasons for making phone calls, like to find out if the magazine is already covering your topic (so you don't have to do too much digging just to be able to query it) or is likely to be interested in it. Or maybe you already have pretty good credentials and just want to sit down face to face with the editor of a magazine you'd love to hit. You won't always get an audience—but at least you won't have been unnecessarily anonymous. In short, the phone is often as appropriate as a letter; sometimes more so. Common sense dictates.

2. Don't just "drop in" on an editor. Well, if you're talking about the editors I know, that's good advice, because they don't usually have the time to make themselves available. On the other hand, what happens if somebody shows up? Sometimes they *do* talk to writers they've never met. It's all a matter of when someone hits them, and what they tell the receptionist. There really isn't much risk—you can (1) get turned away at the door, (2) fail to see the editor, but get to see someone else, or (3) sit and wait for half an hour before (1) or (2) happens. The worst that can happen, in short, is that you'll waste your time; on the other hand, nobody will get angry at you. Magazines don't blacklist people who come in without appointments.

3. Submit no manuscripts; query first. Sometimes that's to keep a magazine from getting too many manuscripts, but most often it's to keep you from doing needless work. But say you have a piece already written—should you query first, then wait for them to ask to see the piece? That depends—are you crazy?

4. Avoid the obvious. That's usually good advice, either because the magazine has already done the obvious, or would rather never do the obvious. (For instance, at *Philadelphia Magazine* we did not get excited about articles on Ben Franklin or the Liberty Bell.) *But:* Suppose your approach is so different as to take the story out of the ordinary? In that case, give it a try—but tell briefly and immediately, in your cover letter or query, why your version isn't just more of the same.

5. The magazine doesn't say that photocopied submissions are okay. Therefore, I should submit only a typed manuscript. Normally, yes—but suppose your original has been lost in the mail? Or is still in transit back from somewhere? Well, you can always retype it. But if you'd like to avoid that step, you can photocopy your copy and send the better of the two along with a little note of apology, making sure to explain that it isn't a multiple submission (that's probably what has the publication worried about photocopies in the first place). Editors aren't ogres, and I can't imagine any editor's turning down a knockout piece just because Xerox did it. However, don't send copies that are hard to write on, or copies that leave a residue on the fingertips, or copies that smell funny as some photocopy machines are wont to produce. Yuk.

6. Don't bother a magazine for an answer regarding your manuscript or query; they'll get back to you as soon as they can. But: It's *your* manuscript or query, so if you don't have an answer within a reasonable amount of time (based on being slightly generous with the timetable as outlined in *Writer's Market),* act as you would regarding *any* personal property. By all means, call. Just be gentle.

* * *

I could give you 50 more examples. Take something as basic as the SASE. Most magazines mention in their *Writer's Market* listing that you should enclose one. Does that mean that when a magazine fails to mention that, it prefers to pay the postage for you? Fat chance; common sense says tha it was an oversight.

If all the above truths aren't so self-evident, that means a little interpretation is called for on your part. You can't just take standard operating procedures and make them the rigid governors of your behavior. Even if the English language were specific enough for people to say, in print, exactly what they mean—which it isn't—that still doesn't mean there would be no exceptions. In fact, language is often *intentionally* vague—just so you *won't* consider it gospel.

When you're in doubt, common sense will usually point you in the right direction. Just ask yourself, "What would I do if I didn't already know what I'm *supposed* to do?" Then do it.

Chapter 12

Writers vs. Editors

I had dinner with a fellow editor recently. This means, of course, that the hard stuff flowed like iced tea (a journalist, to be consistent with the image, must be able to put away a few), and when his tongue was even looser than normal, he leaned across the table and whispered, "I'll tell you something about this business, Spikol. There's no other business in the world where the people who contribute to it know less about it." And he went on to tell, slightly tipsy but making sense, how editors are often blamed for things that are beyond their control—mainly due to ignorance on the part of freelance writers.

The result, he said, pointing to his again-empty glass, is that "many freelance writers have the idea that all editors are about as cold as thish martini," although he looked anything but cold, blubbering in my ear, squeezing my arm and generally making a spectacle of himself. Poor fellow. Freelancers had driven him to the brink.

Well now, I thought, sipping my root beer float, here's something worth writing about.

Because a lot of editors are inaccessible, many of them aren't really aware of how freelancers view them. Editors are looked upon, for the most part, as residing in places far removed from the real world, and in many ways they do. And freelancers are understandably reluctant to write letters to editors explaining how ripped off, mistreated, misunderstood and ticked off they feel, since they figure that this will destroy their chances of ever writing for that publication again. They are, in fact, probably more cautious about chastising one of the many publications that they work for than they would be if they had a full-time job, in which such behavior would certainly be a lot more hazardous. As a result of writing a regular column, I am privileged to get letters from readers who are ticked off and don't mind saying so, since I am not the object of their derision.

With that in mind, and for those of you who'll never write to me, here's what I hear—complete with snappy retorts from the editor's side.

"I sent my manuscript (or query) over two weeks ago and I still haven't heard a word. How can they expect me, or anybody else, to make a living?"

No doubt about it, freelancing is a tough way to earn a buck. But rarely is the magazine trying to make it tougher. First of all, few magazines these days have someone who does nothing but review freelance queries and unsolicited manuscripts; while that may seem rather important to you, it's only a small part of one magazine staffer's much bigger job. So: If that person goes on vacation, chances are your submission will remain untouched until that person returns. Or if your magazine arrives in the middle of a deadline crunch, or during a personnel crisis, or when that one person has fallen behind in his or her other work, that may delay a quick response. Further, if there's a chance the magazine is interested in your piece, the query or manuscript might hang around a little longer until somebody makes a decision. Some ideas are borderline—and those are the toughest, since the editor's decision may rest on a combination of factors, like what else is in inventory, and whether it's worth investing in an article which may or may not see print. And if your manuscript or query had to wait for the first person to read it, and somehow managed to get past that first person, it then has to wait for the editor to read it—and so on. Remember, you're only one freelancer out of hundreds—all of whose queries and manuscripts usually converge onto one person. Three weeks may seem like forever when you're staring at an empty mailbox, but they fly by when you're faced with a growing stack of paper in a magazine's editorial offices.

"They rejected my idea, and four months later the same idea was used."

Depending upon how paranoid you are, you'd describe this as anything from plagiarism to fate. In all probability, the real explanation is somewhere between the two.

Because this is a recurring theme among freelancers, I've devoted an entire chapter to its discussion. For the moment, however, you can accept one conclusion: Magazines rarely steal. They only occasionally accidentally appropriate someone else's idea. Most often, it's a case of another writer's, not an editor's, coming up with your idea.

"They damaged (or lost) my manuscript."

Not unusual, and perfectly reasonable. We're dealing with *paper* here, not steel. That paper is in the magazine editorial department's possession for only a part of the time; the rest of the time it's in a mailbox, in the post office, on a train or plane, in a sack with other mail, in a mail deliverer's bag or tied up in a bundle. And when it arrives at a magazine, it's probably opened on a letter-opening machine. Then it reaches a human being, and human beings, too, have their failings. A human being may spill a cup of coffee. Or accidentally tear something. Or, in handling, the manuscript may become finger-smudged (especially if it was typed on erasable bond). Corners may become bent, pages creased. I don't understand how freelance writers can expect anything less.

Yes, you may have to retype a manuscript once or twice before it ends up sold. That's part of the game. It's not the magazine's fault that paper is perishable. But if you want to ensure yourself against some of the hazards, don't send your manuscript in a number ten envelope. Send it flat in a large envelope with a cardboard stiffener and a similar SASE. That eliminates the folding and unfolding of pages *and* the use of letter-opening machines which sometimes trim off the folded edge and leave gaps in the middle of manuscripts.

"They bought my story, paid me for it, but it never ran. I don't write just for the money; the bylines are important to a writer, and the subject matter deserves exposure."

Of course. You want to see your work in print, and the fact is that a lot of the articles sold *never* get there. You get the money, but that's all you get.

Unfortunately, that's the way it has to be. Magazines rarely know exactly how many pages they'll be able to devote to editorial matter—usually it depends entirely upon how much ad space is sold. Further, they never know when an assigned story may fall through, or when they'll have a 6300-word gap to fill. They *must* overstock; they *must* maintain an inventory of stories. And some of those stories will *never* see print.

When you come right down to it, that's their prerogative. Can you think of any product sold anywhere in the world in which the sale is contingent upon the buyer's being *required to use* the product?

But that brings us to another dilemma. You're very likely selling a one-time use of your writing. (Under the new copyright laws, the only way you can sell more than that is to sign something away in writing, like if you're agreeing that the work is *work for hire).* Are you selling first rights? If so, doesn't that mean that you have a legal obligation to wait until those first rights are used before attempting to resell the manuscript? I believe that it does, although there could ultimately be a statute of limitations on such an obligation. Consult your lawyer.

But look at the other side of it: No magazine buys an article without intending to use it, and not being able to do so is almost as painful to the magazine as it is to the writer, although for a different reason. The magazine has money invested, and in the publishing business today, with production costs and salaries constantly escalating, nobody can really afford to buy a story and not use it.

If it becomes apparent (to you) that your article is *not* going to be used, you can always try to buy it back. Chances are you can get it for less than half what you were originally paid—*if* the magazine really has no intention of using it—and perhaps you can sell it to another market. Remember, very often magazine philosophies change over a period of time; editors change; editorial direction changes. Sometimes a magazine will give you back your manuscript for the asking. (I remember a situation where *Esquire* sold *Boston Magazine* a story they hadn't used and weren't going to use—at one-fifth the price they paid for it.) If, on the other hand, the magazine refuses your offer, chances are they do indeed hope to use it.

"They've had my story for six months. They pay on publication. What do I have to do, wait two years to get my money?"

Yes—if you're lucky. Unless you have an established relationship with, not to mention great faith in, the magazine, selling an article to a market that pays on publication is like selling a bed to somebody and not requiring payment until they actually sleep on it. You probably wouldn't think of doing the latter, so why would you do the former? If you make the deal, it's your responsibility.

"They only paid me $100. I know somebody else who sold them and got $300."

The world is filled with inequities, but the above should hardly be blamed on the publication. You have to ask yourself *why* the other writer got $300. Maybe he or she has been around longer. Maybe your article wasn't as good, or didn't require as much work. At any rate, it isn't a one-way street. If you have qualms about the price, don't accept the assignment—or haggle for a larger sum.

"I did a story on speculation. They rejected it. I don't think it's fair that I don't get anything."

But it is, since you've agreed to do the story on speculation. They promised to look at it, nothing more. You knew that when you began writing. Needless to say, you'll never get rich operating this way.

On the other hand, you just might get a foot in the door. I know of no other way to do that more effectively than to write on speculation, since—from an editor's viewpoint—a bird in the hand is worth two in the bush. But if you strike out, you can hardly blame the magazine.

"I don't understand why I should get a kill fee. I said I would do the story for $600. After I submitted it, they said they didn't want it. Now I'm left with one-third the agreed-upon amount, but I negotiated for $600, not $200."

Somebody said this to *me* once when I paid a kill fee. Well, this is how it works: If a magazine finds a story unacceptable, there has to be an escape clause. There are plenty of purchases where the buyer knows exactly what he or she is buying—like a car or a watch or a typewriter—and it's understandable that the seller, in those cases, expects to get the full amount. Writing is different. There has to be a way out for the publication, because an article is not an article the way a rose is a rose—and a kill fee is the accepted method in the business. Again, look at it from the magazine's point of view: They end up paying $200 for nothing. The writer, at least, can resell the story elsewhere—which should be possible if it's as good as the writer thinks it is.

I haven't covered every possible vice of which magazines and their editors have been accused, but these are the most common. Being a freelancer is, I know, a tough life—but if you can try to see things from the point of view of the magazine, you'll find yourself understanding a lot more of what goes on behind the scenes. And, as my fellow editor pointed out in the restaurant that evening just before his brains fell into his glass, that understanding starts when you read the small print on the contents page of some magazines which says that the magazine cannot be responsible for unsolicited submissions. Well, they *mean* that—and that means that the risk is all yours the moment you toss something into the mail.

Now that you know—pour yourself a drink.

Chapter 13

The Purloined Manuscript

Barbara Lede Stet, a young lady who is wont to give me a lot of grief, came into my office the other day. On her shoulder was a chip.

"Boy, talk about ripped off," she said, waving a magazine in my face. "You people are all alike. I just picked up the latest copy of *True Exaggeration* and there's my story idea, big as life, that I sent them three months ago. Only *I* didn't get the assignment!"

"Tough break," I said, genuinely sympathetic.

"Tough break?" she screamed. "They ripped me *OFF!* How can you call it a tough break?"

* * *

I'll bet there isn't an editor who hasn't been accused of it at least once. Including me. An inexperienced young writer once sent me a query regarding a local musician. He wasn't any great shakes as a writer and we didn't want the story, but, not wanting to discourage him, I wrote back and gave him our reasons—as well as our regrets.

Not more than a couple of months later, I got a second letter in which he was accusing me of trying to steal his idea. He gave me notice that if we ran *any* article on the musician (who had, he said, been approached by a staffer from our magazine), he wanted to get paid the full normal rate for such an article, which he generously pegged at $400.

I knew we weren't doing an article on the musician, so I tried to find out just what was going on. It turned out that, in a quest for New Faces for an annual feature we ran, somebody had gone up to the musician and was going to write a total of two sentences about him—not to mention some 75 other people around town. No article. I then wrote an indignant letter to the writer, in which I allowed myself to wonder what kind of obnoxious heredity had caused his condition.

I've never stolen a story idea, nor do I know anybody who has. I do remember one editor who never answered queries and never sent back on-spec manuscripts and sometimes even forgot to pay authors, but he didn't last long; I'm also sure that there are guys out there in this field who *have* stolen, if only because it's not possible for any field of endeavor to exist without its share of rip-off artists. But, generally speaking, the world of magazine editors is filled with professionals who behave accordingly, and who police the field vigorously to keep out riffraff. I believe that the reports of stealing are greatly exaggerated.

Furthermore, I know how they come about.

First of all, there's no way to protect an idea. This not only means that a publication can use your idea, but that any other freelancer or writer can do the same; after all, the chances of your being the only person to come up with any one idea are pretty slim, assuming that the idea is viable, timely and of concern to the readers of any magazine. In other words, who says it's *your* idea?

For instance, say a writer suggests doing an article on a particular phase of Jimmy Carter's presidency. There are a lot of topics that are fair game there. But suppose the person who suggests doing an article on Carter's Middle East policies doesn't get the assignment—does that mean that the magazine, in eventually assigning the same topic to someone else, has stolen the idea? In other words, if a magazine turns down an idea from one writer, does that mean it can't, in all good conscience, entertain the same suggestion from another writer?

Obviously not: A good idea alone never won an assignment. Of course, ideas count—but the overwhelming reason why most freelance writers receive assignments from most markets is execution, not idea. There are writers I'd assign to write about almost anything, simply because they're so good—I'd know that anything they wrote would be appropriate, intelligent, and of value to readers. By the same token, there are good ideas I've rejected on the basis of a mediocre query—feeling, in essence, that while the idea was good, the writer was not going to handle it in a manner representative of the quality of the magazine.

In short, no magazine could function if it had to give a story assignment to the first person who suggested it. If that were the case, all a writer would have to do to sew up the field is make the most suggestions. But that's exactly where the problem lies. When someone gets turned down for an assignment, or submits a manuscript that is eventually rejected, he assumes that the magazine didn't want the *story*— and cries out in anger when the magazine lets someone else write the same, or a similar, story.

However, maybe it's *you*. Maybe the editor doesn't like the way you write, or considers you a pain in the neck to work with.

Well, that's a low blow. Right, it is. That's why those things are called *rejection* slips.

But any writer would have to admit that an editor has the right to feel that way. And no writer, if the situation were reversed, would feel impelled to purchase a piece of writing that he didn't like just to feel that he could still use the idea.

There are many ways that another writer may end up doing "your" article. And just so you'll understand that rip-offs are not as common as most bruised egos would like to think, here are a few of them.

First and most obvious—the magazine may already have someone working on the assignment. Things have a way of happening like that; there is a certain tide in the affairs of mortals that causes *Time* to put something on their cover the same time as *Newsweek*. Not just understandable things like the Sadat-Begin talks, but inexplicable things like singer Bruce Springsteen. And while you might say that the story you wanted to do about the little photographic gallery that just opened is not exactly national news, that doesn't mean that no one else has recognized its viability as a topic. There's competition out there— folks trying to snatch stories out from under your nose. But it's the *other writer* who's usually doing the snatching, and not the editor. (Maybe you're wondering why an editor wouldn't just say, "Gee, we're already doing that one." Often they do. But other times they'd rather not admit to having a particular story in the works for fear of Little You going to a competitive publication and telling them that you know for a fact that *True Exaggeration* is doing an article on such-and-such.)

Another thing: Sometimes you're too early. You might spot a trend long before it becomes one, and before anybody's ready to believe it. Two months later, when the trend just starts to move, somebody else comes in with a query and sells it.

Or maybe you wouldn't work on spec, but somebody else did. And sold it. Or maybe your query just wasn't enough to get the magazine to assign an article, whereas somebody else came in with a complete— though unsolicited—manuscript. You're not being ripped off; you're merely being usurped by someone who's hungrier.

Often, editors simply forget that they've even been approached. There's a considerable volume of mail that rolls into a magazine office in a single week, even at a small magazine. At the big ones, the numbers of queries and unsolicited manuscripts are probably up in the hundreds. Now who's gonna remember all that?

And most important, with that flood of ideas, who's presumptuous enough to think that he or she is the only one who could come up with any one particular concept? Apparently a lot of people do—despite the fact that there probably isn't anything really new under the sun; despite the fact that while somebody's inventing a portable electric nail-biter in Little Rock, somebody's probably also inventing the same thing in Fairbanks, and somebody else is doing it in Munich; despite the fact that stories, like inventions, just seem to have a time when they become ripe.

Despite all the above, *Writer's Digest,* which functions as a sort of clearing house for those kinds of complaints, has heard its share of horror stories, most recently from the guy who sent two ideas over a period of about six months to a national tabloid. First idea turned down; a few months later, it appears—a rather strange coincidence inasmuch as the subject was a small-town doctor. Next query, same writer, same publication—again, writer turned down. But this time the publication calls the subject on the phone and expresses an interest in profiling him. Now, that sounds suspicious.

What can you do? Complain—but complain to *Writer's Digest.* If a magazine *is* ripping you off, you're not the only one. If you *are* the only one, chances are paranoia is at work. But if *Writer's Digest* receives a lot of complaints about any one magazine, it will know that, at the very least, there's been a breakdown in communications between magazine and writer. Don't complain directly to the magazine; you may just end up alienating people who had no intention of cheating you.

Of course, even with all the stories, proof is difficult to come by. The old saying, "Where there's smoke, there's fire," is used only as a rationale for those who wish to jump to conclusions; the truth is that where there's smoke, there's smoke, period. If there's more than smoke, somebody has to be able to prove it.

And that's the bad news. After all, the fact that your article idea is nonfiction means that it's real and it exists outside your imagination—where others can get it. All you can do is your best—and depend on publications that will treat you fairly. Most of them will. Honest.

Chapter 14

How Much Can You Make?

I have a dream. It's probably the same dream you have, or at least similar to one of them, and it involves getting up in the morning, putting on a new pot of coffee, and relaxing by the window with a cup, watching the denizens of the office buildings trudge off into the snow toward their public transportation.

At about nine or so, I go, dressed in a pair of jeans and a comfortable pullover, to my typewriter, and I sit down and create magazine articles. For this, I earn well into six figures. Of course, I do occasional speaking, but that's charity.

I work three days a week at this.

Remember, I said it was a dream.

Let's face it. If I were going to say anything at all about potential earnings in the magazine field, I'd have started this chapter with You Too Can Earn Less Than a Trappist Monk in Your Spare Time—and Have More Aggravation Than You Get in Your 40-Hour-a-Week Job.

Most freelance magazine writers—were you to divide the number of hours they work into the amount of dollars they earn—probably don't make the minimum wage. In fact, when the American Society of Journalists and Authors polled their members a couple of years ago, the 500 established professionals turned up a median income of $10,000. The career is not designed for those who are —how shall I put it?—upwardly mobile.

So why do they do it? For lots of reasons, some logical, some nonsensical, but all of them good enough to keep freelancers writing. The reasons are easy to identify:

Fame. Advertising copywriting pays more than magazine writing. A good, not great, freelance copywriter with a couple of years' experience can make upwards of $30 an hour, and I know some who won't get out of bed for that. A *top* freelance copywriter in a major market—a city like Philadelphia, which is not even the top of the heap—can easily get around $50 an hour, and I know one who can do double that. But copywriters don't get bylines. They get paid, in a sense, for their anonymity. Magazine writers do exactly the opposite; they subsidize their own ego trips.

A Clear Conscience. Magazine writers generally sleep well, and if they don't it's probably because they're worried about money, not because they're ashamed of what they do for a living. On the contrary, they're proud. Most of their feedback is positive, and allows them to maintain a rather idealistic view of themselves as crusaders—an accolade they're unlikely to have to share with their advertising counterparts. In general, freelance nonfiction writers feel that they're the only trustworthy beings in an otherwise corrupt world, a view I am not inclined to share.

Artistic Poverty. They can wear simple (the only polite word to describe them) clothes and be moody, and everybody will understand: Obviously, they're entitled to, as geniuses suffering for their art. They can feel like part of the working class and be intellectuals at the same time. They can even believe they prefer it that way. They get no pressure to be "successful" on their friends' terms; freelance writers establish their own terms. But, of course, they can't eat them for dinner.

Hope. "I'm glad I didn't become a doctor," one freelance acquaintance told me. "As a doctor, I would've made maybe $100,000 a year. As it is, I'm making $17,000—but the sky's the limit." It's true. You can spend most of your life pulling down modest bucks annually from your writing efforts, but there's always that chance, that hope, that dream, that you're going to sell the article that will become the book that will become the movie that will net you a cool million. And no doctor can say that. Unless it's a doctor who decides to write a book.

That's it. That's *all* of it, unless you want to count the fact that writers *like* what they do. I *don't* count that, since there's no way really to know whether they might not enjoy being filthy rich oil barons or chairpersons of major corporations even more.

Given all the above, we ought to take a realistic look at how much money can be made writing freelance magazine articles, since you're obviously in it to stay—for a while, at least.

First, the ground rules. We're not going to discuss staff jobs on magazines, which are a whole different thing. Not that they're so terrific—but at least they culminate in regular paychecks. The upper-echelon jobs usually go to people who have either (1) worked their way up through the ranks, or (2) proved so excellent on a freelance basis that some magazine couldn't resist inviting them to join the staff. You can file (2) under *Hope,* mentioned previously.

Also, we're not talking about the famous one-in-a-million person who seems to write magazine articles and books with one hand tied behind his or her back.

No, we're talking about people I know personally who represent a part of that work force known as freelance writers—your competition. It doesn't matter that they're all from my part of the country and you may not be—as freelancers, you operate under the same economy: the gospel according to *Writer's Market.* All these people have written for *Philadelphia Magazine,* where I worked, as well as for national markets, and they're used to competing on a high level.

One of them—let's call him Manuel Pica—left Philadelphia some time ago to try his luck in the Big Apple. Pica is a competent, hardworking writer who can turn out salable stuff for major markets with relative ease. When Pica left Philly, he was making about $14,000 a year. In New York, when I last heard from him, he was doing about $20,000 a year, and he wouldn't accept an assignment for less than $600 no matter what. This means he was turning out a lot of stuff for highly competitive markets to make his yearly nut. I can assume that his rate of pay has kept pace with inflation, and noting certain increases in the magazine market since he left Philadelphia, I can peg his current income at about $26,000-28,000 annually. Without even talking to him.

Then there's a fairly well-known writer named Loretta Schwartz. She wrote and sold her first story to *Philadelphia Magazine* about four years ago for $250. Today she won't accept less than $1500 for an article, and usually gets considerably more, the result of her having polished her craft and having won an incredible list of national awards. In any other field, her award-winning performance would have made her a national celebrity. But the kind of articles that Schwartz writes, dealing with the problems of the underprivileged, take a lot of time and emotional commitment. So—despite all her achievements—in 1977, she earned only about $7500. Granted, her star rose considerably after that; she got more national exposure and has just signed a book contract. But if there ever was a case to illustrate that freelance magazine nonfiction is no way to get rich quick, Loretta Schwartz is it.

One writer I know, quite scholarly and with a good enough style to sell regularly to *Philadelphia Magazine* and several national markets, has found that she can make a living from various sources—including marketing. At the moment, she also has a few television scripts in the works and a chance to sell them in the neighborhood of $5000 each. But that neighborhood is in California, since any regular scriptwriter would have to be "on the spot" Out There to make copy revisions. And she's not ready to move. In 1977, she earned about $12,000, of which $5000 came from writing. In 1978, she more than doubled that—she took a job in marketing full-time. She still writes, but she's learned not to count on it.

Writers who can slant can often pull down dollars simply because of that talent. Carol Saline, an associate editor at *Philadelphia Magazine*, periodically hits magazines like *Family Circle, McCall's, Redbook* and so on. Saline freelances the way it makes sense—with a regular salaried position behind her—and this past year earned "about $5000" on the side, not counting what she'll make in her occasional speaking engagements at between $75 and $125 a shot. Further, she's featured regularly on a morning TV talk show for which she earns a few thousand, and she's working on a book—but despite it all, she says, "I'm going to have to work really hard to make much over $20,000." As for becoming a fulltime freelancer: "No way. It would take an awful lot of work to make more than $10,000 a year doing that. In fact, I used to find the effort involved in *selling* ideas took away from writing to the degree that most of my time was nonproductive."

It doesn't sound like there's much money to be made freelancing nonfiction? Good—you're learning. In fact, it's hard to imagine any field that requires such a combination of intelligence and talent for so little pay. But there are pluses as well as minuses.

National magazines, of course, keep their eyes on the competition in their search for talent—and a good story or two in the major markets can lead to several more assignments, especially where new magazines are concerned. When someone wants to start a magazine, you can bet its editorial staff will be poring through other magazines to find writers, although most of the new magazines pay very little. Magazine writers can also make extra money speaking to groups, as Saline and Schwartz do; by teaching at universities or workshops; or by branching out into more commercial areas. (If you can write a magazine article, chances are you can write the introduction to an annual report.)

But without a hot book, or a solid foundation like a staff slot, a high-paying regular column or books, the money will never be *big* money.

In early 1978, *Time* magazine ran an article about the freelance market. Its title, "Grub Street Revisited," gives some indication of what's to come, but it's there in the second paragraph anyway: ". . . magazine writing today has become the slum of journalism—overcrowded, underpaid, littered with rejection slips. . . ."

Time went on to list some of the largest-circulation magazines, including *TV Guide, Reader's Digest, National Geographic, Woman's Day, Family Circle, Better Homes and Gardens, McCall's, Ladies' Home Journal, Good Housekeeping* and *Playboy,* just as I had in my own column in *Writer's Digest* a few months before, using my own selection which included some of those they included. *Time* estimated the going average payment rates in each market, coming up with $2350 for the median article.

Time was being optimistic, however. Using *Writer's Market* and information supplied by the magazines themselves (and reading between the lines in the cases of those that skirted the issue), I make the figure about $1835 per article *at most*—and these are, of course, some of the best-paying markets in the country.

What is really depressing about all this is the arithmetic. Say you can turn out, on assignment, one very good feature-length article and one less ambitious piece each month (that's a reasonable expectation; most writers can do more). Now say you're lucky enough and skilled enough to sell one story a month to one of these top-paying markets— at a monthly rate of $1835. Any writer working today would have to agree that this would be an astounding performance. And say you can knock out a less ambitious article as well each month for $250 average. Okay? You've written a total of 24 articles, sold to the toughest markets in the country every month of the year, and are undoubtedly one of the country's best nonfiction article writers. What do you have?

You have about $25,000 a year. That's all. And if for some reason the *Reader's Digest* assignment, for instance, falls through, you have $3000 less.

Keep your job and write on the side. Take it from me. I was the guy who did the buying, and *nobody* counted on me to pay the rent.

Chapter 15

Understanding the Business

One of the toughest things to face in *any* business—forget writing for a minute—is that the more you learn about it, the easier it becomes to despise it. (I could have said, "Familiarity breeds contempt," but somebody already did.) Anything—*anything*—loses its purity and glamour up close. Celebrities become ordinary people, knights in shining armor become husbands, and careers become jobs.

That's how it is with magazine journalism: Anything held *that* high is doomed to disappoint. To writers trying to break in—and the field is littered with corpses of those who tried and lost—magazine nonfiction writing glows like a streetlight on a winter night: pure, clear, unpolluted. And while all this glowing is going on, there is a soundtrack, too—the words of the First Amendment. Only after considerable exposure does one realize that the glow is an illusion, having more to do with climate than with the absence or presence of pollution, and that the First Amendment is being sung to the tune of "That's Entertainment."

In other words, we all live in constant fear that what was once our impossible dream may eventually turn into just another way to pay the mortgage.

Nevertheless, you want to do something worthwhile with your life; writing seems to be more satisfying than selling shoes (it *is*); you hope that someday you'll *be* intimately involved enough to become disillusioned. If that's the case, you may have to get rid of some of those stars in your eyes—because if you're thinking of magazine journalism solely in terms of the lofty ideals you expect from it, that may be just what's keeping you from making it. In other words, you may be so intimidated by what you *think* magazine journalism is that you yourself are putting it out of your own reach.

The magazine business is a *business*.

The business is, first of all, selling ads. There's hardly a magazine that can exist without doing that; the ads are where the profits come from. Put another way, the freelancer can sell only when the magazine's advertising sales department is selling. Just about every magazine follows a formula: So many ad pages allow so many pages of editorial matter. It's *not* the other way around.

Where I worked, for example, the usual percentage was about 40 percent editorial and 60 percent advertising. That's how the pages broke down. I remember seeing an issue of another magazine, a widely known and excellent one, which seemed to contain more than a normal amount of editorial matter. When I checked it out, it was 65 percent editorial, 35 percent advertising. At the time, I figured they had to be losing money. They were.

Magazines in trouble usually aren't hard to spot. They're something like terminal cancer victims. First they lose weight, then they die. When *New Times* went under, it was hard to be surprised.

Just how much advertising a magazine sells determines how much it can spend. It determines how much a staff can earn as well as what the rates are that it will pay to freelancers. (That's one reason why major national magazines can afford to pay more—their ad rates are so much higher.) Some people think that it works the other way: that you put out the best product you can, sell however many ads you can, and some kind of journalistic magic will do the rest; people will buy you on the newsstand, you'll get new subscribers, and all that money rolling in will put you over the top.

Not true. Magazines can't count on magazine sales to pay the bills. At the newsstand, the distributor takes his cut; the newsstand operator takes his; and there's no way of telling how many copies will actually sell; with luck, the magazine might break even on the raw cost of printing the magazine it sells on the stand. As for new subscribers—they *cost.* Usually they come on at a drastically reduced rate to begin with, and for that the magazine may have to deliver their copies at a loss. In fact, many a magazine has gotten itself into trouble by getting too many subscribers too fast. *

For the magazine, it's a careful balancing act. The attractiveness of a particular magazine as an advertising medium—beyond the specific audience that it reaches, of course—lies in part in something called *cost per thousand.* It's a simple ratio: the cost of the advertisement over the number of readers who read the magazine. For a magazine to sell advertising competitively, it has to deliver a certain number of

---

*This doesn't apply to every magazine. There are exceptions—magazines with tremendous circulations that do not have to depend upon advertising. *Hustler,* at its peak, was profitable without advertising. When you start selling a couple of million magazines on the newsstand at over two bucks apiece, you may be able to make it on newsstand sales alone. The advertising just makes you richer. Indeed, *Hustler* publisher Larry Flynt's 1976 net was $20 million, two-thirds of it from the magazine.

readers, at a certain price, to its advertisers. If readership starts to slip—for instance, if subscribers don't renew—the magazine has to go out and "buy" new readership to meet its guaranteed circulation. That is, it has to use promotional techniques like direct mail to sell new subscriptions. This in itself is a very costly process, and if the magazine gets more response than it expects, it loses money on the production and delivery of those additional subscriptions until such time as it can raise its ad rates to compensate for them. After all, a magazine can't raise its rates every time it needs a little extra money. This is precisely the situation in which ex-*New York* publisher Clay Felker found himself when he launched *New West*—his reliance on unprofitable, cut-rate subscriptions turned out to be his major expense.

But wait. Aren't we supposed to be talking about nonfiction here? Where does the writer come in?

If we keep looking at this from the financial end, the writer is a sort of necessary evil. And even if you resent the word *evil,* the important word is *necessary.* You have one thing going for you, and every publisher knows it: the readers. If the magazine doesn't give its readership something worth reading, both subscriptions and newsstand sales will suffer. In this respect, the writer survives through a symbiotic relationship. The publisher may hold some pretty strong cards, but without writers, he can't play the game. Most publishers constantly fight a war they dare not win.

In fact, Billy Jean King's magazine, *Womensports,* proved that. In a fracas involving some unkind words over a cosmetic advertiser in the magazine—words which appeared in the magazine's editorial matter—the magazine insisted that the editorial staff write something nice about the product. The staff refused and, given an ultimatum, the editor walked out. The magazine was never the same after that.

By explaining some of the business side of the magazine field, I hope to clarify your role a little—and, as I said, take some of the stars out of your eyes. Maybe even diminish your idea of your own task slightly. You're not expected to write the Great American Exposé or a piece of prose that will try the intellectual capabilities of your readers. You're supposed to write something which will help the magazine keep and hopefully increase its audience by giving the readers something *they* want. And even if you are writing the Great American Expose, better keep in mind that nonfiction magazine writing is, above all, entertainment.

One thing that a magazine looks for—even though its editor may not care for the procedure—is an article it can *sell against.* A story about CB radio, for instance, might easily attract advertisers who sell CB units. Many service pieces—articles created specifically to help the reader—offer opportunities to both the editorial staff and the sales department—and you, of course, if you can write them. For some magazines, these articles are staples—they'd go under without them. (See Chapter 30 of this book.)

Some magazines also depend upon peripheral sales to put them into the black. *Writer's Digest,* for instance, sells books, tapes and pamphlets. The new *Saturday Evening Post* (which is, unfortunately, nothing like the great magazine it used to be) sells countless products of its own issue; the bulk of the advertising in the *Post* is its own.

And if you're still not convinced that magazines aren't 100 percent pure, you might ask yourself why some of them put out what is supposed to be a May issue, for instance, in early April. There are two reasons: (1) psychologically, you think you're buying something much more current, and (2) it allows them more time on the newsstand without appearing "stale"—an honest magazine marketer who put out the May issue on May 1 would lose half the month of April on the newsstand *and* half the month of May—because around the middle of May, other magazines would have their June issues on the stand.

In short, magazines—to be understood—must be understood as business ventures. The freelance journalist can't exist in a vacuum. At its best, magazine writing can expose new ideas and create positive social change. At its least—and this is where most magazine journalism is—it simply entertains readers for a few minutes a month, perhaps providing a few insights and some food for thought. As a freelancer, your best shots are in the latter category; it usually takes time and experience and credentials to get to the former. Using a metaphor from another creative field, stop thinking of yourself as Laurence Olivier and start thinking of yourself as Olivia Newton-John. *If you're in it to sell,* stop concentrating on what *you'd* like to sell and start thinking about what *magazines* are likely to buy.

And what's that? Well, what makes magazines sell?

New trends, new fads, new concepts—and any magazine would rather be in the vanguard, even if controversial.

Reader service pieces or features with new product angles—particularly those around which advertising can be sold.

Articles that are fast reads, punchy and unusual. (I once bought one, a very short piece, written by a guy who had changed his name. He wrote a how-to on that subject.)

And, considering how important covers are, articles that might lend themselves to eye-catching cover lines.

All of this may seem bitter medicine, and sometimes I wish there were less commercialism associated with magazine journalism—and with Christmas, that matter. But it's pointless to pretend that things are different, and recognition of how things *really* work can provide valuable little clues regarding what you might be able to sell, as well as give you the confidence to sell it.

And don't get me wrong. There are standards. *New York* magazine does a good job despite—and in some ways, *because* of—its obvious commercialism. A good editor will never run anything that isn't of genuine interest and value to his readers, and the best of them aren't afraid to lose an advertiser here and there for a worthwhile article. Only a bush-league editor or publisher could be convinced to trade away long-range journalistic integrity for short-range economic benefits.

The other variable is you, the writer. This book is here to help you sell your product—but you're the manufacturer. You determine quality. All the "givens" of the business side of magazines can't stop you from deciding what kind of product you want to byline. You might decide to produce something that can be sold cheaply and often, or something that takes a little longer to produce but brings a higher price. Whichever you decide, insist on a certain level of quality regardless of price or frequency of sale. Remember, the old-time craftsman, who knew there was only one way to do the job right, is even more respected in today's world of mass production.

Chapter 16

The Necessary Freelancer

If you've been reading this book in order, chapter by chapter, you've already read that a freelance nonfiction writer who miraculously sold to the top-paying dozen markets in the country in as many months—and who also managed to sell one shorter piece each month for $250—might not earn $25,000 a year. All that work, all that talent—and you still might end up making less than somebody in a semi-skilled trade, even though your performance would make you a superstar among writers.

This doesn't happen because you don't want money. It happens because magazines are fairly tight when it comes to freelancers—and because freelancers are, for the most part, notoriously bad businesspeople. The fact is that if you're good—and you can prove it once or twice to a magazine— you ought to find yourself getting a good bit more than the minimum that most markets quote. But most freelancers are so hard up for the byline that many of them will practically give their stuff away.

As we've said, even at low rates, there are positive aspects to freelance writing, one of them being that you're doing something you really *like* to do instead of performing some mindless, numbing production-line feat. And hope springs eternal: Someday, you just might write the magazine article that becomes the book that becomes the movie that moves you and your family into a nice little place in Beverly Hills.

While you're not holding your breath waiting for that to happen, maybe it would be a good idea for me to rebuild your enthusiasm a bit—give you some kind of honest appraisal that shows exactly where you fit in, how important you are, and how to make the most of it.

First, the bad news. Almost all nonfiction markets are freelancers; your *Writer's Market* shows that. But almost all these markets depend more heavily on staff writing; freelancers are definitely in second place, tolerated because they're useful. Almost any small magazine—even a limited special-interest or regional magazine—could afford to pay well over $1000 for each good-sized article it bought, *if* it could exist exclusively on the work of freelancers. If it had no staff at all, in other words, the magazine could pay those rates and actually end up *saving* money.

Well, then, why don't magazines do just that? There are a number of reasons, all of which affect you whether or not they apply to you personally.

When a publication deals with a freelancer, any editor will tell you, here's what it's up against:

• The end product, unless it comes from a regular contributor, is unpredictable. The magazine won't know, until late in the game, what it's going to get. This is particularly true with a first-time writer.

• The magazine may *never* get its story. Maybe the writer will decide it's not paying enough, or that it just isn't his kind of story, or that maybe something better will come along. If the same assignment goes to a staffer, whose value is his or her dependability, the magazine knows with certainty that it will get the article *how* and *when* it wants it. Of course, this is not to say that freelancers generally disappoint; lapsed assignments are not that common. But it does happen, and it's happened many times to every editor.

• The magazine takes a chance where professionalism is concerned—especially when it's dealing with someone with whom it's not terribly familiar. How can it be certain that every fact has been carefully checked, that every quote is accurate? How willing should any magazine be to put its trust in the veracity of a virtual stranger? And if any legal problem should arise, how predictable is this person's ability to handle himself or herself in court? In other words, when the going gets tough, how does the magazine know that you can meet the challenge?

• There is a general lack of control. When a writer is on staff, the magazine can monitor the work as it progresses, get status reports, confer easily. Not so with freelancers. They can be tough to track down, and telephone or letter communication is not nearly as effective as face-to-face contact.

• Procedures and personnel must be set up to handle freelance writers—like someone to read manuscripts and answer queries and communicate with the writers. A lot of this time is, in terms of generating a usable end product, wasted; most manuscripts *aren't* bought; most queries *aren't* assigned.

• Spec assignments—often necessary for a magazine to find out if a writer can both write and handle the work appropriately—can result in large numbers of freelancers' simultaneously claiming to be working on stories for the magazine. There probably isn't a good-sized magazine anywhere that hasn't run into some definite problems because of this.

• The use of freelance writers can result in the magazine's losing some of its specialness—since the same freelancers, if they expect to eat, are also selling their work to competing magazines. It doesn't exactly thrill an editor to see his competition, particularly in a local market, featuring the same bylines.

Obviously, these drawbacks can't be all that bad, because magazines *do* continue to use freelancers. They have their reasons, too, and knowing them can actually help you define your role in dealing with various publications, and perhaps make you more successful at it. The fact is, magazines would hate to have to get along without you. Here's the good news:

• You cost less than their own staff writers. A *lot* less. Now, that sounds like an advantage to them but a disadvantage to you— however, it's a big reason why you get the work in the first place. To keep somebody on staff requires paying a salary, providing fringe benefits like hospitalization and vacation, giving raises, paying social security, etc. When a magazine pays you, you get a flat rate. It's clean. And easy. So when a publication finds a freelancer who's both dependable and writes well, that person is worth as much in his or her own way as any staffer, and no magazine is about to let such a writer disappear without a fight. If you're good, really good, try to negotiate gradual raises for yourself as you go along. Since you didn't get top dollar when you started (you can count on it), your value should increase as you prove your worth. Some magazines will give you increases without being asked. Others have to be nudged a bit. If they balk, but you know that they'd hate to lose you, just remind them how lucky they are that you don't work for them full-time.

• A magazine that uses dependable freelancers has built-in flexibility—a battery of experts ready to jump in when needed. Make sure you get your stories in on time; establish a reputation for dependability—so if a special project turns up, or if a staff-written story falls through, the publication will remember that you're waiting in the wings

• You have ideas that the magazine doesn't have. After all, a magazine staff doesn't change much; it's the same group of people on a continuing basis. You're not one of them. Because you don't spend all your time in the office, you have exposure that can lead to stories the magazine hasn't thought of. Also because you're out in the "real world" as opposed to the ivory tower of the editorial office, you can write first-person articles from actual experiences—experiences that staffers don't often have. It used to amaze me how few ideas I'd get— or more importantly, how uninspired I'd feel—just sitting around the office. But as soon as I'd get out on the street, or visited a store in which I hadn't been before, or did something different on my lunch hour, I'd bump into a story. That's why I consider a change of environment the number-one condition necessary for creativity: You can't respond unless you have something to which to respond.

• Your style is individual. So is your point of view. Freelancers keep magazines from getting stale. Staffers often develop tones, if not styles, similar to one another. You won't.

• While writing on spec isn't the most profitable nor most businesslike way to work, the freelancer who does it is an asset to any publication, since the magazine doesn't have to invest until the product is proven usable. If you're good, you'll sell whether you have a definite assignment or not—and at the very least you'll get your foot in the door.

I've had two experiences with writers who generally wrote on speculation. One was a newspaper editor from a small Pennsylvania town. I never laid eyes on him, but he was really good—and every once in a while he'd drop a manuscript to me. I rejected him only once. The other experience was a fellow who was employed in the public relations department of a large Philadelphia firm. Once in a while he would query before writing, but mostly e wrote what was on his mind; he'd sit down at the typewriter and bang it out and put it into the mail. I got it fresh, hot off his typewriter, and I bought most of it. What was amazing was that I edited this particular writer less than any other I can think of. I'd change maybe a half dozen words per manuscript.

• Magazines discover "new" talent when they use freelance writers. In fact, some magazines ultimately recruit their staffers from their freelancers. If you're looking for a staff job, freelancing is a great way of establishing your credentials and a track record that could make you appear desirable. You've probably heard lots of stories about kids who went from college to editorships at major magazines, or about housewives who emerged right into high-visibility publishing jobs. Don't believe them. Luck plays a part—nobody can knock being in the right place at the right time—but everything has its price, and the price of making it in this field is hard work and paying dues. However, guts help; for some reason, editors like that lean and hungry look.

• If you have an area of expertise—like business or science—you'll be a real asset to some publications. Few magazines can afford to keep such specialists on their staffs full-time, so you're probably better at what *you* do best than anybody presently on a staff—even if the staffers are better all-around writers. I've had freelancers I would think of for a variety of subjects: medicine, business, science and so on. You'd be amazed how far something as seemingly useless as college chemistry can take you.

Now that you know a magazine's pros and cons regarding the likes of you, the task becomes easier. What's required is that you become 100 percent a professional—get your article in on time (or early, even better); never take an assignment that's over your head; keep clear, concise notes and records of your research and interviews; make yourself accessible to the magazine throughout the course of an assignment, touching base occasionally if you're not easily reachable; and generally educate the editors to your strong points.

Remember, you're selling yourself. This is no time to be modest. But don't exaggerate either. Don't oversell. As the magazine begins to realize that you're a vital resource, you should make it clear just *why* you're as good as you are: You work hard, are responsible, and you do things and take pains other writers don't. If you describe your function carefully, punctuated with explanations like, "I didn't go just to source A to do this, but I went also to sources B and C to double-check and confirm the statistics," it's going to become clear why you're worth some extra money. You'll have to chip away gradually, because you're dealing not just with a tight-fisted editor but with an entire financial structure. But you can win.

One argument, however, always fails. That's when the writer says to the editor, "As far as I can see, you make a pretty good profit around here. I think you can afford to pay me more." Don't try to get higher pay just because you think the magazine has plenty of money; you have no way of knowing what the actual profits are, or how production costs have escalated. Try to get the money based on your own ability. *Deserve* it, *prove* that you deserve it—and then, if necessary, *ask* for it.

Chapter 17

Beyond the First Amendment

I once gave a freelance writer—let's call her Mary Smith—an assignment to look into a particular industry which deals in consumer services. This industry is widely thought of as having a few responsible practitioners and a lot of rip-off artists; the article was supposed to explain the differences and provide guidelines for the consumer, as well as make a thorough examination as to how the con artists within the field operate. The writer came in with a 30-page manuscript, the first five pages of which were a scathing indictment of the entire industry, packed with statements that would have had us libeling just about every business we would have named thereafter in the article. There was not even a pretense at fairness. We sent the story back for a rewrite—a surprise to Smith, since she thought she was going to win a national journalism award.

When Mary Smith returned with a somewhat modified version, we all sat down with a lawyer and went over her manuscript. During our meeting, Smith showed an appalling lack of understanding about (1) her responsibility as a member of the press, (2) the way businesses operate, and (3) what kind of evidence is required in order to make potentially damaging statements. If that wasn't enough, she treated the lawyer as an adversary. It was almost as if she viewed her role as a "journalist" to be beyond reproach, a game played by people who needed nothing more than writing ability as license to destroy businesses and reputations. Despite all that, we eventually ended up with a good, well-documented story—but we were so nervous about the lack of professionalism on the part of the writer, we made a note then and there not to assign her ever again.

In short, the facts are important—but they aren't everything.

Most professions have a code of behavior. In many cases that code is precise to the point of being written down and modified time and again. But even where such a written code exists, there may be differences of opinion regarding interpretation and implementation of that code. Journalism has no such code. It does have an unwritten one of sorts, and it is guided to some extent by the libel laws, but journalists must still be their own watchdogs—because it is easy to be unfair without being libelous and without being liable. In journalism, what is written is often a matter of opinion, not a fact, and it is too often colored by variations in the way that language is used.

For example, suppose the subject of your article is, to be blunt, a physically ugly person who happens to be a plastic surgeon. Does the journalist assume that the choice of profession is partly due to the subject's physical appearance, and that the physical appearance is then integral to, and properly included in, the article? Or that the surgeon hasn't altered his own appearance, and therefore the ugliness can't bother him all that much, and therefore the physical appearance has no place in the article? The answer, if there is one, is probably that the better journalist would assume *nothing,* and so the fact of the surgeon's physical appearance, while it could probably be included in a nonlibelous manner, would stay out. It is less a matter of law than of conscientious professional behavior.

Naturally, to create a *real* code would be a task of mammoth proportions, and might well be a bad idea, considering the propensity that rules have for limiting individual freedom—but the concept does provide a good basis for exploring just what is expected of writers.

The power of the press is formidable, so much so that between two people alone—an editor and a writer—hundreds of thousands of people can be led to conclusions regarding just about anything. If that power is overwhelming, so is the responsibility. That's why people anticipate, in the time-honored tradition, that a writer will be *objective.*

But time-honored or not, that expectation is silly. It is not so silly in terms of just-breaking news, but it is in almost every other case. If a writer is sent out to look into the storm-window business, for example, it is impossible for him to do so without certain preconceptions. If he believed that all storm-window sales organizations were perfectly honest, he probably wouldn't be going out to do the story. He knows, without question, that he is supposed to find out who the crooks are, and how they operate. It's implicit in the assignment. The same is true for just about any other investigative assignment a writer is likely to get—as soon as there is a slant, objectivity is impossible. If that weren't enough, writer A will be different from writer B, and so will their respective interpretations of the "truth." All that can be expected is an attempt at balance—to give the fairest hearing to both sides.

So without objectivity, we're left with the next best thing: subjectivity—or, in another word, judgment.

I remember a situation not long ago where we asked a freelancer—

call him John Doe—to write an article about a politician. He did, and handed it in. It was a perfectly thorough, well-balanced piece, but the writer avoided concluding anything—despite the fact that certain conclusions were staring him in the face. He was attempting to be objective, and consequently the article contained no insights—it went nowhere. We, on the other hand, wanted him to be somewhat subjective, to evaluate the situation for us; we had enough faith in his political expertise to know that he could draw some responsible conclusions about the politician who was the focus of the article, and we had enough faith in our readers to know that they would recognize opinion when they saw it, and would therefore come to their own conclusions. Doe did some rewriting, and when it was done, the politician emerged looking pretty good—better than we had anticipated. We left it at that; it was as close to the truth as we were going to get. We had explored not just facts, but the person behind them—and we found, given the politician's circumstances, that we could understand his motivations, and concluded that he was doing a reasonably decent job in view of them. Subjectivity had served us, and the politician, better than objectivity ever could have. But recognizing this, we also recognized that just as objectivity is no more than a series of facts with no attempt to interpret them, it is still worth more than subjectivity without knowledge.

Our first writer, Mary Smith, started out seeing things in terms of black and white—no grays—and so she indicted virtually every business in a certain field of endeavor. John Doe chose grays; he saw neither black nor white. In the human experience, there are gradations ranging from pure white to solid black; people are never as identifiable as the goodies and the baddies in B westerns. Yet, journalists too often make sweeping generalizations because of incomplete examination, or fail to make them out of fear. The source of both of these errors is usually a basic lack of information.

So maybe that should be a part of our code. If you're going to write about something, *know your subject.* Too often, writers naively approach businessmen (particularly on the corporate level) as exploiters, politicians as implicitly corrupt. Anytime you're seeing things in those terms, back off and squint a little—try to see where the grey areas turn into white and where they turn into black.

Not that I'm knocking what you'd call *gut feeling.* It can be a good barometer when you're onto something, but there are, as the saying goes, two sides to every story. If you're doing an article which takes a particular point of view, you have an obligation to check out the other side. First of all, it helps you insure that you have your facts straight. Second, it provides balance and builds credibility. No two people on opposing sides of any issue feel the same about it, and rarely can they sympathize with one another. Depending upon whom you listen to, you could be moved in one or another direction. Your job in providing a fairly complete, comprehensive picture for the reader, however, is to get both sides. This is probably the toughest part of our unwritten code—for a journalist, having been so indoctrinated that he has assigned a protagonist-identification to those on one side of his story, to come full circle and be willing to give the other side the full benefit of the doubt. I have rarely seen this happen; many journalists, like people who find lumps, prefer to ignore the suspicious little growth and hope it will go away.

Here's a good real-life example of why this is important. A freelance writer was doing an article about a prisoner. From the outset, perhaps because the prisoner was so atypical and wrote such convincing, intelligent letters, the writer was sold on his innocence. When she turned her manuscript in, it did indeed look as if the fellow sitting behind bars had been wrongly accused and convicted. We were, however, skeptical, not just because a jury of 12 people had found enough on which to base a conviction, but because writers have a tendency to *want* just that sort of thing to happen; when you have a convicted prisoner who turns out to be guilty, you don't really have much of a story.

So we had her go out and check the *other* side of the story—the prosecuting attorney, the detectives involved in the arrest. This time, our writer came away convinced that the prisoner might well have been guilty of the crime (of course, there was still no way to be sure), and a pretty good story bit the dust.

Another thing: Every story starts somewhere. Some pieces may originate with a tip—a phone call or a letter to you or to an editor who will then assign you to check the story out. The tipster may sound convincing, and you'll want that story so bad you can taste it. But rarely will such a story come your way for 100 percent altruistic reasons. Often, it's a case of somebody's having an ax to grind. So you have to ask yourself why the tipster called in the first place. It may jeopardize your story, but it's part of that unwritten code.

Somebody may call offering certain sordid details regarding the operation of a business. Scratch the surface and you'll probably find a disgruntled employee or ex-employee. Or maybe a dissatisfied customer or a competitor.

Or somebody may call and say that you should do an article on the corruption inside some governmental bureau. He may tell you he's just a well-meaning citizen who wants to see clean government—and he may well be—but he might also be someone who's had problems with that particular bureau.

A couple of years ago a narcotics dealer came to me and offered to spill everything he knew about the dope traffic in this country—names, places, the works. He didn't want any money. He didn't, in fact, seem to want anything, and that made me nervous. In the course of conversation, we found out that he was soon coming up for trial, and our guess was that he hoped the publicity resulting from a magazine article would get him a change of venue or, at least, a "good citizen" public image.

Does it make a difference? Isn't the story the important thing? Yes—and no. It depends entirely upon how much you can believe and how much you can use. You'll have to find out, first of all, whether your informant does have an ax to grind, and you'll have to determine just how much this might affect what he tells you. And you'll also have to consider that eventually somebody will point out, for instance, that your main source for the article was a guy who got fired from his job; and that has to cast some doubt on the credibility of the article you're doing about his former place of employment. This doesn't mean you shouldn't do the story. It simply means that you must be doubly careful to check the facts on both ends. You owe at least that much to all concerned.

The only way to protect yourself from being used by a source is to check *other* sources, talk to *other* people, for corroboration. If you can get the same information from some less impeachable sources, and if you can document it, you're on safer ground. It's not as difficult as it sounds; almost anybody who turns you onto a story will usually be able to lead you to others who can offer additional information. If your informant can't do that, watch out—he may be the *only* one who's seeing the demons.

There will be, in addition, certain obligations that you incur with your sources, and any writer's code of conduct should include a healthy respect for those without whom the story could not have been written. Take the source who wishes to remain anonymous. Should you provide him with that anonymity? Yes, if you get the info on that basis. It's a matter of integrity—and besides, if you blow his cover, you blow your reputation. You're in a position of trust at this point, and you might just as well be a priest or a psychiatrist.

But there's only so much you can do. Laws vary from state to state, and recent court decisions have made it clear that it isn't always possible for a journalist to give unqualified protection to a source— unless that journalist is willing to go to jail rather than divulge it. That's the bottom line: They can put you away, unless your state provides a fairly ironclad shield law that offers protection to sources. If you're not willing to go to jail, you can't promise *absolutely* that your informant won't be identified. You can, of course, indicate that the chances are extremely slim that he'll ever be identified, but you can't *guarantee* protection, despite the fact that few journalists have heard the steel doors clang shut behind them and that few issues are really worth a court's taking a case that far.

Necessity's being the mother of invention, there *is* a way to protect your sources—and under certain circumstances, it might be the *only* way to do a story.

That way is, simply, not to know too much. I know somebody who once did a story just that way; he got a tip regarding a prostitution racket. Since he considered prostitution a relatively harmless crime and realized that the police would make only a token effort at investigating him as a result of his article, he told the tipster that he didn't even want to know his name. He arranged to meet the guy at a bar, avoided watching the route they took to get to the prostitute's house, and told the prostitute he didn't want to know her name. Later, when questioned by the police, he told them everything he knew—*everything*. It wasn't much; they were with him for less than five minutes.

How you feel aeout this comes down to what you think is the lesser evil. I know only that he got the story and protected his source without commiting perjury or going to jail—and if you think any run-of-the-mill article is worth doing either of those things for, you should have your head examined before you type another word.

In another situation, I had an opportunity to buy an article from a Philadelphia police officer about the behind-the-scenes details of a particular situation which got a lot of local press. Immediately, knowing that he could lose his job if his identity were discovered, I gave him a code name—and never used any other name in relation to him. We kept our transactions as infrequent as possible, and I made it a point to know as little as possible about him. Not long ago, I purchased another article from him, under his pen name, which is the only way that I know him. If I had to produce him in court for any reason, I simply couldn't; I wouldn't know how to go about finding him. He is as protected as anyone could be.

Another rule deals with off-the-record quotes. If someone gives you some information "off the record," you have an obligation not to use that information in your story. You may be able—with the permission of the person being interviewed—to use the quote without attributing it, like, "A source close to the governor revealed. . . ." But sometimes the nature of the quote itself will identify the source, so be careful. Further, as mentioned elsewhere in this book, not everyone knows—or agrees on—the definition of "off the record." Before you proceed, make sure that both you and your informant are talking about the same thing.

Under these circumstances, you may wonder why an off-the-record quote is of any value at all. It's valuable because it can lead you places where you might not otherwise have gone. (Remember the secret contact, "Deep Throat," in *All the President's Men.*)

By the same token, there may be a time when your interviewee allows you to quote him on the condition that he can see the final-typed version of your article. If you make a deal like that, you're duty-bound to honor it. If you have no intention of honoring it, don't make it. (Sometimes, to obtain an interview from a reluctant witness, it will be sufficient to promise that you will let him hear the quotes of his that you'll be using. There's nothing wrong with doing that, and it can't compromise your final product—unless he insists on revising his quotes, which then becomes a matter for your discretion.)

If there is no written code, perhaps it's because there can't be. The issues are too complex. Journalism must be its own watchdog. As a profession, I think it does a good job of policing itself.

As for you, the writer: You have the power of the press and the protection of the First Amendment. Your sources have nothing but your word. Betray them and you betray yourself. This may be difficult to remember when, someday, you have to weigh the public's right to know against the promise of keeping something off the record. Do you keep the promise and keep private that which you *know* should be made public? By now, you should know the answer.

Needless to say, it can be a very tough business.

Chapter 18

Reading Them Their Rights

Years ago, the *Miranda* decision changed the American system of jurisprudence. You couldn't, the Supreme Court said, ask a person any potentially incriminating questions unless the person knew that his answers could be used against him. He had, in fact, the right to remain silent.

The basis for this was not a matter of fair play, but the Fifth Amendment of the Constitution. The key phrase is, ". . . nor shall (any person) be compelled in any criminal case to be a witness against himself. . . ." And while *Miranda* does tend to hamper the law enforcement authorities in some respects, it's apparently worth it; the old rubber hose just ain't what it used to be. Of course, this decision has the same Achilles heel as yet another judicial premise, the one that says a person is innocent until proven guilty; suffice it to say that we often *assume* guilt when a person is merely accused, and we're even surer of that guilt when somebody takes the Fifth. But not officially, because the accused has a right to know in what way information that he willingly supplies may be used against him.

Maybe there should be a *Miranda* decision for the press, too. There isn't. You can go up to anybody, ask him any question, and then, with few exceptions, print his answer. You can even *selectively* print *a part of* his answer. You can, in short, make a person appear intelligent or stupid, straightforward or evasive, innocent or guilty—depending upon the context in which the quotation is used. For proof, just look at the term "no comment." If taken at its face value, it shouldn't be used at all. And yet, it's *often* used in a particular context that may load it with implications:

> *"Mr. Jones, the district attorney is saying that you murdered your wife. Is that true?"*
> *"No comment."*

For the most part, people being interviewed by the press would be better served by simply ignoring the interviewer completely than by saying, "No comment."

Why isn't the press bound by its own version of *Miranda?* There are many reasons, two of which stand out. First, the person being questioned by a writer or reporter is not testifying in a court of law; even if a person should admit, under such circumstances, having committed a crime, and even if that admission should appear in print, the readers cannot hand down a sentence, nor can the law use that admission to prove guilt. In fact, the quote conceivably couldn't be used in court at all, since the person had not been warned of his right regarding self-incrimination prior to making the statement, and also had not made the statement under oath. Second, the press itself has a basic constitutional freedom which, in case after case, has been given the benefit of the doubt. The freedom of the press, guaranteed by the First Amendment, is thought to be so important that it sometimes has permitted apparent infractions of behavior that might not be tolerated in other bodies. (In a recent decision in the US Court of Appeals for the Second Circuit, in fact, a judge issued a decision which may allow the press to become even less accountable—it weakened the 1964 *New York Times* vs. *Sullivan* case, in which it was decided that a public official may win a libel case only if he can show malice or reckless disregard for the truth on the part of the defendant.)

With the press receiving such preferential treatment, one must ask: Does the person being interviewed by the press have any rights? He does. But there is no law which says that he must be *informed* of these rights.

Despite that, many journalists do believe in providing ground rules for certain types of interview situations—perhaps because the cards are so heavily stacked in their favor, perhaps because a sense of fair play prevails.

For instance, does a person have to submit to an interview by the press?

No, he doesn't. And anybody who's used to being interviewed knows that. Public officials—to use an understandable example—will sometimes be notoriously evasive when it comes to speaking for publications; they can either decide not to answer at all, or not to answer the specific question, or to inquire about the health of your kids. But what about the local cab driver who's asked by the press why cabbies sometimes take the long way around when they pick up a fare at the airport? Or the local tavern owner who's asked why his drinks cost half a buck more than those at the place down the street? They don't have to say anything, but often they don't know that—or, worse, are afraid *not* to say anything because that means they'll have to trust your interpretation of that refusal. Maybe that should be the first thing you tell an interviewee: that he doesn't have to say anything at all, and that he won't be treated with hostility if he doesn't.

Generally speaking, people who aren't accustomed to being interviewed are both nervous and intimidated about it. Sometimes they'll say things they regret, things they wouldn't have said if they'd been less anxious. Do they know about "off the record"? Not if you don't tell them. The fact is, anybody who's agreed to be interviewed deserves the right to be able to strike certain comments from the record—as long as that decision is made reasonably soon after the words are said. And interviewees should know that they can do that.

In fact, here's where you might want to get a little more specific. What, exactly, does "off the record" mean? If a whole conversation is off the record, does that mean that not a word of it will ever appear in print? Or that parts of it might appear in print without the speaker's being identified? Or that the information might appear in print, but not as a quote and without attribution? Or that the quote will appear intact, but a euphemism like "a person we'll call John Smith," or "a highly placed source," will be substituted? Or that the information will be used strictly for background? There's a lot of confusion here even among pros, so if somebody gives you information off the record, or agrees to talk to you off the record, you ought to make it clear exactly what the term means to *you*.

Sometimes things get a little hazy. I know of one case where a guy was interviewed officially (I've changed the actual situation here, but the chain of events remains substantially the same), said what he had to say, and thought that the interview was over. He offered the writer a lift back to town, and they chatted on the trip. It was there, in the car, that the writer got her story—but the interviewee, who'd been kind enough to offer the ride, didn't know that until he saw it in print. All of which comes down to another thorny question: When is the interview over? Does the subject have to worry about being quoted an hour later, a week later, a month later, if he happens to bump into the reporter on the street or see her at a party?

Here's another example. Say there's an idealistic assistant DA who agrees to be interviewed about his boss, a tough, powerful district attorney. The assistant thinks that he has a sort of duty to talk to the press, and ends up primarily praising his boss because he truly believes that the man is a good, competent and responsible leader. But he also has a reservation or two, the way most people do about those for whom they work.

When the article appears, only the negative comments are used. If the assistant DA's political career survives, by some miracle, he'll certainly never talk to the press again.

It may be said that the assistant was incredibly naive, that he should have known that he might be quoted out of context—or even that he should never have agreed to the interview in the first place. Well, I maintain that he's not expected to know these things, and if we are saying that common sense dictates that a person should not talk to the press, what are we actually saying? That the press can't be trusted? That anybody stupid enough to allow us to exercise our First Amendment rights deserves to be made the patsy?

It can happen to anybody. I once attended a question-and-answer session with a group of freelancers where the conversation was cordial and mutually respectful for almost two hours. There were also, at one point, about ten minutes of hostility. When the article covering the session appeared in a local underground newspaper, it told only of the hostility.

Lots of interviewing takes place with a tape recorder present, and most writers will tell the person being interviewed that he can, at any time, request that the recorder be turned off. But even that is a ploy that often works to the writer's advantage; while it appears that the writer is bending over backwards to be fair, in practice the interviewee will forget that the tape recorder exists. There's an expectation—perhaps an unreasonable one—on the part of the interviewee that the writer will know, by the way the conversation goes, just what's meant for publication and what isn't. That's probably at least a little true, assuming that writers are observant students of human behavior. But most writers won't, on their own, eliminate such parts of the conversation.

* * *

Okay, let's say that you're a decent type who doesn't want to mislead or confuse or trick or take advantage of anybody, and you'd be inclined to establish certain ground rules prior to the interview. It sounds easy. It is, if you're interviewing the local butcher about how to select the best steaks.

But suppose you're doing an investigative assignment where you're not only trying to find out the truth about something (a truth that you know will not automatically be forthcoming), but are not even telling anyone you're a reporter? I know of a case where a publication, unable to obtain public-sector information (due to a hostile political climate) which should have been available under the Freedom of Information Act, stopped sending reporters to the government agency and started sending "students" and "housewives." Of course, they were *all* reporters, and they obtained the information formerly denied them as reporters. It was easier than going through the legal procedures to rectify the situation, and what they did was perfectly legal. Assuming that there are many people who have reasons for not wanting their activities made public, the press occasionally must resort to guerilla warfare.

There are plenty of laws regarding what you can or can't print, but not regarding how you can go about getting the information. That's because it's assumed that the press is involved in a quest for truth, on behalf of the public's right to know. If it turns out to be otherwise and a person is wrongfully defamed or libeled, that person has recourse through the courts. The obligation of the reporter may be unwritten, but it's clear.

There are, then, times when one must be circuitous—and times when such behavior is unnecessary and gratuitous. The problems begin when reporters or writers, shielded by the First Amendment, use their constitutional guarantees in situations where such guarantees accomplish little except, perhaps, for embarrassing people or intruding upon them in unconsequential areas—situations in which, were the positions reversed, the reporters or writers would themselves prefer to be treated with a little human kindness, a little discretion.

The press is, and must be, permitted to be its own watchdog. But it's only through a responsible exercise of its power that the power can remain undiminished.

It is, as they say, up to you.

Part II

Chapter 19

First Writes

The article was just about perfect, and that made it—to me, anyway—one of a unique category, a classification to which, over the past couple of years, I had assigned hardly any. It was a special piece of writing, and when I finished reading it, I handed it to my wife.

"Here," I said. "Read the first page, and then, if you can stop, *stop*."

She couldn't, and my reaction was confirmed. It was practically a perfect piece of magazine nonfiction, an on-speculation manuscript which was purchased immediately and appeared in print soon after.

It is rare that any manuscript will so engage my attention that I cannot, from the first page, put it down. Which brings up the next question: Suppose the first page had been less than intriguing. Would the rest of the manuscript have suffered in any way? In other words, was that initial takeoff part of the momentum?

Almost certainly. And that's one reason why I usually put so much emphasis on the importance of the lead, or opening, of the article. From an editor's point of view, the lead functions like the bait in a trap: It draws the reader in and occupies him in such a way as to make him unaware that the door by which he entered has closed tightly behind him. From the writer's point of view, of course, there is only one reader, one audience, to be concerned with: the editor. Ultimately the editor decides if the magazine's readers will get to read the story in question. So it stands to reason that if you give the editor something he or she can't put down, you'll probably make a sale.

What constitutes a good lead? What makes the beginning of a story so seductive that readers find themselves, in just a few sentences, enmeshed to a degree where they are hardly conscious of reading at all? That depends on the publication, and it varies as much as do the different kinds of magazines. One editor's lead is another editor's boredom. It would hardly do for a magazine like *New Times,* for instance, to start an article like this:

> In 1975 some 154,000 porpoises were killed by fishermen seining yellowfin tuna in the Pacific; most of them suffocated in the three-quarter-mile-long nets. No one wants this to happen. Many fishermen need the porpoises as beacons to locate tuna, because the fish typically swim under and behind the porpoises. . . .

But such a lead is appropriate (if less than thrilling) where it appeared—in the *Smithsonian*. For, while both *New Times* and the *Smithsonian* are nonfiction magazines, the way they handle their subject matter is vastly different—as it should be for two very different audiences.

How long is a lead? In newspaper writing, it's often the first paragraph, or even the first sentence. That's because newspapers have to move fast—set you up, pull you in, and then keep you by quickly supplying all you want to know, almost all in one swift operation. In magazine writing, the goal isn't any different, but the pace is: You don't have to say it all in a paragraph. It might take three or four paragraphs to fully develop the lead. It might take six or eight. If a newspaper did that, you'd be getting what they call an "in-depth feature-length" article.

That's the first thing to remember: A lead isn't any specific length. It is, rather, determined partly by necessity (in that certain information will have to be transmitted) and partly by the amount of time a writer wishes to invest in hooking a reader. Regardless of subject, the optimum amount of time is the amount of time that any reader will reasonably spend getting involved—a criterion so dependent upon the subject and the writing that it hardly pays to try to make any kind of rule at all.

If you had to have one, it would be this: *Shorter is better, but never at the risk of making it shorter than necessary.*

I remember one article written for me on assignment where the writer made a fatal mistake. He had a dramatic lead—so dramatic, in fact, that he allowed it to take over. The lead was far too long; the writer gave in to his every artistic or poetic whim and made it that way. Result? The length of the lead dissipated the dramatic effect. The *writing* was good, but by the time I reached the guts of the story, where I was about to learn something concrete, I was already tired of the subject. Further, because the lead had so much drama, it turned out to be more interesting than the subject.

And that's the second thing to remember: Your lead, while it ought to be compelling, should not be *more* exciting than the stuff that will follow it.

Before we talk about what else a lead should have, let's take a look at one. This one's from the first serious magazine article I ever wrote, and it's as good as any to use as a sample:

> Linda is an attractive, friendly looking redhead with a great smile, and if you had seen her on that particular day in August, standing by a parking meter, her hands full of packages and a nickel between her teeth, trying to get the nickel from her mouth to the meter, the last thing you'd have done would have been to punch her in the mouth.
>
> But somebody did.
>
> Four kids walked up to her and one said, almost nonchalantly, "I'll help you with that nickel, you white bitch," and let her have it. Then they ran away.
>
> This happened about 15 feet from the corner of 12th and Rodman Streets. That's where Linda and I live.

What that lead was supposed to do was *keep readers reading*. At best, if it was a successful lead, it would do some (or even all) of the following things in the pursuit of that goal:

Give the reader a stake in the action. That's first and foremost; you're not going to hold readers' attention if there's nothing there for them to care about. In one way or another, you have to get the readers involved, get them to relate to what's going on. They have to *care*.

State the case without overstating the case. I would never read an article that promised, for example: "What you're about to read now will change forever your preconceptions about small planes." Why not? After all, lots of people fly—why wouldn't this lead work? Because, in addition to other problems (that preaching tone, for instance), it promises too much. Readers aren't suckers, and that kind of sideshow exaggeration makes it clear that the writer either lacks perspective or has a large ax to grind. Further, in a line like the one above, you've already robbed your readers of any sense of surprise, of discovery—you're lucky if they read it at all.

Try to appeal to basic human interests. My foregoing sample lead gets the reader to identify with the heroine, to share the outrage. It also promises to discuss a particular lifestyle which the reader can look forward to leading vicariously.

Promise to let the reader in behind the scenes. This ties in directly to the one above: Readers are voyeurs, and voyeurs like to look in on provocative situations from the relative safety of their armchairs. This story sounds exciting.

Promise new information. Readers like to learn things they didn't know before, gain new perspectives. The reader has to feel that reading the article will be *worthwhile*.

Promise to entertain. This is tougher than it sounds; it's where the *quality* of the writing comes in. No matter what the lead says, *how it says it* determines whether the readers will be inclined to read further—again they should feel that *what follows* the lead will be even more interesting than the lead itself. The readers must be drawn in not only because of the benefits they'll receive, but *because they'll enjoy the trip.*

Be direct. Don't beat around the bush. Some writers feel that by cleverly concealing their subject, or by dangling some kind of journalistic carrot in front of the readers' noses, they'll intrigue them into staying with the lead (and therefore, with the story) longer. This kind of high-school newspaper thinking generally gives way to my least favorite kind of lead, which goes something like this:

> He's not nearly as big as you'd expect, nor nearly as threatening. And the moment you look at him, you know that his reputation is probably exaggerated. He sits behind a large desk, twirling a pencil between his fingertips, smiling his smile. As you read this, he is probably on the verge of boring you to death. . . .

That last sentence is mine. Of course you're bored; how can you care about anyone if you don't know who or what he is? Writers who write leads like this figure that they'll keep you for a few extra seconds—really get you entrenched. In my case, the reaction is just the opposite.

Be appropriately dramatic—not too much, not too fast. The timing in a lead is important. Take this one:

> Miller had hardly made himself comfortable in the small, secluded booth at the Lucky Dragon Cafe when a gun was suddenly thrust in his face and fired point blank. Miller jerked back in his seat, looked amazed for a split second, then fell forward into his won ton soup. . . .

While this lead seems to have all the makings of an exciting story, something about the way it's handled robs it of impact: The deceased got that way too quickly. If I had first been told how this guy left his wife and two kids that morning, and how he decided not to tell them how frightened he was, and how he went to the Lucky Dragon because he didn't think his pursuers would find him there—by the time the gun went off, maybe one or two paragraphs *later,* I would have been anticipating something dreadful and, more important, worrying about it. Then, and only then, should the writer have blown Miller's brains out.

I'm sure that this list isn't all-inclusive; further, I'm not at all certain that all editors would agree with it, given the different demands of different markets. But I believe that if you keep most of what's here in mind when you sit down to start writing, you will, at least, get your articles read.

To develop a real sense of what happens in the opening paragraphs, try looking at leads a little more closely from now on. Remember the one I wrote for this chapter? I wrote it with *you* in mind.

Chapter 20

The Ego and I

There are, I believe, three time-honored methods of kicking off stories which symbolize a beginner at work. There's *Once upon a time* (ages 4-9, James Joyce excepted), *It was a dark and stormy night* (ages 10-14, and Snoopy), and *I could hardly believe my eyes* (ages 15 through adult). Of the three, my nomination for the worst is the last, an opening almost impossible to follow with anything of genuine interest. The last time I received a manuscript that started out in that general manner, I knew before I finished the sentence that I was going to reject it.

There are a few ways that sentence could have been saved. One would have been if someone famous (or infamous) had opened with it. It still would have been awful, but the words "I" and "my" would have had some significance: the identity of the person expressing it. And there are eyewitness accounts of events that would have salvaged that sentence—the Hindenburg disaster, the People's Temple tragedy, the A-bomb on Hiroshima—but any one of these could survive almost any opening sentence.

For an unknown writer dealing with a typical sort of magazine-type nonfiction situation, however, "I" is simply the first person; it has *no* additional connotations. There are right and wrong times to use it.

The writer's voice is a very individual, personal thing, which explains why the first person is celebrated not only in literature, but in poem and song as well (try to name three 20th-century ballads, quickly, that don't contain the words "I" or "me"). Many things can be said better in the first person. But there are also writers who never use the first person—those who write for *Time,* for instance—and yet the writing is fast-moving, lucid, thorough, and the lack of the first person does not seem a loss at all. In fact, one doesn't even notice it.

The first person, then, is hardly essential; a writer of nonfiction could conceivably go through life without using it once. But when used properly it has certain advantages, not the least of which is that readers get the impression that they are closer to the experience and to learning exactly what's in the mind of the writer.

You'll note that I say, "get the impression." Simply because a story is written in the first person is no guarantee that it is any more candid or personal that if it were in the third person. And the reverse is true: The third person is not any less subjective. I can sit down and write my first-person experiences with a psychiatrist, and the reader will get only *my* impressions of a psychiatrist-patient encounter—impressions which could, and probably would, be vastly different from someone else's. But if I write about somebody else's experiences with a psychiatrist, it's still going to reflect *my* reality—that is, how I interpret what I've been told by the other person. This is the case whether I write in the first person or the third person; I'm still the writer, and no greater objectivity is automatically achieved by the use of the third person. In fact, in magazine nonfiction, objectivity isn't even a goal.

Some years ago, the first person was not as common in magazine journalism. You'd see it in adventure and confession mags, because that was their stock in trade: "I Was Tracked by the Giant Grizzly"; "I Fell in Love With My Son-In-Law." There have always been first-person magazine articles. I have a few old *Life* magazines from the '40s which contain some first-person pieces; one is an eyewitness account of the first ten days of World War II; another is an American agent in Italy, writing under a pseudonym, telling about the rise of fascism there. These people had earned the right to use the first person by virtue of having lived through something, but even at that, these pieces were not *typical* of what was being done in magazines. Typical was a relatively detached description of the action through the writer's eyes and ears—but the writer wasn't there, if you know what I mean. In order to write in the first person back then, you had to have certain credentials—you were a nurse coming home on a ship loaded with wounded soldiers; you were the pilot of a plane in a bombing mission. If all you were was a magazine nonfiction writer, you were virtually anonymous, at least until you got your spurs: A few did eventually achieve star status and inherit the right to use the first person. But nonfiction was a ragged stepchild, and its writers were merely reporters. People who wrote fiction—they were *authors.*

The New Journalism of the '60s changed all that. Suddenly every magazine was potentially a confessional. Suddenly the writer's innermost thoughts were permitted to see print, often without justification or substantiation. Women wrote about having their tubes tied. (So did men.) Magazine journalism became more than writing the news or the stories behind the news. It was often the writer as hero and, not surprisingly, the hero had a part in the story. It is not uncommon these days for magazine articles to include the activities of the journalists—written by those same journalists—as they track down their stories. And many, many writers have blossomed in a field that suddenly has a place for talented people who like to write about themselves: about their divorces, abortions, new houses, homosexuality, old age, college days, illnesses. Today, when writers lose their jobs, they mail away stories about the indignities of trying to collect unemployment compensation.

Just as there is no story that can't be written *without* the first person, most any story can be written *with* it—in the hands of the right writer. But it is not a matter of *can* or *can't;* it is a matter of *should* or *shouldn't.* And that is often an area in which even editors will disagree. There may be those who will generalize, "I'm getting tired of all this first-person stuff"—but they'd be the first to get excited about a powerful piece of first-person writing.

When should one use the first person? That's a matter of judgment, of course, and the writer has to make the decision. I hesitate to give you any rules—after all, *I'm* writing this in the first person and certainly can't claim objectivity—but I think that most editors would agree with the following guidelines. Ignore those you want to ignore, but at least consider them all.

The number one mistake that most beginning writers make is to write in the first person automatically, just because it feels comfortable, when the fact is that the reader doesn't know *you* and doesn't care about *you.* I put the word "you" in italics because that emphasis is important: The reader might be interested in *your experience,* which is not the same thing at all, but the reader can't be interested in *you* until he finds out who *you* are. That opening line, "I could hardly believe my eyes," is not only without impact (since we don't know who "I" is and therefore have no idea what would make that person incredulous), but is also downright annoying, since it doesn't deliver any information that makes us want to continue reading—and is presumptuous enough to think that we will anyway. On the other hand, if that same line came to us in the first person halfway through an article—after we "got to know" the writer—the line could then have some impact.

Sometimes the first person actually gets in the way; that is, the story would be better off without it. Profiles are often like this. I have seen profiles handled both ways—with the writer in the first person playing his role as pursuer/interviewer, or with the writer apparently nonexistent (and virtually anonymous). Which works better? It depends upon the writer, but generally I would rather read a profile that allows the subject to come alive on its own merit without being involved in paragraph-by-paragraph competition with the author's autobiographical impressions. Very often the use of the first person turns out to be the conclusion of an ego trip for an author: Assigned to do the big story on the big personality, the author will want to talk about his acts of one-upmanship, of catching the subject off guard. Such articles are often vendettas, particularly in cases where the subject has refused an interview, and we find ourselves privy to an on-the-trail-of article in which we are constantly waiting for the writer to catch the ghost. Of course, that never happens. Much better, I think, to keep the first person out of profiles—or to bring it in only where absolutely appropriate.

That's something writers don't often think about: that they can write just *part* of a piece in the first person, staying out until the time is right to step in. In such a fashion, Guy Neal Williams, in his writing of "The Mushroom Pickers" for *Philadelphia Magazine,* wrote more than half his article about the exploitation of migrant workers on the mushroom farms of Pennsylvania without using the first person (while there was no way that Williams could have done this story without being there, he wisely didn't include himself until he was an actual participant). And then, suddenly and unexpectedly, Williams wrote:

> Midway through the research for this article, after hearing wildly contradictory statements from farmowners, crew leaders, social workers and mushroom pickers, I decided to try the work myself. . . .

At this point, Williams really *did* become part of the story, one of its characters, a participant in the action. He was not only a reporter anymore; he was a mushroom picker. *It was appropriate for him to become a part of the action.*

As for me, in case you're wondering: I'm almost always part of the action. That's how I write, and I'm comfortable with it, and apparently people are comfortable reading me that way. I like what happens to dialogue; I like letting the reader behind the scenes, behind the eyes, into the mind. Here's a fast exchange from an article I wrote called "The Vasectomy":

> I remember asking my family doctor about the operation, and how he hesitated, and how he then said, "They're having some second thoughts about that operation."
> "Oh?" Outwardly I was nonchalant, but inside I was praying. *Come on, give me the bad news. Tell me why I shouldn't do it.*
> "I don't know just why," he added.
> *Oh.*
> But he gave me the name of a urologist, and I called him.
> "We don't do them anymore," he said.
> "Why not?"
> "Well, I'd rather not say."
> "Listen," I pleaded. "This is my *life.* If there's a reason why I shouldn't be getting a vasectomy, I'd like to know about it."

> There was a silence. "Well, it takes a lot of discussion. We have to spend a lot of time talking to patients about it. It ties up too much time to be worthwhile."
>
> Apparently, he never met the doctor who did mine. . . .

Another example for an article I did about divorce; the article started here:

> The phone rang. It was Harry. He and Fran wanted to come over. It was Saturday night and we had no plans, so we said okay. It would be good to see them. It had been a long time.
>
> "What time will you be here?"
>
> "Give us about half an hour. By the way, this is our last night together. We're splitting. We thought we'd commemorate the occasion with you."

And finally, you can get into things that nobody else can write: like these recollections of growing up in an article I wrote about Atlantic City. The girl was 12, I was 14:

> We went together, off and on, for about three years, and I remember spending one entire summer trying to get up the nerve to touch her breast. I was obsessed with it; in fact, my fingers would curl at the very thought. But Lisa never noticed any of these efforts; she was always a perfect lady; she would never see that my fingers were actually an eighth of an inch from touchdown. Once they managed to make what you'd call a soft landing, fingertips only, encircling the breast entirely without actually touching it; I had cornered the elusive prey but could not get up the nerve to go in and make the capture. . . .
>
> Forget all that poetic stuff about coming of age in South Jersey. Remember an entire summer spent with a hand wavering over a size 32B like a 747 over a fogged-in airport, never to land

I present you with these so that you will understand how I love the first person, and so you will know that I'm not passing any judgment on it that would arbitrarily limit its use. I use it all the time, breaking every rule that I would be inclined to give you.

But there is a danger in using the first person—the danger of sounding preachy or pompous, the danger of the narrator's becoming the hidden agenda. Some writers tend to sound self-conscious in their use of the first person; commonly, you'll see the following in an otherwise fast-moving article:

> When I asked Smith about the new offshore wells, he told me, "It's too early to tell; we've got considerable exploratory drilling to do. . . ."

when it could just as easily, and more effectively, have been:

> As for the significance of the new offshore wells, Smith says, "It's too early to tell. We've got considerable exploratory drilling to do. . . ."

In the above case, the first person clearly gets in the way, the article suddenly becomes an interview, and we are unable to use the present tense which, in the latter example ("Smith *says*"), allows the story to sound more current—unless we do it with *When I ask* and *he tells me,* both of which bring the narrative into the *actual* present tense — that is, limits us to a you-are-there.

Sometimes writers include themselves in stories to their own detriment, their observations tending to reveal their lack of experience:

> As we walked through the gray, endless halls of the detention center, I was amazed at the feeling of darkness, the unrelieved monotony of the architecture, the narrow confines of the cells. . . .

Better this way, more specific and less personal:

> The halls of the detention center are gray and practically endless; they wind through the darkness, past the narrow confines of cell after cell, in unrelieved monotony. . . .

The difference is obvious: The first version makes the writer sound inexperienced; the second, while making essentially the same observations, tells the reader absolutely *nothing* about the writer—which is better, since the naivete is not noticeable.

Of course, the word "oppressed" instead of "amazed" could certainly help this situation, and there are occasions when I would lean toward the first instead of the second—but only on occasions where the first person is significant to the plot. However, sometimes writers use the first person because they don't know how to avoid doing so. I remember one article that went something like this:

> As we sat in front of Miller's fireplace I asked him what he'd been doing since we'd last met. "I'm working on a movie script," he said, nursing a beer. "I have a few people looking at it." He tossed it off with the same casual attitude I'd observed in him before; in fact, he then asked me what I'd been doing in the intervening year. . . .

This is where a lot of writers get into trouble; they believe it's necessary to include *everything,* and that gets them into a position of feeling that they have to include themselves, where they were and what they were doing. The above paragraph is better this way, and allows the inclusion of some details that might have been eliminated for reasons of length:

> Miller sank deep into a beanbag chair by the fire and took a long sip of beer. His attitude was studiedly casual: "I'm working on a movie script," he said. "I have a few people looking at it." He did not seem particularly interested in talking about himself, but that was characteristic. . . .

Thus we eliminate the first person entirely—but the reader doesn't feel cheated. Miller does not suffer, either, from the exclusion.

* * *

Naturally, everybody wants rules—and I'll supply a few—but there really are no hard-and-fast rules regarding the use of the first person in journalism. The most important considerations are not *when* or *who*—but how effectively the writer handles the first person.

In fact, in any hierarchy of recommendations, that would be number one. Use the first person:

1. When it makes the story, or part of the story, more effective.

2. When it doesn't intrude. If you are the most interesting character in the article, use it; if you're the least interesting, don't.

3. When your credentials or experiences qualify you not only to be the writer, but to be one of the players; that is, just because you're a mountain climber writing an article about mountain climbing doesn't mean you have to be in it; however, if you climbed a particular mountain on the particular expedition about which you're writing, it would be more appropriate to write in the first person.

4. When something about your experience is unique, and nobody else could have written the story. One article I received recently was by a woman who grew up in a household where the mother was seriously ill. She told the story in the first person—told how it changed her life and that of her father and her sister. The article was even stronger *because* of the first person.

5. When you're famous, and people want to live vicariously through you.

In all these cases, you'd probably be safe using the first person. But that doesn't necessarily mean you'll *want* to. And it doesn't necessarily mean you should.

Remember, suicide notes are always in the first person.

Chapter 21

Quotations, Part I

A quotation, like a pun, should come unsought, and then be welcomed only for some propriety or felicity justifying the intrusion.
—Robert W. Chapman
The Art of Quotation

Ah well, Chapman, you obviously never had to deal with City Hall. These days getting quotes is part of the job, and nobody just sits around waiting for a good one to come unsought. But the necessity for justification of the intrusion—there we agree.

If you could've written magazine nonfiction in the '70s, Chapman, quotes* would've been an important part of everything you wrote. (Actually, a terrific essayist can get by with nothing but narrative, but for most of us—not including you, of course—quotes are *de rigueur*. I mean, let's not try to kid anybody.)

There are two basic kinds of quotes. Most typical is the single-source quote—the statement from one person who's either responding to an interviewer, hurling an invective at an interloper, or speaking unguardedly and being overheard (a moment of silence here for Earl Butz). It can be a piece of flotsam picked up from another source somewhere—a clipping, a speech, a report—usually plucked for its ability to enlighten the reader.

Then there's dialogue.

Dialogue is worth a few paragraphs because it's so easy to handle inappropriately. In nonfiction, dialogue may appear as an excerpt from the transcript of a trial, or portions of a tape, or a verbatim por-

---

*Quote is a verb. *Quotation* is a noun—or an adjective in the case of *quotation marks*. I know this, but I use the word *quote* interchangeably with *quotation*. This is not a misuse that I have invented, but an occupational affliction that I do not care to correct.

tion of a conversation between interviewer and interviewee, or a part of a conversation overheard, or partaken of, by the writer. For that reason, dialogue is fairly uncommon in nonfiction: Most relevant conversations aren't overheard, and those that are aren't that interesting or that revealing. (Besides, it's hard enough to find one interesting speaker, let alone two.)

Fiction, of course, is something else. The writer calls the shots, so dialogue becomes a tool of exposition—as good or as bad as the writer involved.

Because dialogue isn't all that common in nonfiction, readers expect a lot from it when it does appear. They expect something particularly revealing, or particularly funny—and if they don't get it, they're bound to wonder why the dialogue was included at all. Further, because the writer is often trying to reconstruct a conversation at which he was not present, and would often like to force the dialogue to provide additional details, the dialogue can come out sounding stilted indeed. Everybody knows how conversation unfolds, and a reader may not know how to write dialogue—but he'll know that it's wrong when it's wrong:

> When Morgan reached the service station, he walked right into the service bay and said to the mechanic, "Remember me?"
>
> "Oh sure," the mechanic reportedly replied. "You were the guy who came in here last week with the '74 Chevy and wanted to know if we did state inspections, and I told you we did but you'd have to come back. . . ."

You could quite successfully write nonfiction for the next 50 years, never use dialogue, and never miss it. On the other hand, sometimes it can really add something:

> A very concerned gentleman called next. His dog had just uncovered a nest of about five newborn baby bunnies and he had been forced to adopt them. He was asking me, the rabbit expert, for some pointers. We started chatting like two television mothers.
>
> "I use evaporated milk cut with water," he said.
>
> "Why bother?" I replied. "I use Enfamil Nursettes. Prepared baby formula. It's ready to use—just heat—and it keeps practically *forever* in the refrigerator."
>
> "Sounds great," he said, "I'll try it! Now here's one for you: baby rabbits are prone to constipation when they're on milk. One vet said that we should stroke their genitals to help keep them regular."
>
> "Suit yourself," I replied.

In that case, the dialogue *does* capture the essence of the conversation, and something would be lost if it hadn't been used. But it is the sort of dialogue that the writer can most easily overhear—in that he was one of the parties involved.

Quotes of any kind are "loaded." The mere appearance of quote marks around a word or phrase—as in the sentence before this one—calls attention to it, singles it out, and there isn't a reader alive who doesn't anticipate that a quote will be more significant than, say, a piece of description nearby in the story. So powerful are quote marks that their very appearance around a word can even change the word's meaning; in fact, there have been libel cases decided just because of the way quotation marks were used. Here's an example of how that could happen:

> When we arrived for our appointment at his hotel, Smith met us in the lobby. There he introduced us to a rather attractive blonde "associate" of his, who sat there and looked pretty but didn't say a damned thing the entire evening. . . .

The appearance of the word "associate" in quotes indicates to the reader that the writer feels that there is something unusual about such a description, and that the word is not one that any reasonable person would have chosen to describe the woman. It is almost a certainty that Smith could collect damages for this use of quotation marks, or at least give the publication in which it appeared a run for its money. Further, there's a good chance that the blonde "associate," if such a description tended to make her recognizable to anyone, could also collect.

Quote marks give a statement currency, and for that reason they should be used discriminately, normally reserved for the kind of information which is revealing in nature. For example:

> "Quote marks give a statement currency," Spikol says. "For that reason they should be used discriminately, normally reserved for the kind of information which is revealing in nature."

The foregoing is appropriate to have been quoted: It says something significant and expresses a particular point of view which reveals something to the reader. On the other hand, something further back in this article—

> "There are," Spikol says, "two basic kinds of quotes. . . ."

is an arbitrary statement at best, and a silly comment to grant the power of quotation marks—unless you are trying to make the point that the speaker is sort of pompous. It isn't significant and is precisely the sort of thing that, when quoted directly, slows the reader down. Not only is it dull, but the reader stops trusting, convinced that this particular writer lacks any sense of proportion.

An article can also bog down when quotes are used ad infinitum, paragraph after paragraph, without a break; my personal limit—unless the quote is particularly revealing—is about three paragraphs. Less, if possible. It is difficult to maintain reader interest when the writer allows a character to run away with the show.

How, then, *does* one handle a long quote? By paraphrasing:

> Spikol says that there are basically two kinds of quotes that concern writers: the single-source quote, and dialogue. The former, he says, can take various forms. . . .

Of course, sometimes one uses direct quotes because what is being said is so important that the writer doesn't *want* to paraphrase it, and that's appropriate. But it doesn't make sense to direct-quote information like—

> "Store hours," Millner says, "are 9 to 5. . . . ."

—when one could just as easily say:

> Millner said that store hours are from 9 to 5. . . .

—or, better still, since the information imparted isn't likely to be questioned:

> Store hours are from 9 to 5. . . .

In other words, develop a sense of what is *worth* quoting. Rarely, as a nonfiction writer, will you actually be on the scene when an important occurrence takes place. More likely, you'll be there after the fact, talking to eyewitnesses or maybe just to people who have learned second-hand what happened. You could conceivably quote an article (and a reader) into the grave if you quoted every source. But fortunately, certain things can be taken on faith, many comments are suitable for paraphrasing, and certain information can be presented as statements of fact, the results of your research, confirmed by witnesses and "unloaded"—containing no built-in rationales as to why the information would be subject to dispute.

One criticism you hear—and you hear it often—is people complaining that they've been quoted out of context. The writer, either not understanding what was actually said, or deciding to use a quotation to support his own point of view without regard to the actual meaning of the quote, selectively includes it in his article—despite the fact that its meaning is changed by its position in the article. This business, taken to extreme for the sake of illustration, could end up coming out like this:

> Of course, there has been much controversy concerning the issue of abolition, and even the President seems to have his doubts that ending slavery was worth all the lives spent during the War Between the States. In fact, he was quoted recently at Gettysburg as having said, "The world will little note nor long remember. . . ."

Naturally, you're not expected to quote anybody *en toto*. You can select bits and pieces as you wish. But if you quote out of context, you have an obligation to explain the context.

* * *

I said before that most nonfiction needs quotes. And most of it does. But that doesn't mean that most nonfiction leans *heavily* on quotes. The fact is, most magazine articles contain fewer direct quotations than you might imagine—even articles you've read and seem to remember containing a lot of quotes. Go back and read them again. Most will be primarily narrative, reflecting what the writer saw and heard. If it *seems* like there were a lot of quotations, that's because the quotes were chosen judiciously and used effectively. Words in quotation marks have power beyond their numbers.

Chapter 22

Quotations, Part II

"O that he were here to write me down an ass!"

That's Shakespeare, *Much Ado About Nothing.* It seemed appropriate—first of all, because of the quotation itself; second, because if you're going to write about quotes, how can you not at least give lip service to the guy who has managed to commandeer more pages in John Bartlett's *Familiar Quotations*—usually referred to simply as *Bartlett's*—than anybody else in history?

Now, while you'll never catch up to Shakespeare in terms of being quotable—unfortunately, he scooped the world on many of the sayings that were worth saying—you still have a shot at *Bartlett's.* All you need is the right quote. If you're really brilliant, it might be something that you yourself say. But even if you're not, you might, with a little luck, *quote* the quote that will end up becoming familiar enough. It all depends on how you present it. And, of course, on what's being said.

If you have people speak in an article, you have to describe *how* they speak. Most common is the word *said,* but when does that get tired? Quite simply, when it gets tired. When that happens, there are lots of words left to choose from: *added, emphasized, reiterated.* Of course, only *said* is neutral; even *replied* has an additional connotation and indicates that the person being quoted is not merely *saying* something. Nevertheless, most of those words are relatively harmless; nobody could deny, for instance, that he *added* something. On the other hand, some words can be trouble, particularly if overused. If you have your character in a position where he *grimaced, complained, shot back,* and *retorted,* he is going to sound like a nasty person indeed, or at least one with a relatively short fuse, which could become the basis for complaint later, unless the descriptions were justified.

The word *said,* while it is free of those worries, carries with it an additional consideration. It is *past tense,* and its use makes a statement seem less current, less spontaneous, less pressing. Of course, you could argue that *grimaced* and *complained,* etc., are past tense, too, but they usually describe one-time occurrences that properly belong in the past tense. However, most quotations don't reflect a single position on a single question at one specific point in time, but an *attitude* on the part of the interviewee. And common sense will usually tell you which of these attitudes will not change overnight. For instance, in—

> "Obviously," Roberts said, "the welfare system in this country doesn't work as well as it should.". . . .

—the word *says* could more appropriately substitute *said,* since the quote indicates a relatively permanent attitude rather than a one-time response. On the other hand, a sentence like—

> When questioned about his role in Murray's firing, Smith shouted, "You can go to hell!" and slammed his office door. . . .

—would hardly be appropriate with verbs couched in the present tense, unless you were writing the entire narrative in the present tense.

Said, in short, makes the *thought* seem like past tense—a one-time response to a situation—whereas *says* indicates a probable on-going attitude.

One last word: In any exchange between two people—in any dialogue, that is—it won't be necessary to use a great many words to describe *how* something was said. Often it can be left to the readers' imaginations to determine how it was said, assuming that the parties to the dialogue have been identified in such a manner that we know who's doing the speaking at which time, and assuming that the readers know what situation exists between the two speakers.

Quotes can be tricky. How they're used can greatly affect character development, for instance, that sense of "getting to know" the people involved. Quotes can put an article to sleep or they can wake it up. A great quote has no predictable life span; chances are it will be picked up again and again. But put a good quote in the hands of an amateur and watch what happens.

For instance, here's a common failing, something I find in most manuscripts:

> "The city officials don't care what's going on. They don't want to bother with making sure that the program runs properly, that all citizens get equal treatment from it, that the people who are conducting it are fair and impartial. As far as I'm concerned, it's a total flop," says Charles LeRoy, chairman of the board at Mercy Hospital.

What's wrong with that?

Well, there's nothing wrong with the quote itself—but we don't find out who's saying it until the quote is over. That's like not being able to see the face of your blind date until after the good-night kiss. Better this way:

> "The city officials don't care what's going on," says Charles LeRoy, chairman of the board at Mercy Hospital. "They don't want to bother. . . ."

Better still:

> "The city officials," says Charles LeRoy, chairman of the board at Mercy Hospital, "don't care what's going on. They don't want to bother. . . ."

For my money, the earlier in the quote the person is identified, the better. *But get the quote started.* It's more effective than going entirely in the opposite direction of the first illustration, which would be tantamount to doing the following (which is, incidentally, often done):

> Charles LeRoy, chairman of the board at Mercy Hospital, says, "The city officials don't care what's going on. . . ."

In that case, there's no reason to be interested, nothing to keep you hanging. There's no rhythm.

Not all quotes come from interviews. Magazine writers are great users of newspaper clips, books and other sources. When you lift a quote from these sources, should you credit the source?

Most of the time, yes—for two reasons. One, the reader will want to know at what time, and under what circumstances, a quote was given. Two, and this is a professional matter, the person who did the original work should get credit. There's a peripheral benefit, too: Sometimes the mention of a source enhances the article's credibility, since it indicates that you've done some research.

However: If the comment was made in a public forum, such as at a press conference, or during a speech, or as part of a trial rather than in a personal interview, I think it's ethical to use the quote without crediting the medium in which the account appeared. As for wire service stories—if the quote was particularly revealing or important, I would probably be inclined to want to credit the wire service itself, since the newspaper in which the quote appeared would have little to do with it—although a newspaper could edit a wire-service report in such a way as to diminish the clarity of the original report.

* * *

Now that you know some of the mechanics involved, let's talk about what is appropriate to quote. Naturally, when somebody tells you that something is off the record— provided that he does so at the time and not as an afterthought a week later—you're obligated to keep it off the record. (This is discussed more fully in Chapter 18, a necessity since there are various interpretations as to just what "off the record" really means.) But how about the stuff that goes *on* the record? When you show a direct quote—that is, in quotation marks—how direct does it have to be? Word for word? Or is it enough to paraphrase what someone said?

That depends upon who you are. If you're Sally Quinn, quoted in *More*, the media monthly before it merged with the *Columbia Journalism Review*, you would never, say, fix bad grammar if a person used it as a matter of course, but you would fix it if it happened inadvertently. If you were Jack Newfield of the *Village Voice*, quoted in the same article, you wouldn't mess with the grammar at all because you'd think it added color. On the other hand, if you were either of those two people, you would not even use a tape recorder, a fact which, if you were *me*, would make you wonder why people who are such sticklers for getting every word right would make things so tough on themselves. In sum, different quotes for different folks.

I almost always use a tape recorder. I believe that paraphrasing a quote is okay when it's not a particularly significant quote, but if I'm going to put something in quote marks, I want it to be as close to the original as possible. Like Quinn, I do fix language, unless the language is customarily spoken poorly—and sometimes even then. For instance, a lot of people drop their "g" when speaking in the gerund (or, if you prefer, speakin' in the gerund), but a paragraph of that would have the speaker soundin' somewhat illiterate, y'know, which he or she might not be at all. One of the problems is that the printed word is *always* out of context in that we can't see or hear the speaker—and it's too easy for a writer to allow the small failings in speech to remain in the copy whenever he wants to make someone appear less than brilliant. I mean, if someone pronounced a word with the accent on the wrong syllable, how would you handle that—print the word phonetically and hyphenated, with accent marks, to get the idea across? I know, for instance, a very perceptive and successful entrepreneur who often uses the word "emulate" when he means "emanate." It is the only such characteristic I have observed in his language; it would be unfair—that is, it would not accurately reflect either his intelligence or his use of language—to quote him directly as he spoke.

Sometimes I paraphrase when I don't want to—for example, if I ask someone a question and get an "uh-huh" answer, in which case there is no quote, but information has been transmitted nonetheless. So a question like "Do you like school?" and an answer like "Yeah," becomes *John Bowers says that he likes school,* which is not a direct quotation and doesn't pretend to be. (You can avoid such responses from interviewees by coming up with better questions, incidentally, questions which require more extensive answers. One could just as easily ask, "It would seem to me that school would get in the way of your extra-curricular activities. How do you handle the conflict?")

As for tape recorders—I think they're the perfect quote collectors. Only they're *not* perfect. They can break, batteries can go dead, you can forget to turn them on. Of course, better tape recorders will indicate when something isn't functioning 100 percent properly, but there's still the human being who must monitor such indications: If you don't push the battery test button, you're not going to know if your batteries are dead, and if you don't check the cartridge occasionally, you're not going to know if the damned thing has stopped. However, even with all those negatives, I *still* wouldn't dream of not taping. Even if I take notes as well.

As noted, all this depends upon who you are. I've heard of writers who have uncanny memories—they can walk out of an interview with a few penciled scribbles and remember everything that was said. I've never met one of them. I do know writers who *think* they can do that; it seems they're often the ones who are accused of misquoting.

Those who allow themselves to be interviewed deserve to be quoted accurately, in the words they used, so that no nuance of meaning is changed. Too often, writers edit quotes to make them read better, more concisely, more logically—or even presume to know better than the interviewee just what he or she intended to say. That's often necessary—but before putting quotation marks around *anything,* one should give it some careful thought.

Fortunately for Shakespeare, he wrote everything down. Otherwise, a rose by any other designation might be just a decent-smelling flower.

Chapter 23

Putting It All Together

Dear Ms. Jones:

Thanks for letting us see your manuscript. The subject was right on target; in fact, if we'd been able to stay awake through the piece, we'd have bought it. . . .

Editors don't write that kind of rejection note. But every once in a while, an editor *will* receive an article that contains all the logical information, goes from logical start to logical finish, yet seems to resist every effort on the editor's part to finish reading it. This article always gets a fast return trip to its writer, and editors are often at a loss to explain just what the writer did wrong. But the result is boredom, and while a writer can be many things—controversial, heavy-handed, opinionated—and get away with it, nobody who writes for a living can afford to be boring.

Of course, no writer, no human being, *intends* to be boring. And no writer would submit a manuscript if he knew it was going to put an editor to sleep. The writer is, after all, an entertainer, obliged to keep you reading, and to keep you entertained. Whether the article is deadly serious or downright frivolous, the writer is on stage—not able to afford an untimely hesitation, a false start, a sudden hush, *unless* it is appropriate to the moment.

In that sense, the writer has to have the instincts of a stand-up comic. A *good* one.

Successful comics achieve a sense of balance, a sense of knowing what's important, of knowing how to start a joke in such a way as to get the audience's immediate attention, gradually giving them bits of information (and just enough of it) to make them eager for the punch line—and then, finally, zinging it to them and leaving them rolling in the aisles.

As a writer, you too must open with a lead that will immediately attract a reader, the equivalent of the comic's opening enticement, "A funny thing happened to me on the way here today." Of course, that *specific* line is about as compelling as "Once upon a time"—it's too predictable. The clever comic, however—and the clever writer—will tell us an intriguing opening story or anecdote that will really involve us and make us hungry for more. The lead is simply that which gets the readers started—and gives them enough of a stake in the action to keep them interested. From there on, it's a matter of combining two kinds of information: the concrete and the abstract. The concrete, for instance, could be the case history, the unfolding of the part of the story that focuses on human drama and emotions to get attention. Comics do this when they talk about their spouses or mothers-in-law or bosses, or what it was like growing up in their old neighborhoods; they know they will strike universally responsive chords by doing so. The actual joke—whether you've heard it or not—is effective because it's loaded with connotations an audience can identify.

Take, for instance, Guy Neal Williams' "The Mushroom Pickers" in *Philadelphia Magazine.* Here's how Williams started his story:

> In Toughkenamon, a sleepy farming village in Chester County, there is an old, rotting white house within sight of Route 1. Five olive-skinned men sit silently in front of the house, drinking beer and cheap wine as they watch carloads of tourists and picnickers pass. Although it is a blisteringly hot summer day, one of the men, a forlorn and ragged man of indeterminate age, shivers and coughs horribly. He has few teeth, his face bears the stubble of several days' beard and he wears a single gold earring. He sips his wine, coughs again and spits a frightening mixture of mucous and blood. Another man goes into the house and returns with more wine and a battered guitar. He strums it and sings a quietly bittersweet Spanish *doloroso.* It is a plaintive song about a young man very much like himself, far from home, away from his family and his lover; he has fallen in with bad company and he fears for his life.
>
> The listless summer breeze does little to cool the men and it does even less to blow away the stench of sweat, decaying food and manure that seeps from the house. A voice from inside calls out and the toothless man goes in, still coughing and spitting blood. It is his joyless and expensive turn with the whore inside. The other men wait for theirs as they go on drinking, moving slowly and deliberately toward an oblivious rest. They drink and try to forget they will soon return to the cold, dark ordeal of their work.
>
> The men are mushroom pickers and the crumbling white house is their home. They are Puerto Ricans and illegal alien Mexican migrants. They live and work in filth, constant fear and abject poverty.

Williams' lead is captivating; so evocative is his summer day, you can practically hear the buzz of flies. More important, Williams has our feet in the concrete of his story. So it is now time for him to switch gears, to add to the abstract side of our understanding. That's the kind of information—background material, figures and statistics— that often bogs a story down, but which is no less important than the part of the comic's monologue where he fills you in, as entertainingly as possible, with information you need to understand the punch line of the joke. However, he knows that he can't belabor it.

> Chester County—just two miles west of Philadelphia—is a lush, green area of farmlands, historic battlefields, game preserves and small country towns, and while the city's urban sprawl moves inexorably toward West Chester, Kennett Square and Chadds Ford, the peaceful isolation of the rural life is not yet gone. There is little besides clean air and country quiet to attract urbanites to Chester County—the area has little industrial development, limited housing and inadequate public transportation. But Chester County also has the cash flow and sound economy of a fairly heavily developed area, primarily because of the local mushroom industry.

Now we've learned that there is a great contradiction between how the area *looks* and the way things actually *are*. It's implicit that we're going in behind the scenes, and we're anxious to do that—and that makes this a good time for Williams to force-feed us some figures, quickly, about just how many people are affected:

> Mushroom farming is one of the mainstays of Chester County's economy and cheap labor is the mainstay of mushroom farming. Virtually all of the pickers in the roughly 300 local mushroom farms are migrants, the cheapest and most expendable form of labor. There are an estimated 3,000 migrant mushroom workers, 2,000 Puerto Ricans and upwards of 1,000 Mexican illegal aliens. The majority are illiterate or semi-literate single men who live in barracks provided by the growers. And sometimes die there.

By this time, we are not only beginning to have an appreciation of the horror of the lives of the mushroom pickers, but also of the enormity of the mushroom industry. At this point, Williams could have given us substantially more information about the industry—facts regarding annual production figures, farm operations and so on. But he didn't; he knows that to do so at this time would cause us to lose interest—just as the comic, if he is going to keep us listening to his monologue, must never forget to keep us focused on the characters that inhabit his world. Williams returns to the part of his story that involved us in the first place, the human element, because he knows that's what will keep us. And not until after he does that do we learn—some paragraphs later— the kind of information that will make this even more essential to read: that 75 percent of Pennsylvania's mushroom farms are in Chester County, and that Chester County is just about the mushroom capital of the world (in fact, most of the nation's total production of mushrooms comes from Pennsylvania). We learn that Estaban, the toothless man, if he's the average migrant worker, will live only 49 years—but that he can expect less because that coughing and spitting blood indicates mushroom lung disease. By the time we reach an explanation of just how the mushroom farms work—information that would have bored us minutes earlier—we're anxious to find out all we can about this industry that seems to exploit its workers so cruelly, and therefore we won't think twice about reading the remainder of a very long article. "The Mushroom Pickers," incidentally, won a national journalism award.

The similarities between the comic and the writer don't stop there. Both are storytellers, and the more obvious their moves, the less convincing and surprising their conclusions. Transitions are important to both of them, although much more so to the writer; an old-time comic, to get from one joke to the next, might say, "Speaking of my mother-in-law . . .''; but that would be awfully heavy-handed on paper—something the writer must watch out for.

The essence of pacing and structuring nonfiction is, in a way, second-guessing the reader—that is, giving him *as much* information as he needs (but no more) *when* he needs it (but no sooner). Avoiding overkill is important; too much of the same kind of information—too many statistics, for instance (many writers have a tendency to lump all the hard facts together in this manner, preferring to get them "out of the way" and then to get on with the "juicy" parts of the story)—is enough to make a reader forget the human drama and wonder why he's reading the article in the first place. The reader's attention span is short; the writer must be acutely sensitive to this and, each time he feels that he's going down, switch gears so as to reinterest the reader. That is what's known as a sense of timing, and I believe that most writers really do know when they're becoming boring—even if they don't always know what to do about it. In fact, I believe that they often would rather *not* acknowledge their own misgivings when to do so would mean going back and punching the keys again; they'd rather ignore the problems, get the manuscript out of their hair, and hope that the editor won't be fussy or demanding. But editors, who are part audience and part talent scout, *do* notice the imperfections. When a writer lays an egg, it's as obvious to an editor as it is to you when a stand-up comic fails to get a laugh—and most often it's not the material, but the presentation (for proof of that, study a Johnny Carson monologue sometime; you'll see that his "bad" jokes often get as much audience response as his "good" ones).

It's a careful balancing act: What interests people most is people; what interests people least are abstractions, like numbers and statistics. This naturally wouldn't apply to someone who is reading an article for the statistical information it contains, but it does apply to the average nonfiction reader who wants to know not just the facts in a vacuum, but how the facts influence the lives of people. By the same token, too many case histories and too little of the context in which they take place can make us care less about the people; they simply won't seem real without some hard numbers to back them up.

Perhaps this is the hardest knack to develop: A sense of proportion and equilibrium. The facts are necessary, even if they tend to slow down the action. The action is necessary: Without it, nobody will care enough to read the facts. Like a good stand-up comic, the writer will set us up, providing just enough information to keep us interested and not dwelling on the trivia that gets in the way of a successful delivery. And the lively writer gives us details with which we can strongly identify—packaged in a framework that has a good sense of beginning, middle and end.

The end is important. While the comic can look at his watch and say, "I see my time is up . . ."—a writer must conclude with clout. Save a good quote, round out the central idea of your article, and give the reader a sense of finality, not the feeling that you've simply run out of words.

One last thought: The similarities are figurative, not literal. A writer's work will receive the greater scrutiny (the words do not disappear with speaking); a writer's ideas will be less independent of one another. (You can't, in other words, throw a string of one-liners together and have an article.) But the *challenge* is the same. Keep that audience—even if the audience is an audience of one, and an editor—fascinated.

Chapter 24

Moving Right Along

Not long ago, I had an 11th-hour job to do: cut some lines out of a story—fast. We were sitting right on deadline, and one article ran roughly 30 lines too long.

Now, there are three generally accepted ways of eliminating lines of copy. One is to steal them from artwork: A photograph which is two columns wide and runs the equivalent of 20 lines deep, for instance, may permit tighter cropping from the top or bottom. Cut off five lines in depth and, because the photo is two columns wide, you save ten lines of article. Another way is to eliminate widows—which sounds like something the Mafia would do, but simply refers to those annoying final words that spill over to make an extra line of type, keeping paragraphs from ending evenly. You get rid of widows by taking out another word (or words) in the paragraph, but it's time-consuming and expensive: If you stole 30 lines that way, you'd end up having to reset 30 paragraphs of type. The last and most efficient way is to make large cuts in the article; there are almost always paragraphs, or large chunks of paragraphs, anyway, that won't be missed.

In the case in question, I was going to do it via the last method. No sweat, I figured; I'd done it a hundred times. Twenty minutes later, though, I began to worry. The article was impossible to cut. I'd found only six lines—one paragraph—that could be eliminated.

The article was just too "tight" to cut. I ended up eliminating a sidebar instead.

What's the point? Am I telling you to construct your articles so that editors can cut them more easily? Not on your life: Despite any inconveniences, it's an editor's delight when an article hangs together so well that you can't find a single paragraph to eliminate.

How does an article like that happen?

The secret is something called a *transition:* the passage, within a piece of writing, from one thought to another. How transitions are handled can and does make the difference in readability—because they determine how easily and naturally an article flows from paragraph to paragraph. A rough transition is like a bump; one sentence you're one place, the next sentence you're someplace else—and either you don't know what you're doing there or you're painfully aware of how you got there: choppy writing. Smooth transitions, on the other hand, get readers to the next subject without any awareness that the subject has changed at all; they feel that they're reading a logical extension of the previous thought. And if you've ever wondered what makes an article just plod along instead of reading quickly, chances are the article consists of paragraphs stacked one on top of another with no transitions of any kind, rough or smooth.

At their least, then, transitions get you where you want to go—and supply an apparent reason for going there. At their best, transitions make any article read like a masterpiece of logic, with one subject or avenue of thought following another so naturally, so spontaneously, it seems to the reader as if the road taken is the only plausible one to explore next.

Perhaps the best way to show transitions in action is to go through an article, locate the transitions and see how the writer made the switch from subject to subject. To illustrate, I'll use an article about pool—pocket billiards, if you will. You aren't going to be able to read the article, but I can tell you how it came together and what happened to it along the way—how the transitions occurred.

The article opens with a good lead—enough to establish a reason for the reader to stay with it—and, shortly after the opening, takes the reader to a rather rundown pool hall. It is to be the longest scene in the story, a description which ends with this:

> ... And while the tables are in disrepair, the slate beds—the playing surfaces—are in decent shape. There's a lot of coming and going, but not many people hang around to shoot. Mostly, they come in to use the bathroom.

Now the transition:

> You have now been to a pool hall. Let's proceed to the billiard parlors. What's the difference? The same as the difference between a housewife and a domestic engineer. . . .

This first transition, you'll notice, is actually rather heavy-handed: If you were paying attention, you felt the "bump." Fortunately, the other transitions that follow are not as obvious. Take this next one where, after talking about the generally accepted negative image of pool halls, the paragraph *sets up* the transition that follows it:

> It takes a certain amount of courage for, say, the fellow next in line for promotion to the new vice presidential slot at the insurance company to tell his gray-haired, gray-suited, gray-faced superiors that he intends to stop by the pool hall and run a few racks, and would they

care to join him? But even if he has this kind of self-confidence and sense of self-worth, there is still the time-honored bugaboo: a talent at pool is the sign of a misspent youth. . . .

Here's the next sentence—and the transition:

> Actually, the game has a tradition, if not respectability, behind it. They were playing something like it in France in 1440. . . .

At that point, the article has shifted *logically* into the origins and background of pool, and the article now traces the game from the 15th century to early 20th-century America; all of which ends with one elderly, dignified and wealthy gentleman:

> . . . "They had high stools," he remembered, "and when I was just a young fellow, people used to come and sit on the stools and eat their lunches and watch the games. . . ."

That wraps up the history and sets us up for a description of the average pool fan—and here's the transition that gets us there:

> Most people who maintain any sort of devotion to pool usually started out playing it in their youth, since only youth (or great wealth) affords the kind of free time that enables one to invest himself into the pursuit of such an unmarketable skill. . . .

Now follows a little more of that—the last paragraph of which naturally leads to a discussion of proficiency, like this, and again sets up a transition:

> . . . although it is certainly possible to pick up the game in mid-life and become proficient at it in time. . . .

Now watch this transition immediately after the above:

> But it's not easy. The game is not simply a matter of . . .

We're smoothly into a discussion of the kind of talent it takes to shoot pool, which will take us, some paragraphs later, into a *general* discussion of those who shoot it best:

> So when you see someone shooting pool really well who looks really stupid, he is probably smarter than he looks, but perhaps took a wrong turn somewhere in life. Or a right turn, depending upon how you look at it.

Which leads to a *specific* discussion of those who shoot it best:

> A few of these exceptional players are known to show up at various Philadelphia area pool halls. . . .

The article now discusses a couple of local players, including one who played against several-times world champion Luther Lassiter—a perfect opportunity to talk about the pool *halls* instead of the players, like this:

> Lassiter doesn't show up much around Philadelphia, which is good news for those who play the occasional tournaments at some of the clubs. . . .

The article goes on to talk briefly about a club or two, then the piece compares the image of pool halls with the reality, winding up a description of one billard parlor with:

> ... and this is an extremely cordial pool hall. ...

Now the transition:

> Which would surprise you only if you've based your opinions on popular stereotypes, or on *The Hustler*, that 1961 movie which did for pool what *Up the Down Staircase* did for teaching. ...

By now, the article has supplied a reason to spend quite a bit of time exploring local pool halls—and the reader has been enticed to actually want to know how these places differ from one another. Naturally, as Freud (a lousy pool player, incidentally) insisted, everything finally comes around to sex, and this story does, too, sliding into the subject with some talk about the more modern pool halls with their piped-in music and carpeting, and the fact that more women are frequenting pool halls these days. In fact:

> If you visit the Cue and Cushion today ... you will realize that nobody looks as good shooting pool as a woman. ...

The article talks about how women shoot pool, and how men can still beat them, and how some tired old stereotypes are still honored in certain pool-hall settings. This leads to a female psychologist's claiming that the game has symbolic sexual overtones, which then leads the article into a game between two men, both of whom are interested in the same woman—a game which takes on added importance for that reason. It's a perfect way to get into pool hall gambling:

> Most times, of course, the stakes aren't quite so high. ...

Now, to complete the transition:

> Ostensibly, gambling never takes place with the knowledge of the operator of the pool hall. ...

Now the article delves into gambling—therefore, hustlers. We read about one who is quite good but not smart, and consequently doesn't make much money. The series of paragraphs ends with:

> He doesn't lose, you understand, but he'll never get rich.

Which brings to the reader's mind: Who *does* get rich? And not coincidentally, the next sentence is the transition:

> If you could create a hustler, a bionic pool shark, he'd look like Wally Cox. ...

The description that unfolds, of course, is a rather pointed one of a predator—and this article is, after all, a sort of upbeat one about pool. So rather than leave a wrong impression, the threat is deflated:

> There are very few of these people around anymore. The ones good enough to do it lose their anonymity too quickly. So the field is glutted with amateurs. ...

And then the article ends. We have been swept along from beginning to end.

But don't think that all this happens simply because the writer planned it that way. An article has a life of its own, and transitions, at their best, are the natural consequences of a logical unfolding of the article. Most transitions *aren't* planned. As you write, you'll simply find yourself moving logically from one place to the next—and you won't even notice that you're writing transitions. That's what it finally comes down to: Transitions are as much called for by the *story* as they are by the *author,* in the same way that once an artist starts painting, the canvas itself—the spaces still unfilled, the colors already there—tells the artist what's needed. As you read your writing, you should be able to spot only those transitions that are rough, or missing altogether. And that's when you have to build them in, create a flow that doesn't naturally exist—or, at least, didn't happen naturally.

Let's suppose you have to go from one point to another and there just isn't any way to do it naturally. There's no logical transition staring you in the face; you're going to have to invent one. Is that okay?

Sure, as long as it doesn't *sound* invented. Remember, it shouldn't be noticeable *at all* as a writing device.

Say you've boxed yourself into a corner. You know that you've finished with the subject at hand, and now you'd like to cross the street to the next one—but damned if you can find a break in the traffic. That's where the self-contradiction (often just the word "but") comes in. You make a statement, then take exception to it. Say a paragraph ends like this:

> As the crime wave diminished, both the city and the deployment of foot patrolmen returned to normal.

That sentence has a feeling of finality about it. So how are you going to (1) hold your reader, and (2) move him along to the next subject? Maybe like this:

> But—as one shopkeeper says—normal in the city is still frightening. "They say it's over," says Charlie Field, a sporting goods store owner, "but there's still a holdup a week among small businesses. . . ."

Or:

> But is normal deployment enough? Charlie Field, a sporting goods store owner, doesn't think so.

Or:

> But if everything is quiet at police headquarters, it's another story at [and here you can fill in whatever you want, practically, including your own bathroom, providing the connection isn't too ridiculous].

By using these self-contradictions, the writer establishes an artificial tension that enables the article to move with impetus into the next segment. Sometimes all you have to do is *think* "but" or "despite all this" or "whether that's true or not" or a number of other variations to yield a good transitional sentence. And remember—there's nothing to stop you from going back to the previous sentence and rewriting it to *set up* a transition. Like this:

> The crime wave diminished. And both the city and the police department made the mistake of thinking things were back to normal. . . .

When you write a provocative sentence like that, you don't have to worry about a transition's working; it's practically guaranteed. In fact, the next sentence could start out as innocuously as the one below and still be loaded with anticipation:

> On a Saturday morning early in April, Charlie Field unlocked the door of his sporting goods store for business as usual, disarmed the burglar alarm, and threw on the lights. . . .

Because of the setup in the previous paragraph, the reader knows something exciting is about to happen, and would actually experience a sense of disappointment if the writer didn't come through.

A thought which is, appropriately enough, a setup for another transition—mine—so excuse me while I move logically along to the Sunday *Times* crossword.

Chapter 25

Ad Libs

When people know you by reputation, they tend to think that you've always been what you are. When I go to a particular doctor, for instance, I think of him only in terms of being a doctor. But the fact is that the man was in the printing business for many years before he decided to become a doctor, so he was a printer and a businessman first. I don't know how much of himself from that era he brought along to his current profession, but I suspect he brought a great deal; I don't think anyone has a choice in that.

At the moment, I'm a book writer: that is, I'm writing this book. Before that, I was a magazine editor and writer. But I didn't write my first magazine article until many years after I'd written dozens, maybe hundreds, of ads. One day I sat down, wrote a magazine article, and that changed my life and switched my major orientation away from advertising and toward journalism—or toward "real" writing, at any rate. That was only eight years ago, when I was 35. Now I'm 37. Shows you what writing did for me.

Nevertheless, I've kept a hand in advertising as well, doing free-lance jobs here and there over the years. In fact, these days I'm spending about half my week in advertising, which is more than it's been in the recent past. It pays well, it's fun, it's as least as honest as journalism—but, like journalism, the amount of integrity depends on the individual, not the profession. Further, it wasn't until I started writing magazine articles that I really began to appreciate what all the years of writing ad copy had done for me. While I'm not recommending that you go out and get a job in advertising just to learn what I did, I am saying that advertising will teach writers some of the most valuable disciplines they'll learn anywhere—disciplines that will serve them well in just about any writing field.

That last thought probably sounds like it's right out of an ad. And in a sense, maybe it is.

First of all, what do advertisements and magazine articles have in common? Not much, it seems—not on the surface, anyway—except that they're both comprised of words—and that, you might argue, makes magazine articles about as much like ads as they are like menus or the minutes of a meeting.

But they do have quite a bit in common. For instance, ads usually contain headlines—a series of words to trigger one's interest and get one involved—and those headlines therefore perform for the ad roughly the same function that the title and opening paragraphs perform for an article. When the copywriter is given an assignment to execute an ad, it's his or her job to come up with the best possible headline. Sometimes that headline will shock or startle, sometimes make a simple but powerful statement, sometimes ask a loaded question—but at its best it will do so in a catchy manner that promises to educate and entertain so as to ensure readership of the rest of the ad. The best ad headlines are saturated with this quality; through them, even people who are not about to buy the product in question will be able to enjoy the ad and learn something by reading it so that when they *are* in the market, they will think of that product. Of course, readers don't consciously take time to decide whether the ad is giving them the motivation necessary to read. It happens spontaneously.

That's exactly what the lead to a magazine article should do: Get you to read, spontaneously, the rest of the article.

Another principle of advertising that could help writers is conciseness: Taking 100 words to say something that could be said just as well in 50 is a waste of 50 words. That's something ad copywriters learn early. People driving past a billboard have only a few seconds to read it. People flipping through a magazine will thumb right past an ad unless you nail them with a *few* well-chosen words. The most effective and best-remembered advertising headlines in recent history are those that have gotten the message across with economy of expression: "Only her hairdresser knows for sure," "We try harder," and so on. It's the real thing.

If you don't believe that a super lead—combined with a good title and subtitle—can make a difference, try to stop reading this one that appeared in *Esquire,* by Richard Reeves:

> **Title:** *The Last Angry Men*
> **Subtitle:** I began a search for heroes—for men who stood up to the system. I wanted to find out why they did it, what they accomplished.
> **Lead:** "Hey, Dick," I asked my friend Richard Cohen, "whatever happened to that guy Hanrahan?"
> "I don't know," he said.
> "Did he go back to the *Post?*"
> "No."
> Cohen obviously did not want to talk about John Hanrahan. They

had been friends, pretty close for a couple of years when they were ambitious young reporters covering Maryland politics together for *The Washington Post.* Cohen had gone on to become a cityside reporter and columnist. Hanrahan became assistant Maryland editor. They parted ways on October 1, 1975, when the *Post's* pressmen vandalized the paper's pressroom and went on strike. Cohen crossed the picket line and went to work. Hanrahan did not.

Naturally, you won't often have control over the title and subtitles. In fact, you'll hardly ever come up with the one that's used, since those elements are usually controlled by the editor. No matter. Most people will read the first few lines of an article, giving you the benefit of the doubt. That's one way in which you have a little edge over the ad copywriter. But that lead had better be something else, and Reeves', above, is pretty good. As is the subtitle. And the title.

At least, he caught *me.*

Now take a look at the beginning of this chapter. It's an interesting enough lead, but maybe it's a little slow. There are plenty of ways that it could have been shortened. Perhaps it would have lost a small philosophical insight, but maybe it would have gained interest— maybe the trade-off would've been worth it. At any rate, it could have been said:

> Long before I wrote a book, long before I wrote a single magazine article, I was writing ads—dozens, maybe hundreds of them, over a period of several years. Then one day I sat down. . . .

Surprise. You really wouldn't have missed that first paragraph at all, right?

Ad copywriters know something, then, that writers of nonfiction should realize: If you want somebody to read what you have to say, you have to *earn* their attention.

You might assume that because what you're writing about is important, or because it contains information that will be useful to the reader, it will be read. But think of the ad copywriter who knows that the refrigerator he's writing about is the best on the market—it offers features no other refrigerator offers, contains energy-saving devices that will reduce a buyer's electric bill. Doesn't he have something worthy of attention? Of course he does— but, because he's writing an ad and because people don't automatically believe ads, he realizes that he has to *work* to get the reader's attention. Further, he knows he's *competing* for that attention.

But is that all there is to it? You attract a reader's attention and involve the reader in the copy, and then the reader will understand that the copy is important and continue reading it to the end? Not exactly. I remember receiving an article about a local university from a pretty good freelancer. It was well written; the sentences were smooth and crisp—but the article was easily twice as long as it should have been. I was asleep by page eight, but I knew that was going to happen by page five. The article was slow getting off the ground, the interviews were too detailed, the quotes too long. The article was tedious, and I wasn't about to spend a couple of days cutting it. I rejected it, even though I was more than interested in the subject. (I'd attended the place in question.)

On the other hand, I'm reminded of a political piece that I got from another freelance writer. It covered a battle between two candidates for an elective office, complete in about 16 to 19 double-spaced type-written pages, though it could easily have run twice that length. I bought it. I have very little interest in politics and do not normally want to sit down and dig in to a political article, but this one grabbed me from the beginning—and my criterion for a political piece is that if it can keep *me* interested, it can keep *anybody* interested. Unfortunately, most beginning writers lack that kind of perspective and spend 15 pages discussing an issue which no normal reader would be willing to read about for more than five. Articles of this kind seldom get to the editing stage, since the editor, who is also a reader, finds it dull one-third the way through.

You, for instance, may be a great train buff and would like to sell a 20-pager about traveling on trains. Well, swell, if you're really one of the world's most fascinating writers—otherwise, don't expect to sell it to a market that has to interest a wide range of people, most of whom couldn't care less about trains. But if you did a ten-pager on trains instead of a 20-pager, you might just sell it. And make more money for less time at the typewriter.

Besides, that's the trend. Magazines are leaning toward shorter pieces today because space is at a premium, and your chances are better if your articles are shorter.

And maybe that's the biggest advantage the ad copywriter has going for him: He's limited. If the client can afford to buy a large space, like a full page, that means that the copywriter has a lot of space in which to get the message across. But if the client can afford an ad only one-third that size, the message must somehow be told in the smaller space. And the simpler the message is, the more effective it usually is.

But the ad copywriter doesn't simply make his story as brief as possible. He makes it as brief as possible *keeping in mind the goal, which is to give the reader enough information on which to base action.* The copywriter's job is, most often, to cause something to happen—either the person is supposed to fill out and mail in a coupon, or go out and see the product in a store, or call about the service, or go out with money in his hot little fist and actually make the purchase. An ad that's too long will lose the reader before the punch line is reached. An ad that's too short will rob the reader of sufficient information on which to base a decision.

As a magazine article writer, you have the same problems. Though you might say you're not trying to sell anything, you *are* trying to sell—a concept, a belief, a point of view, or even something as basic as a restaurant you'd like your readers to try (or avoid). And you make similar decisions. It's impossible to sustain a couple of dozen manuscript pages on a movie review, for instance; but do you know where six pages would be too much and four would be just enough? Can you, in other words, keep your copy trimmed to a minimum without trimming it to the point where it loses charm, style, and just lies there, perfunctorily factual?

It is that balancing act which the successful copywriter can perform—and that the magazine writer, to be successful, has to learn—and it's been my experience that many beginning magazine writers pack almost *all* the available information into their articles, even though we'd be happy to settle for lots less. When a copywriter tries to sell a car, he doesn't drone on endlessly about the drive train or the carburetion system—that would be, as the old advertising maxim goes, *selling the steak*. The copywriter wants to *sell the sizzle*. That is, nobody's going to buy steak if you describe precisely how they got it from a cow, and what it looks like with the muscle and bone and tendon and gristle showing. But show it covered with mushrooms, onions, and served up rare in its own juices—that's *sizzle*.

While the magazine writer can hardly write an in-depth article on "sizzle" alone, rarely does the reader need the whole steer. If you're writing a profile, for instance, it's usually unnecessary (and boring beyond belief) to backtrack through the subject's entire life. I remember getting one like that; not only did I have to live through the brat's formative years, I also had to live through them *chronologically*—and nothing's more tedious than articles about babies unless it's articles that start out, "From the time he was a small boy, John Smith loved boats." We want to start out where the article is pertinent to us—say, with Smith's attempt to cross the Atlantic in a sailboat last summer at the age of 74. We want the high points; we want those anecdotes and stories and illustrations that will add to our understanding of the subject *today*. We want selectivity that entices the reader to dig in.

If you've ever read a really good ad, there's something else you've probably noticed: a certain flow, a quality of each sentence's and each paragraph's leading into the next. A good ad follows a logical progression, and that's because a good copywriter will know just when to answer certain questions or deal with certain topics. A successful ad, by the time you've finished reading it, won't have answered *all* the questions, but it will have answered *enough* of them so that you'll be intrigued into taking the next step. As a magazine article writer, you want to be more complete, answering all the questions that would normally pop into the head of the most interested reader—but do it with the logic and transitions of the copywriter.

Isn't it great when the writer seems to have anticipated your every question and answers it just when you get hungry for the answer?

Done well, it's like this: The lead opens with anecdotes illustrating the life-styles of various gay parents and their children. Hmmm . . . interesting topic. That gets you started. Then you wonder just where it's occurring in cities in your part of the country, notably in suburbia. And just about that time you find yourself wondering how pervasive this kind of thing is, and the writer then broaches a statistic—not a very complicated one, but enough to answer that question: "It's estimated that gay parents now comprise one out of every x-many married couples with children in the world today." Well, you think, that's quite a statistic. Now you're beginning to relate that to the paragraph just read, wondering what set of circumstances contributes to such an arrangement. Guess what? The writer starts to tell you.

At the end of it all is the end of it all. The final thrust of both the ad copywriter and the article writer is to leave the reader with a particular conclusion or feeling, or the urge to go out and do something more. The effectiveness of the article would, of course, be seriously hampered if the conclusion lacked an appropriate resolution. As would that of the ad.

All this won't happen through sheer luck. At its best it's a writer's instinctive reaction to what he himself is writing. I have a feeling, in fact, that if more writers trusted their own instincts, there would be more good writing around; but then there's always going to be that majority of writers who don't have much in the way of instinct, or have buried their natural inclinations out of respect for what they've been taught, and use little literary tricks to get themselves from thought to thought. And their products are somewhat predictable, hackneyed, overwritten and dull. In sum, a bad advertisement for themselves.

Chapter 26

Little White Lies

Here's a fictionalized (but not fictional) situation: An editor gets a story from a freelance writer. The story is nothing short of excellent, but there's one hitch: Too much of the article cannot be substantiated. While the editor knows that the writer is trustworthy, and that he has reported things exactly as he learned them, so much of the information is off the record, from sources who are afraid to be identified, that the potential for a lawsuit is as compelling as the story itself.

The editor has a choice: not run the story, or take a chance, or *fictionalize*. Say the story is about a home-remodeling outfit in a suburb. Seeing the potential problems, the editor says, "Let's make it a storm-window dealership in New Jersey." It's worth a laugh, and the editor gets it. But he is not kidding. Not much, anyway. He knows, as everybody in journalism knows, that the device is often used: the fictionalization of a character or sequence of events to get a publication off the hook. The magazine tells the story—it's a true story—but the main characters are disguised. Nobody can sue for libel; by the same token, the readers learn that situations like the one described *do* exist, and the readers are made wary of it, so the magazine makes its point. Only, of course, not as powerfully as it might.

The illustration above may seem a bit far fetched, but it is a fact that the farther one strays from the truth, the less effective one's words become. Truth *is* stranger than fiction, and the best fiction of all is that which gets the reader so involved that he will forget that the story is not from real life. It stands to reason, then, that when you have the truth, it's best to use it.

Of course, the truth, once revealed, may endanger your source—or prove potentially damaging or embarrassing to others—and so your source might not wish to be quoted by name. That's when you turn that person into "a highly-placed informant," or "someone intimately involved," or "an observer who is close to the situation." Or any one of a variety of what we'll call *paper masks*. You've seen them used. You believed anyway. If it had the ring of truth, it probably *was* true.

While this device may sound like a convenient way to get the writer off the hook, it has its dangers. Like any other liberty, the fictionalization of a person or an event can be abused. The political observer quoted as a "knowledgeable source" may, in fact, be a kook. Which means that you are even more responsible to ensure the veracity of your informant, since you've eliminated the possibility of anyone else's doing so.

Fictionalization is used always as a method of protection: sometimes to protect the publication and the writer; more often, to protect the source.

Say a woman gives a candid interview about her extramarital affairs. The writer must disguise her at the risk of jeopardizing her marriage; this is the kind of fictionalization which is almost always agreed upon before the interview.

Another example: A writer goes into an institution—say, a nursing home—to investigate abuses. In the course of her investigation, she talks to some residents who supply her with necessary information. But while she can leave the home, her informants are stuck there. She knows that there could be reprisals against them if she goes back to her typewriter and writes the story using their real names. In this case, she would most likely elect to fictionalize.

Or say a social worker has effectively entrenched himself between some juvenile gangs, a position from which he has been able to accomplish substantial good. In order to bring the problems he sees to the attention of the public, he arranges to take a reporter to see the gangs, talk to them. Knowing that the gangs don't want the public involved, and knowing that the gang wars will continue endlessly unless the problem receives a public forum, the social worker introduces the reporter as just another social worker. When the magazine article appears, the name of the real social worker—and his occupation—have been changed; perhaps he has become a priest or a neighborhood businessman. With appropriate disguising of other incidents that would "blow the cover" of the social worker, his relationship remains intact.

This is a common device, one that you can find in any magazine. Most often the writer will call attention to the fact that the character has been disguised, in fact, sometimes that tends to strengthen the credibility—after all, if we're disguising someone's name, there must have been someone there *to* disguise: "Emily (not her real name) has been an alcoholic for eight years." Or, when it helps the credibility of the story to be more specific—"Emily Flint, 25, a blonde mother of two, has been alcoholic ever since she moved to Center County eight years ago." The falsification may be followed directly by its rationale: "Emily Flint is not her real name. However, because of fears of losing her job and causing embarrassment to her children, she wishes to remain anonymous." Very often, particularly in highly personal or lifestyle pieces, only a first name is used; sometimes, as in articles that describe medical issues, a first name and last initial only are used, like Sue F. And sometimes a name isn't even necessary, depending upon the depth of the characterization. When someone's importance to the story is minimal, as in an off-the-record quote that marks the only time the character will speak, it's usually sufficient to refer to the speaker as "one of the workers involved," or "a close friend of the chairman," and so on.

Sometimes the writer will have a specific opinion and will actually *create* a character to get it across rather than editorialize. This may or may not be taking more license than the situation would dictate; however, it should be remembered that the writer will, by the time he has researched a story, have had opportunities to see both sides of the story with more clarity and objectivity than those involved. And he might well write something like this: *While the public has accepted the strike as a fact of life, at least one observer has noted that there may be grounds for an injunction against the strikers.* The writer himself is the "observer"—who has now been sufficiently involved to have a point of view and, in fact, may be better informed than those about whom he is writing.

But all this is a matter of discretion. It would certainly be unfair, you would think, for any writer to emphasize a minority point of view without referring to that of the majority, yet that kind of thing is done all the time, resulting in stories built upon selected quotes calculated to force the reader to a particular conclusion. If you're going to fictionalize, balance becomes even more necessary, since fictionalization in and of itself can be enough to jeopardize your credibility. I have seen, too often, how preposterous quotes left unbalanced make entire articles seem like fiction; while the writer feels he has built a strong case, the quotes themselves indicate a process of selection and elimination that tells the reader not to trust the writer's judgment.

What it comes down to is this: Your readers will accept only a certain limited number of fictionalizations before they begin questioning their veracity. *You* may know that they're real quotes from real people, but your readers have no such assurances. The way to maintain the reader's trust and keep your own credibility alive is to use as many *real* names as you can, interspersing them in such a way as to give support to the statements made anonymously—assuming, of course, that the comments in questions are supportable. If they're not, you probably shouldn't be using them.

Here's an example: Six people are interviewed, with a promise of anonymity, about a city health clinic's abusive handling of cases of venereal disease. To any informed and halfway-sensitive reader, let us say, the clinic's attitude will seem fairly outrageous, and the reader may be led to think that the interviewees are exaggerating. At this point, it's a good idea to interject a comment from a local physician who has dealt with the clinic and knows something about its reputation for handling VD cases. Such a quote instantly establishes the credibility of the statements—as well as the probable existence of the witnesses.

If all this smacks of manipulation, that's because most magazine writing is. There is hardly an article in any magazine anywhere that won't be impelling its reader toward a singular point of view, or at least toward an understanding of both points of view with a decided emphasis on one. That is the presumed difference between magazine and newspaper journalism; magazines generally have more flexibility to interpret and to allow the writer's personal opinion in coming to conclusions; newspapers generally leave such editorializing for the editorial page (although even that has changed considerably in recent years as newspaper "feature" reporting has grown up and become more and more distinct from newspaper "news" reporting). The magazine method is perfectly ethical, incidentally, as long as the writer is not trying to persuade his readers that the article offered is totally objective. But even if he would try to do that, he would, most likely, not be believed; most readers are more sophisticated in this area than most writers would like to think.

At its best, fictionalization won't seem fictional. If your article holds water—if the locations are real, and the sequence of events is real, and if the story takes place in an atmosphere of realism—a pseudonym won't throw the readers into a tizzy. In fact, given the circumstances of a particular story—given that the reader has been brought to understand the dangers implicit in the use of actual names—the use of a pseudonym may even heighten the realism.

How much fictionalizing is appropriate? This is, as we said before, a matter of discretion, of achieving a balance through the use of supportable facts and real quotes. But:

• You don't fictionalize unless you have to. That's rule number one.

• You can't build your *entire* case on fictionalized quotes; no reader will buy it. Good supportive materials—like news clips and interviews with recognized authorities—will make for a better story.

• Using a fictionalized quote doesn't take you off the hook if the quote turns out to be libelous—no matter how accurately you quote someone, a libel passed along and recorded is no less dangerous than a libel invented—and it could be a lot more difficult to defend if you can't bring your anonymous source into it. The key is not to stop using quotes, but to make sure they're defensible. If you promise someone anonymity, that becomes even more important—since not all states have laws that would enable you to keep your source out of court.

If you've promised anonymity to an interviewee in exchange for some quotes, don't describe the interviewee in question so distinctly as to give away his identity. This may seem obvious, but even small details can be giveaways. For example, the following quote offers no protection unless *all* the details have been disguised: "A 42-year-old company vice-president—let's call him Harry Smith—says that Cornell Gooding, president of Gooding Metals, told him during a golf match at the Sequoia Country Club that he intended to resign." Gooding would have to be an idiot not to know who "Harry Smith" is, and others would probably be able to venture some fairly educated guesses.

On the other hand, you don't want to disguise things so much that you alter reality beyond one's ability to handle it as truth, because truth has a way of *sounding* like truth. The farther from it you travel, the tougher it is to return.

Lastly, having a quote, anonymous or not, doesn't give you license to use one that's irresponsible. The same qualifications apply for fictionalized characters as for real ones: If they're not good sources, if you can't trust them, don't use the quote.

* * *

Closely related to fictionalizing a single character is creating a composite; that is, rolling several characters into one. Say you spoke with Millie, Molly and Meg about their divorces, and the three divorces came about for fairly similar reasons. Each of the three women has given you some good quotes—but you know that to introduce all three women would be beating a dead horse, as well as boring your readers to death. So you throw them together—a quote from Millie here, a quote from Meg there—and they all come out in a woman named Martha. (You might be less likely to do this if you are permitted by the women to use their real names—in that case, your article might be better served by identifying the real people, if it will deliver in reality what it loses in readability. It's a matter for your discretion. But if the women *require* anonymity, you might as well create a composite unless there are good reasons for retaining their individual identities.)

On the other hand, if you require the support of numbers for your article—if you need several quotes from several sources to give the premise of your article some weight—it might *not* be a good idea to reduce three proponents of a point of view to one person.

One final word. Anonymity is often frowned upon as an act of cowardice. That's why most magazines won't print anonymous letters. Anonymity means that somebody has something to hide. Readers are automatically less receptive to pseudonymous characters in an article, and writers who use too many paper masks are certain to obliterate reality.

Used judiciously, the truth will most often be its own best defense.

Chapter 27

Truth Is Stranger Than Fiction

The difference between fiction and nonfiction is supposed to be that fiction is fictional and nonfiction is not. That should, follows the logic, make nonfiction *fact*—but whoever created the term must have had a reason for describing it as a non-something instead of a something, just as our judicial system has a reason for finding people "not guilty" instead of "innocent."

Further, while people say that truth is stranger than fiction, nobody ever says that *fact* is stranger than fiction, which could indicate—as I believe it does—that there is a difference between the facts and the truth.

You're confused. Actually, it's not confusing. It's simply that nonfiction *isn't* necessarily fact, and sometimes nonfiction is almost entirely fiction, and the truth is something we get when we're lucky enough, or conscientious enough, to hit on it; it's certainly not a requisite.

For these reasons—and we'll get down to specifics soon—magazine nonfiction writers live in the best of all worlds. They don't have to worry about creating characters or plot or dialogue from scratch. And there's a market waiting for their articles that's probably 20 to 40 times the size of the fiction market. If there's an argument for magazine fiction—and I've heard them all—it's that fiction is the most fun and offers the broadest creative challenge, since the writer calls all the shots and gets to manipulate characters and story line and dialogue, etc., 100 percent.

But the nonfiction writer, while limited to a factual unfolding of the story, has tremendous creative advantages *because* of the facts—built-in characters and a real guaranteed-to-work plot that permits more fictional techniques than you'd ever expect. This can be especially important if you're a writer who avoids the tougher type of article because it always comes out paragraph after paragraph of facts, without much drama. There are probably tools you're not even using—

tools you may not, in fact, know you own. Even newspaper writing, once strictly reportage *(Include as little color as possible, kid. Don't slant the story or lead the reader to a conclusion about anything.),* has been influenced by these tools. Take, for example, a few story leads from the front page of *The Philadelphia Inquirer*—picked at random on the day I wrote this. Remember, these are the first sentences of front-page stories:

> Tired and hungry, Edgardo Ortiz had just returned home from his night shift at work early last Saturday morning when he heard the banging of nightsticks against the front of his Feltonville rowhouse.

> Private William Cook was wounded when an M-16 rifle discharged in his face as he crouched in a foxhole, and he can barely see out of his right eye.

> Up until yesterday afternoon, Maria Colantino had been certain the city's public school money problems would be solved and, in fact, that's what she kept telling her teaching colleagues at Hunter Elementary in North Philadelphia.

These are a far cry from the who-what-where-when-why-and-how of the old newspaper "inverted pyramid" style. The reason, pure and simple, is that newspapers have started to realize they are in an attention-getting battle with magazines and television. They're not just in the news business; they must *entertain,* too.

Of course, a magazine article based on any of the foregoing news stories would not start out the same way. The newspaper has to tell the news quickly; it has no room, and no time, for elaborately-crafted leads. It must get the essential facts into the lead even if the form *has* changed. Newspapers have learned that they can "grab" readers with solid, suspense-building openers—but they know it had better be a one-two punch. In each of the foregoing leads, the reader can sense that the crux of the article is coming up fast—probably in the next sentence.

Magazines—except for newsmagazines like *Time* and *Newsweek*—don't pretend to deliver the news, let alone do it in an objective manner. They are delivering good, fast-reading articles—about real people, places and things, yes; but *subjectively.* Not just *what* happened, but often with a great deal of speculation as to why and how it happened: The story *behind* the story. So magazine writers have, and are expected to have, opinions—and the reader who reads a magazine article *knows* that he or she is getting a slanted version of what happened. It's not fiction—but it may not be fact, either.

Today's nonfiction writer, in short, has to make nonfiction more interesting than fiction. This means turning a pile of pigment into a painting: How one uses the stuff, and knowing when to quit, determine the outcome. The artist, not the model.

Yet many fiction writers refuse to write nonfiction because they're convinced it would deprive them of their creative expression. That's silly. Nonfiction presents the writer with one of the toughest creative challenges of all: to write something that's stranger than fiction, yet stays within the bounds of responsible fact interpretation.

This cannot be done without techniques that we usually accept, however, as the province of fiction.

The fiction writer is quick to point to "description," for example, as his area of expertise, something that he uses to surround his reader with mood, feeling, the appearance of a place or thing. Isn't a nonfiction writer limited here? Nope.

Here's a paragraph from a story I wrote for *Philadelphia Magazine* a few years ago about a family in a changing neighborhood. You can find similar passages in practically any magazine:

> I know the neighborhood—knew it, anyway. Years ago, I lived there, and I never went back until one night this past January.
>
> At night, it looks about the same. Winter nights have a way of scrubbing things clean; the air is distilled, silent, crisp, and street lights are starlike, faceted by the brittle air. The lawns, even those untended, stretch before the homes like navy blue rugs. And the sky is pitch black, the foil against which all of this is placed, a dark velvet flatness protectively blanketing the little rows of homes that reside in tandem below, as uniform as piano keys.

You can do *anything* with description in nonfiction that you can do in fiction. But what you're describing has to *be there*. You're talking about a real place.

There are times when the nonfiction writer actually writes fiction. Say it's a guy having an extramarital affair. The writer can't use a real name because that would certainly be an invasion of privacy—except in the case of a Wayne Hays, for instance, whose affair was conducted at taxpayers' expense—so he creates a fictional character and a fictional name for him. Then, as pointed out in an earlier chapter, there's the composite character—you have three women, all of whom have had problems getting a high-level job because of sex discrimination, and for the purposes of your article, one woman will do. But each of the three women has something worth including. So you roll them into one. The *one* is fictional—she doesn't exist—but she's based on fact. You can take liberties like that with magazine nonfiction, and those liberties aren't much different from what you might do in fiction.

The fiction writer will argue that nonfiction can't hold a candle to fiction when it comes to dialogue—and that's true. It is the *handling* of language that makes the biggest difference between nonfiction and fiction. In fiction, there is often page upon page of conversation. Nonfiction writers don't use dialogue as often because they *can't*—they're rarely there to hear it. Much of what they do is reconstruct, and reconstructing a conversation, even when based on a description by an eyewitness, is loaded with pitfalls. It depends too much upon memory, and could prove dangerous should one of the participants deny his involvement in an embarrassing conversation.

But where fiction writers have dialogue, nonfiction writers have monologue: quotes from an interview. And they can be dynamite. I remember in particular a story which appeared in *New York* magazine early in 1972, and I know from people who have read that story that it's never left them. In it, author Herb Goro told his now-famous tale of "The Old Man in the Bronx," much of it in the words of the Old Man himself. Listen to these quotes, and try to imagine a patchwork quilt of them interspersed with just enough description. This is the Old Man now, talking about his younger days and the woman who eventually became his wife:

> "After I went with her a couple of weeks—I don't know what came over me—I wanted to give her a kiss. I started to have too much feeling. Do you know what she done to me? She hit me. That night I never slept. I had a friend, Goldberg, about 50 years old. Me and him used to peddle together. I went over Sunday morning to see him. I said, 'What made me do it? I met a girl and I wanted to give her a kiss and she hit me. I shamed myself. Now I am sorry and I don't know what to do. I can't go back to her, I can't eat and I can't work.' 'Well,' he told me, 'go back and talk to her. Tell her you're sorry you did it.' "

And again, the Old Man, nearing the end of his life:

> "Ninety years a man and all I do is eat and sleep. I've been in the hospital eight, twelve weeks. I know it's a long time. I can't do anything any more. People don't want to hear me and I can't hear when somebody else is talking. I don't think. Why think? What I think now never can help nothing no more. When a man comes to my age he's done. He's got no strength. He can't talk right. He can't see right. So he does what he can do. He can eat and he can sleep and that's all. He prays maybe God will take him away, maybe he'll be better off in the next world. I pray to God every day God should take me. Nobody can know me no more. The doctors, the nurses, they don't know what kind of man I was. Who could look at me lying in bed and know what I was? Who listens to an old man?"

There are times, of course, when you *can* use dialogue— even take liberties with it. You can embellish dialogue in which you've participated, provided it's the sort of light dialogue where accuracy isn't important and you're not going to get anybody angry. There are other things that can be done—like creating small pieces of fiction to spark up a factual piece. I'm not endorsing the practice, and I don't approve of it, but it's done all the time. Most nonfiction writers do a harmless bit of inventing almost every time they sit down to write.

You can also create an imaginary dialogue without betraying the trust of the reader:

> Of course, something like this could never happen. You know that and I know that. But does the guy from the IRS know that? Here, just for the sake of argument, is how such a conversation might unfold. . . .

At this point, you're writing fiction.

What else do you want? Flashback? It's used all the time. If you were to start a profile when the main character was five years old and taking her first dance lesson, you'd probably lose the reader in the first paragraph. If you start the article with her about to audition for a nationally-respected ballet company, you wouldn't. Halfway through the piece, though, you just might want to talk about the early years, and you'll flashback.

And so it goes. Find it in fiction, and chances are you can use it in nonfiction. And because the plot is already there, waiting for you, you'll be able to give greater attention to the character development, local color, pacing and all the other things that go toward making an excellent piece of writing. You'll be able to use your imagination to its fullest—even experimentally.

And that, strangely, is where the fiction buff will fault you most of all. Nonfiction, you'll hear, doesn't take all that much imagination. It's a skill, not an art. Where does the inventiveness of the author come in?

Here's another excerpt, this one from a story by Mike Mallowe, which appeared in *Philadelphia Magazine,* in which he had to reconstruct for the reader a bizarre murder at which only the murderess (Winnie Ransom) and the murder victim (Peggy Sweeney) were present:

> Peggy Sweeney was screaming. Screaming and wailing and coming back from the dead. Back from the dead. Just like Sharon Tate. Like Sharon Tate must have screamed at Charlie Manson. Like a mad woman. Winnie Ransom couldn't see past the blood or hear the screams. This time Peggy Sweeney really was dying. Winnie couldn't save anybody.
>
> Peggy started struggling to her feet, cut wide open and bleeding. Her intestines were exposed.
>
> Out in the hallway Winnie remembered passing a hammer or hatchet. Something to make her stop. Stop the screaming and the blood. The hammer was right out in the hallway. Just a few feet away. Anything to stop the screaming.

I wish I had room here to give you the rest of this—what came before it and what came after. It was absolutely spellbinding, every paragraph. And it was *true.*

There's the key. It was *true!* It really happened! This is what's so fascinating about nonfiction that can never be true of fiction. You're not reading about a murder that you can put back into the bookcase and forget by morning. You're reading about something that really happened. And it'll probably stay with you forever.

That's nonfiction.

Chapter 28

Last Writes

You gotta have a finish.

Think about it: How many story leads can you remember? Hardly any, right? But an ending, handled properly, can often be more memorable than any other passage in the article. The ending is the grand finale, the knockout punch, the unsung hero of magazine journalism.

At least it should be.

The first serious magazine article I ever wrote, back in 1971, ended with a lengthy paragraph in which I sort of hoped that people of different economic means and races would someday find a way to live together. While it sounds dreadful as an ending, and typically early-'70s as a sentiment, I thought it was pretty good, given the context of the article, a piece about a now-classic confrontation: a middle-class neighborhood on the fringe of a depressed area.

I remember showing the finished piece to Alan Halpern, the editor of *Philadelphia Magazine*. He took his pencil and slashed out that last paragraph. I almost died. He might as well have chopped off my index finger.

I'll tell you the ending to *this* episode— later. For now, let me just say that an article does not end when you simply run out of things to say; instead, you should sum up, in a single thought or quote or anecdote, the main point of the article with *power and polish*. Strive for a strong—unforgettable, if possible—statement that will leave your readers feeling, thinking, even taking action.

Often, the ending of an article is the beginning of . . . something else. You give your readers something that will stick to their ribs the way successful endings in other media do: top Broadway plays, great movies. There is one final moment that will be better than all other final moments in that it will stay with your readers, burned into their hearts and minds—and through that final image, the point of the story is not *made* (it has *already* been made by this time), but *etched* into the consciousness of the reader. It is the last strike of the hammer, the final imbedding of the die.

Of course, the ending of a lighter, fluffier article doesn't have to work that hard, in that way. But the superlatives still apply: It should be the *best* ending compatible with the story.

Telling you what consistutes a bad ending is easier than telling you what makes for a good one, so we'll start there. A bad ending is, first of all, not a matter of taste—not any more than is a bad apple. You'll recognize one, if you're unlucky enough ever to find it in print, by one of the following characteristics on what must, by necessity, be an incomplete list.

1. The ending dilutes the point of the story, making you feel that you've somehow wasted your time reading it:

> Of course, police brutality represents the very worst of what we might expect from any system of law enforcement, in that it denies citizens, some of them undoubtedly innocent, due process. On the other hand, there is the police view as stated by one detective who prefers to remain anonymous: "With this Miranda decision, sometimes the only way we can get a confession is to beat it out of them."
> He, too, has a point.

2. It preaches, usually jeopardizing the credibility of the writer by belaboring a point already made:

> Until we find a way to keep the police from mistreating suspects, you will not see the American justice system working as it was intended—and any confession must be greeted with suspicion.

3. It tells the reader what to think, the article probably having failed to present the facts that would allow the reader to draw the logical conclusion—and so is heavy-handed:

> The next time you read about a confession gotten by the police, you'd better stop and think twice: Just how did they get it? Maybe with a blackjack?

4. It leaves too much unresolved.

> Miller, in signing his confession, admitted guilt. A month later, at his trial, he claimed to have been beaten. The question that remains is, Was justice served?

5. It ends weakly, without impact—often an attempt at the dramatic that failed:

> On the way out, I passed by one of the interrogation rooms. And suddenly, I knew what Nazi Germany must have been like.

6. It ends on a wrong note, managing to say something a little different from the rest of the article:

> Just before I left, one officer told me, "It's a tough job. Sometimes my wife doesn't see me for a couple of days in a row. The hours are long and hard. Sure, sometimes we get carried away trying to do our job. But nobody's going to do it for us."
> When I left, I was glad I wasn't a cop.

By now, you have some ideas as to what the article covered by those endings must have been about. How might it have ended better?

> But all the excuses can't justify a Wallace Simms. On the evening of Sunday, April 10th, police took Simms, a carpenter suspected of murdering Nancy Peters, from his home where he, his wife and three children had been watching television. As the horrified family screamed and pleaded, Simms was handcuffed and brutally shoved into the back of a police car.
>
> The next day, after 17 hours of interrogation, the police got their confession. A day later, Simms died of internal injuries reportedly suffered when he "fell down a flight of stairs" at police headquarters.
>
> On April 30th, another man confessed to the Peters murder.

Surprisingly, the best endings are often there on the page staring at you when you've finished that "final" draft—just a few paragraphs in front of your original ending. That's what happened with my first article for *Philadelphia Magazine*. Once I got over the shock of seeing my beautiful prose snipped from behind, I looked at the article over Alan Halpern's shoulder and realized that, yes indeed, squatting right there a few scant lines above my X'ed-out ending was a *better* ending—also mine.

So the next time you can't quite end a piece, try chopping off paragraphs from the end until the story ends itself. Even the best artist can apply a few brushstrokes too many on occasion.

Sometimes you'll have to hunt further for an ending. Often it will be in the middle of an article someplace—an anecdote or quote you've already used which could be moved to the end and make a terrific windup.

And if you can't find the ending in any of those places, or in your head (another possibility), go back to the beginning of the article. It's often possible to find in the lead a way to write the ending, coming full circle. But, be careful that it doesn't seem contrived; you're looking for power, not predictability.

In one *Philadelphia Magazine* story, "The Forgotten Children," freelancer Loretta Schwartz writes about a state institution and describes a scene with a 16-year-old mentally-ill child. The scene could have appeared anywhere in her story. But, by putting it at the end, she managed to leave her readers with a strong graphic illustration of all that her story tried to say:

> For 15 minutes David led me, and we walked back and forth across that nightmare ward, holding hands, turning whenever we came to a wall or locked door. Every now and then David spoke. "I want to go outside. I want to go home. I want to have a warm bubble bath," he said. And as I listened, I realized that this "unreachable" child had not only made contact but somehow, miraculously, had articulated his most basic human needs—almost as if he knew that they were the very things that might save him.
>
> I was told I had to leave. I heard the screams of anguish and the

door shut, locking him in. I saw his young face pressed against the barbed wire—and then I knew that those were things he would *never* get.

The article, by the way, won a National Magazine Award.

Endings can be tough, even tough*est*. Sometimes a story will almost write itself—you'll sit there and do little more than pull pages out of the typewriter—but comes the ending, you'll know that you're in trouble. I've agonized over endings for periods of time far in excess of their proportions in the finished article, and I don't know anyone who hasn't. It's seldom easy.

I remember one time when it was very difficult for me, and when I finally did get it down to the *thought* I wanted, it was still difficult to get the right words for that one thought. It was an article about a writers' conference and one girl there (this was right before it was illegal to call young women *girls)* seemed to show a lot of promise. The article was not very optimistic, however, and it was important to achieve just the right tone for the article's end. I went through:

> *Girl from Massachusetts, I'm making it a point not to remember your name. I never want to know the end of your story.*

> *Girl from Massachusetts, I did not remember your name. I don't want to know how your story will end.*

> *Girl from Massachusetts, I did not write down your name.*

> *Girl from Massachusetts, I will remember your face, your eyes, your dress, your hair, but I will not remember your name. I never want to know how your story ends.*

Shucks.

> *Girl from Massachusetts, I will remember your face, your eyes, your dress, your hair, but I did not make it a point to remember your name. I never want to know how your story will end.*

> *Girl from Massachusetts, I will remember your face, your eyes, your dress, your hair, your poise, your energy waiting to have its day, but I. . . .*

and then, finally:

> *Girl from Massachusetts, I will remember you: your face, your eyes, your dress, your hair—but I will not remember your name. I do not want to know how your story will end.*

For the article writer, there are few kicks more enduring than a great close to a good article. It's worth rereading that "final" page a few times before you send the story off to an editor, and, if you have any doubts, rewrite it.

And if you think *you've* got it tough, consider Ernest Hemingway. When he was working on *A Farewell to Arms,* the novelist supposedly rewrote the finish 39 times.

Chapter 29

How Many Drafts?

Barbara Lede Stet was discouraged. "Jeepers," she said, "I don't know if I have what it takes. I must've rewritten this piece three times."

"So?" I replied.

"Well, if I was a natural writer—I mean a real born-to-be-a-writer type person—I think it would just *flow* out of me."

"Sort of as if you took a literary diuretic, right?"

"Right. I mean—"

"Why don't you shut up, Barbara?"

That wasn't a real conversation. I save up my hostility for my writing. In real life, I try to explain that different writers have different methods, and that Barbara and her counterparts of the many drafts are no less talented than the person who can sit down and write good prose word by word and have it appear exactly that way in print. In the business of writing, only one thing counts: the way the final product reads when it reaches the reader.

I can relate this to the column I write for *Writer's Digest*. It is never a one-draft proposition. I am usually lucky enough to accomplish it in two drafts, but it sometimes goes to three, and a couple of times (when I must not have known what I wanted to say in the first place) it has gone to four. And if that sounds like a lot of work, it doesn't compare to the work that I usually invest in a major, feature-length article—which I normally don't expect to get done in less than three drafts and, more often than not, will go to four or five. And even that may not be enough in the case of an ending or other key paragraphs.

This would be a tremendous amount of work were it not for my secret weapon: the typewriter. I am a fast typist, somewhere between 80 and 100 words per minute. My typewriter is a self-correcting IBM Selectric, too, which is twice as fast as standard electrics. What I lose in rewrite time I make up in speed. In fact, when I write a first draft, my objective is essentially to get all my thoughts down on paper in roughly the order in which they'll make the most sense, figuring that I can always do the cutting, build in the flow and smooth out the transitions in a subsequent draft. I work much the way a sculptor does: first a pile of clay with a rough shape approximating the subject, then a gradual improvement of line, a gradual adding of detail. But I get it all down *fast* to begin with, and that way I don't lose anything.

Needless to say, not everybody can type fast. Not everybody can type, period. I know at least one successful freelancer, a woman whose work has appeared in many major magazines across the country, who can't type. She writes her first draft in longhand, and has her teenaged daughter type the finished product for her. She rarely does more than two drafts. She's used to working that way (despite my constant pleas that she should learn to type, which I'm convinced would make her more prolific) and feels that longhand is less rushed, gives her time to reflect on what she's writing while she's writing it. For her, it works.

And not everybody is comfortable, as I am, doing three to five drafts. In fact, there is one danger associated with doing a large number of drafts, a danger that can't be eliminated: After a while, you begin to lose any objectivity you might have had about your own piece. It starts to bore you. If you've rewritten it five times, it stands to reason that you've probably read it no fewer than ten.

Maury Levy, whose work has appeared in *Oui, New York* and *Womensports,* usually does one draft. His first version, with small editing changes, is his final version. In Levy's case, it may be that necessity is the mother of invention: He is a lousy typist. So Levy thinks his stuff through, word by word, and puts it on paper with two fingers.

Another writer I know does it all with scissors. First there's a frantic pounding-it-out on the typewriter, then a more carefully-considered slicing apart and slapping back together. It's hard to believe that out of all those slivers of paper will come a story—but it does.

Who's right? There is no right. Different strokes, as they say. If you can do it in one draft, you're either good enough to get it right the first time out, or you don't have enough taste to realize that you really should've done three drafts. If you do six drafts as a matter of course, you might be heading for an ulcer. Or a nervous breakdown. Or the Nobel Prize in literature.

Regardless, here are some helpful tips to make your work more effective and less time-consuming:

1. Try to arrange your writing schedule so that you can build in a respite between drafts. A day is good, two days better. This enables you to get away from your article long enough to forget the parts you've memorized. When you come back to it fresh, you'll approach it as though you were reading it for for the second time instead of the tenth.

2. Get your research done before you start writing. Rewrites are difficult enough without having to make massive changes because you didn't do your homework, and a lot of writers—particularly those without much experience—get excited about a story and start writing it before they should; by the time the end comes around, after all the backtracking that this system makes necessary, the inspiration is gone—usually to the detriment of the article. When you sit down to write your first draft, make sure you have the information that will enable you to get it out of the way. That alone will cut down revision time substantially.

3. Feel free to work from an outline. I don't usually use any kind of outline myself, but that is not to say that I haven't occasionally used one to good advantage. It depends on how clear the article is in your mind. If you can think of it as a continuum and have a feeling for how the various characters and events can be interwoven, you don't need an outline—and that, I think, is ideal. If it's a confusing pile of data, however, you might want to prepare an outline. Outlines are no substitute for understanding, though, so go back over the information until it all hangs together in your mind. *Then* write.

4. Don't reread your article each time you finish typing an additional page or two. That will just add to the total number of times you'll be reading it; consider the mathematical proportions of typing and reading page one, then typing page two and reading pages one and two, then typing page three and reading pages one, two and three—by the time you're finished, you'll hate your own article. And don't try to perfect each page before you go on to the next, since that will create havoc with the pacing—not to mention your deadlines. Mike Kimmel, a writer of my acquaintance, says he *can't* stop working on a page until it's 100 percent right—so he works getting each page letter-perfect before going on to the next. He produces some excellent writing but, as he admits, nowhere near as fast as would be possible if he could break the one-page-at-a-time habit.

5. Don't do your editing at the typewriter. Try for a change of scenery. And more importantly, a change of seating. Writing is a sedentary task, and sitting in one position all the time will not only provide you with muscle aches and a sore back, but may put you into a stupor as well. I write at the typewriter, but I edit myself anywhere else—standing by my drawing board, sitting around a swimming pool, enjoying a drink in the living room or a cup of coffee in bed.

6. Don't be afraid to cut and paste. Rewriting is a combination of rereading and editing. Each draft offers additional opportunities for altering the position of elements, and if you come across an anecdote or observation that makes for a better lead, switch it to the front of the article and try it out. Second and third drafts are excellent times for knocking out extraneous sentences, quotes and so on, too.

7. Don't throw away your earlier drafts until you're done with your final draft. You won't necessarily *improve* just because you *change*.

8. If possible, have a good reader give your final draft a once-over. When I'm in doubt, I ask my wife to read my work; she's an excellent critic and a good editorial influence. But I wouldn't let my mother read it. She'd love *anything* I did. Moral: Don't let your mother be your critic, unless she's my wife.

Now you know. There's nothing wrong with you just because you do ten drafts, and there's not necessarily anything right with you just because you do one. Take it from me.

I've just finished writing/typing my first draft of this, but by the time you see it there will have been a couple of other drafts. And you'll *read* a much better piece than I just *wrote*.

Chapter 30

The Service Piece

You don't get too many guarantees in life, and I'm not about to offer an ironclad one—but I can *practically* guarantee that just about any decent writer who takes this chapter seriously can make some money as a direct result of it. Maybe you.

Now that's what I call a strong lead.

The idea behind all this came to me on a dark and stormy morning. There, on my desk as I arrived, was a thick envelope. Since I'm always afraid of thick envelopes (I'll never forget that story about the guy in England who had his arm—or was it his head?—blown off when he opened one), I asked my lovely assistant at the time, a mother of three, to unwrap it. I closed my door and waited.

Lucky for her, it wasn't a bomb. Just a manuscript and a few other intriguing odds and ends. And while it's true that a lot of the manuscripts received in this business *are* bombs, this one wasn't.

It was what is commonly referred to as a service piece—that is, an article at least partially dedicated to helping readers select something in a particular category, giving them as many facts as possible to help them make that selection. The writer of this particular piece, a fellow named Bill Ordine, went to a great deal of trouble to put together a service piece on golf courses.

Sounds dull, doesn't it?

But it wasn't. First of all, Ordine checked out more than 20 local courses. Then he wrote an article with a good lead and gave a blow-by-blow description of each course—not hole by hole, which would have been unutterably tedious, but the best holes, the most beautiful holes, the toughest holes. He either praised or damned the condition of each course, exploring why the courses were that way and what could be done to improve them. He talked about ambience, topography, aesthetics.

Then he made a chart which gave every necessary vital statistic for each course—from location and phone number to the number of yards to the availability of electric carts to the fees.

That would have been enough. But Ordine even had a freelance artist create a map showing the location of the courses, using golf flags to pinpoint each.

I bought the package.

From the standpoint of a magazine staff writer, service pieces are probably the least fun and bring the least recognition. Nobody wins any awards writing them, and they don't exactly make the kind of waves that good investigative reporting can.

But from the readers' point of view, these pieces are terrific. I remember the reader reaction received by a local paper in Philadelphia after running a piece on eyeglasses. The piece compared just about every optician in the downtown area. In each case, somebody actually went out and shopped for the same lenses (the frames varied depending upon availability). What the article showed was that it was possible to save a very large amount on the *same* pair of glasses—and it named names and showed just how much each optician charged for basically the same job. The piece was extremely effective and, believe it or not, was much talked about.

And that's the main function of service pieces. By the time you know you're paying too much, it's usually too late. By the time you get out to that golf course, you're not going to turn around and go find another—you're going to play it. Service pieces keep readers from making mistakes and enable them to get the best deal the first time around.

Loosely defined, a service piece is one that gives the reader information regarding the use or purchase of items, services of facilities. A how-to is not the same thing. This chapter, for instance, is a how-to, but it's not a service piece. In a service piece, you're not telling the readers "how to" do anything. You're simply doing the legwork for them.

As we said, most magazine staffers don't particularly like to do these pieces. And that makes them duck soup for freelancers.

Naturally, it's always best to query before you do any article. And it's best to get a definite assingment, if possible. But if ever there was an article that was worth doing without querying, or on speculation, it's the service piece. First, you can usually be fairly certain that no one else is doing it. Second, it's the kind of thing that most publications want and can't get enough of. It's not surefire—nothing is—but it's a good bet.

If you're interested in doing service pieces, concentrate on local markets. It's tough to do them for national markets because people don't shop nationally, and while you might be able to do a piece on airlines or mail-order houses or something like that, I don't recommend it. Stay local with this kind of thing and you can have a steady income, and what's better than eating regularly? More important, many a freelance writer has found the service piece a great way to get a foot into the door.

Okay, you say, where's the catch? Why aren't freelancers climbing over the transom to do these pieces?

Some are. But there's one major drawback to the service piece: It's time-consuming. You'll have to check your facts carefully, and there are going to be at least as many of them as you'll find in a typical investigative piece. The chances are slim that you'll end up with a fee commensurate with the hours you put in if you don't know how to get organized. On the surface, service pieces seem like a tough way to make a buck, and that's what discourages many writers from trying to crack the market.

But that surface appearance is a little deceptive, because the way to do this kind of thing is to organize yourself and your time before your start—and then take it step by step.

First, pick your subject. Timing is important. You don't do a golf piece in October. Ordine sent me his in late March, just in time to schedule it easily for a warm-weather issue. Conversely, I once received a piece about a boat-stealing racket which told readers how to avoid being victimized. The piece came in just a little late. I told the writer to resubmit it, and he did, but I didn't actually buy it until almost a year later.

Next, don't pick a subject that's beyond you—you're in no position, for instance, to do a service piece on car dealers; so many variables are involved, and so much of the information is dependent upon service after the sale. Don't try to be *Consumer Reports;* choose a subject in which you've had some experience. That way, your article can include the kinds of personal insights that really inform readers. Bill Ordine, for example, *is* a golfer. He doesn't say that in his copy, and he never told me that, but it's obvious just by reading him—and that gives him much more authority.

Once you've selected your subject, make a list of all the things that you think are important. Create a chart. An article about squash courts, for instance, might list the courts down the left-hand side—names, addresses and phone numbers—and the following categories across the top: number of courts; membership fee; court fee; guest fee; cost of lessons; hours of operation; and comments to cover anything that doesn't fit logically under its own category.(You don't want to create a category for a variation which will affect only one or two, maybe three, listings).

Now use the phone book. The yellow pages will tell you who's who in the field about which you're writing. Depending upon the kind of information you need, you can either (1) call the places and get the vital statistics, or (2) create a questionnaire and mail it to them to fill out, explaining that you're doing an article for a local publication and would like to include them. I haven't seen a commercial enterprise yet that won't cooperate when it'll be getting some free publicity, although I do remember a proprietor's becoming so nervous that he almost dropped his phone. I have a feeling his business was a front for a bookie joint.

Sometimes everything can be done on the phone or through the mail, depending on your subject. In the squash article previously mentioned, which was, in fact, published, the chart was constructed entirely over the telephone—but there were no ratings involved. If you're going to evaluate the services or facilities or merchandise offered—which might well make for a better service piece—you're probably going to have to visit the places in question. That's where the time-consuming part comes in. In fact, you must go out and actually "shop" in order to make accurate and fair comparisons. You can get quotations on the phone, sure—but you can't see what your money is buying.

This brings us to the most important aspect of service piece writing: accuracy. If you get a few facts wrong, chances are you won't get another assignment. In this sense, using a questionnaire gets you off the hook—you can always prove that it wasn't *you* who made the mistake—whereas a phone conversation can be misleading. You ask how many whatzits the shopkeeper carries; she tells you she has hundreds of them. But you may be talking about styles, and she may be talking about the actual number in inventory. Be careful.

Remember, too, that the best kind of service article won't be read exclusively by those people who are interested in the subject. The janitor's wife, in other words, *will* read about mink—so the problem, as in any other article, is to *make* the subject appeal to as many readers as possible.

Here's the lead to Bill Ordine's golf article. For the record, I've been on a golf course exactly twice in my life, consider the game a waste of time, hate it, and still found myself intrigued into reading his article. Ordine started out this way:

> Cobbs Creek Golf Course is a lot like Mrs. Spiegelman. Mrs. Spiegelman was a quiet, elderly lady who lived in my old neighborhood in South Philadelphia when I was growing up there.
>
> Cramped in the cattle hold of a livestock transport, her family had sailed from Germany at the turn of the century along with the "huddled masses" of a dozen other countries in search of the American Dream.
>
> For the Spiegelmans, the dream was fulfilled quickly. Within a generation they were the proud owners of three of the best Bavarian bakeries Philadelphia has ever known.

They prospered and flourished and were able to build for themselves a mansion of a home and enjoy most of life's luxuries, but they also shared their fortune with needy friends and were gracious patrons to their church. They were the new aristocracy of a generous democracy.

But the Depression hit the Spiegelmans hard. They didn't have the financial staying power to endure the lean years—they lost everything.

The fall came when Helga Spiegelman was still young, at a time in her life when she wore her wealth with a grace and charm that inspired admiration rather than envy.

When I knew her, Helga Spiegelman was old and gray. Some, seeing her on her way to church, considered her a pathetic sight in the faded and threadbare dresses whose cut and fashion were three decades past.

But Mrs. Spiegelman, despite her frayed hem and worn heels, still possessed the high cheeckbones, crystal clear eyes and the proud, erect carriage that reminded one of Katharine Hepburn playing some regal matriarch.

And in that way, Cobbs Creek Golf Course is a lot like Mrs. Spiegelman. . . .

Service pieces may or may not be right for you. If you *want* to do them, it's probable that you can quickly develop a reputation as an expert shopper—there are a few people who actually do this kind of thing consistently and make out pretty well at it. Most local or regional publications feel the need for service pieces, particularly those publications with a "city survival" angle, and few of them ever really get enough. I've seen good service pieces on dance studios, natural childbirth centers and hospitals, hotel rooms, theater seats, places for romantic interludes and many other categories of persons, places or things—and as many of them that have been done, there are millions left to do. Remember, your local publication has hardly scratched the surface; the field is wide open, relatively untapped, and ready for somebody who wants to tell the world where to find the best deal on—you name it.

Chapter 31

The Profile

"I just wrote a profile," Barbara Lede Stet gushed at me over the phone, virtually bubbling when she told me the name of the personality. It seemed that she had been lucky enough, or persistent enough, to have touched some sort of responsive chord in the soul of this hard-to-pin-down celebrity, had seen him and talked to him, and now she had written a profile on him. Or so I thought.

Bring it in, I told her. And 15 minutes later, she did. Our conversation sounded like this:

> Q: Gee, Barbara, what *is* this?
> A: It's a profile of so-and-so just like I said.
> Q: This is a profile?
> A: It's *not a profile?*

Good question. For what Barbara had brought me was a question-and-answer interview, which is, for my money, usually the most boring kind of writing possible even when it's good—except, perhaps, when it's done the way *Playboy* does it. And I'm not even so sure of that, since the question-and-answer format itself is so unimaginative and overdone.

But whether a Q&A can be interesting and provocative is not the issue here; the point I'm trying to make is that there's a substantial difference between an *interview* and a *profile*. Even if the terms are occasionally used interchangeably by beginning writers, the fact is that the two types of writing bear little resemblance to one another.

An interview is a conversation with somebody—most often face to face, but sometimes over the phone. It may be reproduced without much editorial comment (as in the Q&A format), or as a single-sequence story with editorial comment and quotations from the subject (newspapers often do this when a star comes to town). Or it may be *part* of the research for an article—one of many interviews, and one whose subject may not necessarily be important or integral to the article.

A profile is something else: It is an article whose main subject is a particular person, and it is rarely based exclusively on *an* interview or on interviews with that person.

In fact, profiles are probably at their least expository—and writers at their laziest—when written with information supplied by their subjects. After all, no subject—particularly one with some sophistication at dealing with the press—will supply information that might be damaging or embarrassing; the only anecdotes the writer will get will be those that the subject wishes to share. And, assuming that the subject is in public life, he or she will almost certainly be adept at handling the press; that ability is, at least in part, how celebrities get to be celebrities in the first place. Most public figures can be very likable and effective in person; no writer should go out to meet one without having done plenty of homework.

And what is that homework? In a profile, the subject is a human being—and that means one who has traversed a certain number of years, entered and left a certain number of neighborhoods and institutions, and come into contact with a certain number of lives—in other words, the subject has left a trail which, if it could be traced back from the present, would lead to a total picture of the subject's life. When writers write biographies, serious books that cover the entire lives of their subjects, they are as comprehensive as possible, attempting to find out that which has never been discovered, and to give greater meaning to all that *has* been discovered.

The difference between a *biography* and a profile, of course, is not merely the length, which would seem sufficient to necessitate a different treatment; rather, it is *focus* that makes the difference. A biography deals with the entire life of the subject, whereas in the profile (which is, incidentally, a device of magazines) the focus is current. The question, *Why are we interested in this person?* is always answered, *Because he is such and such today.*

In answering that question, several others should occur: Is the subject everything he seems to be? That is, does that image, that veneer of, say, sensitivity and forcefulness, really represent the person, or is that simply what he has decided to show to the world? You can't find out just by speaking to your subject, which is all Barbara did.

How did the subject get that way? Don't just ask, "How did you get to be so talented?" or "How did you get interested in acting?" That tells only the professional story. Try to find out what makes the subject tick—what drives him. Try to gain his trust and his sincerity. In those terms, Barbara was the taken, not the taker.

How does the world react to, and perceive, the subject? Not just coworkers and professional colleagues, of course, but other observers—from the media to the guy who runs the elevator where the subject works. Sometimes a simple question like, "Say, isn't that so-and-so?" can bring forth a torrent of gut-level reaction—and perhaps some good anecdotes and other useful information, too.

How does the subject perceive himself? This is probably the only question the subject can answer—but don't expect him to do it accurately. He won't say, "Actually, I'm a fraud, but I'm working on it." A fraud couldn't say that.

What can we learn about the subject by analyzing his environment—the people, places and things with which he surrounds himself? Barbara never got to see her subject in those contexts. What would his '79 Rolls Royce have told her? What would a '74 Volkswagen have told her?

None of those questions can be answered by discussions, no matter how frank, with the subject alone. Nobody would or could be that candid. In fact, even if the subject answered every question you might ask, holding nothing back—even if he were as candid with you as he might be with a psychiatrist—you would be getting the story from only one point of view. And the best magazine profiles are those in which the subjects are positioned in their worlds by a hundred different threads.

That was the strength of Nora Ephron, who wrote a number of profiles early in her career. It was not uncommon for her to do dozens of interviews. (I recall reading somewhere that she once talked to 90 different people for a single profile.) While that will seem like overkill to virtually any magazine writer (if not in terms of data gathering, then in financial terms, since no job could possibly pay enough to make 90 interviews economically feasible), that sort of thoroughness—or insecurity, perhaps—was at least partially responsible for the high reliability factor in Ephron's work.

But it's hard to imagine a standard magazine profile's requiring anything approaching that sort of depth. In fact, I remember a situation where an unnecessarily large number of interviews contributed toward torpedoing an article. In that case, a writer with a penchant for thoroughness conducted over 50 interviews for an article that actually required no more than a dozen. That in itself wouldn't have been bad if the writer had been able to toss out most of what he'd collected, but—having it—he was unable to either whittle it down or create a hierarchy of importance. He ended up trying to use almost all the interviews, and this resulted in an article that was disjointed—a shotgun rather than rifle approach.

The point is, then, that numbers aren't the important thing. How many interviews you'll do will depend upon how many you *have* to do before you find yourself knowing more about your subject than some of the people you're interviewing. There's a temptation to load up a profile with quotes, to try to impress the reader with the depth of research—but sometimes that breaks the tempo, drags the story down. A profile shouldn't put people to sleep. A biography sometimes will—since it is expected to be all-inclusive, and parts of anybody's life can be routine, even boring. But not a profile.

For a biography, of course, one must go back in time—not just months, but decades. For a newspaper interview, we don't usually have to go back in time at all. For the average magazine profile, because we're dealing with a person whose importance lies predominantly in the present, a few paragraphs about the subject's early life are usually enough; one would hardly try to track down elementary-school teachers.

The profile writer should go after three types of research: previous written material (like profiles and interviews and newspaper clippings); other records (like corporate filings, Dunn and Bradstreet reports, records of liens against property, professional or business affiliations or memberships, college transcripts, etc.); and interviews with people who know the subject and can relate to the subject's current life. While the written materials and other data will supply a fund of background information and give the author leads to follow, it is the interviews that will make the subject come alive for the reader. You can know all the known facts about a person, but nothing can replace the impact of his mother's saying, "My son is not a very nice person," or a colleague's saying, "He's impossible to work with."

(There are, of course, things that simply cannot be stated in an article even though they may be true; just what can and can't be printed is a matter of the public's right to know. While just about every magazine has a legal department to oversee such considerations, it might not be a bad idea to familiarize yourself with terms such as *invasion of privacy, defamation,* and so on, some of which are covered in Chapter 32 of this book. The fact that you are quoting someone else does *not* get you off the hook.)

Interviews are particularly important when one must write a profile for which the subject refuses to be interviewed—something that often happens when the figure is either reclusive or has an inkling that the profile might be unflattering. This can lead to the in-search-of profile, where the subject may never allow an interview (which is, of course, his right). Sometimes that kind of article will include sequences involving the writer's attempts to track down the subject; whether that slant works depends upon the ability of the writer and, for that matter, just how tough, interesting and revealing a chase he had.

One which appeared recently in *Oui* was called "Ten Minutes with J.D. Salinger," by Greg Herriges. The actual interview with Salinger, a recluse if ever there was one, is probably the least interesting part of the piece, and Herriges realized that the *most* interesting parts were his attempts to track the writer down, all of which were without the knowledge of Salinger. In fact, the piece would've been better had Salinger tried to avoid contact; as it worked out, Salinger was relatively receptive, if only for a very short time, and didn't have much to say; the article therefore expires rather than ends, even though it does so with a rather bittersweet sigh. At any rate, Herriges is to be congratulated for turning a dull, anticlimactic interview into an appealing in-search-of type of article.

If your request for an interview is rebuffed, that doesn't mean your article *has* to read like an in-search-of article. If that's the approach you want to take, fine. But if you would rather not concentrate on your search, there's usually no need to call the reader's attention to it. You can use quotations uttered by the subject during press conferences, for instance. Or comments which have appeared in newspapers—like "Spikol, quoted in *The New York Times,* . . . ." Or outtakes from speeches. Or quotes picked up from other magazine articles, so long as you credit the source, and as long as you're certain that your subject did in fact say what you're quoting him as saying. Whatever, if you intend to use any information which would appear to be inflammatory or potentially damaging to your subject, it's incumbent upon you to try to contact the subject and give him a chance to rebut. And you should keep a record of those attempts—a phone log and, of course, carbon copies and receipts from registered letters.

Should you tell the reader that you couldn't reach your subject? In a critical profile, yes, since you'll want to go on record with the fact that you tried to reach the subject and couldn't. But in any well-written profile, except for the in-search-of variety, the reader will hardly think much about that, since you'll have interviewed so many people *around* the subject, both friends and foes, that you'll sound like an intimate acquaintance. In a profile, those interviews are as important— maybe *more* important—than talking to the subject.

By the time you're done with the collection of data and the writing of the profile, you'll have a story which might not necessarily have an ending. Profiles are like that. What you've done is swooped down on a subject and caught him at a certain point in time; naturally, you'll have to swoop away and leave him there to act out the rest of his script. About all you can do is speculate a little about your subject's future—and, if you've done your homework, you'll probably be able to do that with some insight, as in:

> The future looks bright for Spikol. Since he won his Oscar for his outstanding portrayal of the singing priest in the remake of *The Bells of St. Mary's,* he is likely to be blending his many talents from now on.

And then, if possible, close with an anecdote, something that personifies and sums up your subject:

> It is 11:30 on a Thursday night in early February. Spikol wearily climbs the steps to his third floor office, turns on the light, sits down at his IBM, and begins. "The quick brown fox," he sings, sounding just a little like Sinatra. . . .

Chapter 32

Libel, Part I

> The First Amendment . . . presupposes that right conclusions are more likely to be gathered out of a multitude of tongues than through any kind of authoritative selection. To many this is, and always will be, folly; but we have staked upon it our all.
>
> — Judge Learned Hand

Judge Hand's statement is a cornerstone of the philosophy of the free press: that it is essential for American journalism to carry a wide variety of points of view about those people and institutions whose activities are grist for the mill. It is understood that the reports may be true or untrue, but there is a difference between intentional and accidental lies, between deliberately misleading innuendo and statements and simple, honest misunderstanding. True or not, it is thought to be better for the press to have the freedom to raise certain issues, and to express opinions on them freely, than to be restrained by virtue of being able to print only the truth, especially since the truth is only recognized as such after it is defended as such. And further, truth is not usually the province of one side or another of an issue, but usually rests somewhere between the two extremes, and — in that sense — lies even help us find the truth.

An example: You have written an article which accuses a corporation of intentional discrimination in its hiring practices, which is illegal. The corporation decides to sue for libel, saying that it may have few blacks and few women in its executive strata, but that the condition exists for reasons other than the systematic program of discrimination with which you have accused the corporation. In this case, the facts may be clear — but the *truth* may be harder to get at.

Curiously, what has come out of the courts is a wide variety of precedents that are useful but hardly the last word. Despite the celebrity of the libel action, there are libel actions being brought constantly, and there is probably not a publication in the country that is free of the threat of such a suit. And some of the landmark cases come from everyday, run-of-the-mill stories that contain a small factual error or ambiguity in language.

For instance: *You can tell an intentional lie and not be held liable for damages. You can tell the absolute truth, and be able to prove it, and be held liable.*

When I first heard those statements, I found them staggering. Tell an intentional lie and get away with it? Tell the truth—and have to pay for it? What kind of journalism is that?

As a writer, you'd probably like somebody to give you a list of everything that's libelous. You could then look at the list and say, "Well, now I know what to write and what not to write, so I'm safe." Unfortunately, that's impossible. First, the libel laws vary from state to state (although all states generally agree on the formal requisites of libel); second, it is not always easy to distinguish between what is *privileged*—in other words, fair game for the press—and what may be the press sticking its nose where it doesn't belong.

However, you don't need a list. You need only a few guidelines. And the first guideline is simple. Don't automatically be afraid of libel.

Libel means injury to reputation. A libelous publication is one which exposes a person to hatred or contempt or ridicule, or which tends to cause any person, organization or group of persons to be shunned or avoided socially and/or professionally and/or in their business or occupation. That should give you the idea: Attack somebody's reputation in print and you'd better be ready to defend your right to have done it.

The mere fact that some uncomplimentary information has been published is not automatically a guarantee that someone can successfully sue you. There are defenses to a libel action. And while this chapter and the next can't take the place of a course in libel law, we'll try to present guidelines sufficient to avoid basic libel problems. But because writers, like libel laws, vary, I leave you with that age-old warning: One who attempts to be one's own lawyer has a fool for a client. In other words, *when in doubt, check it out.*

First, let's take a look at what libel is.

To create a libel, you need three things. *The libel must be published. The person being libeled must be identified.* And finally, *there must be a harmful effect.*

Let's say that I decide that I dislike you sufficiently to write you a letter about it, and in that letter I say that you are incompetent, not trustworthy, probably psychotic, a torturer of children, a Nazi, a person totally diseased in spirit—and therefore, I no longer love you and am breaking our engagement. Is that libelous?

You might say no, because it's only a letter. However, letters can be libelous—and this one could have been if I'd sent a copy of it to all of our friends. That would constitute publication. However, in this case the correspondence has been between you and me, and I haven't shown the letter to anyone else—so I haven't "published" it.

There was a case where a man (it wasn't me) sent a letter to a New York widow in which he offered her five dollars for a date and pointed out that they could have "a good time." The letter wasn't particularly obscene, although it was a trifle suggestive, but the woman decided that she had been publicly insulted and sued for libel. She lost—the letter hadn't been published until she herself put it in front of the postal authorities.

In a 1964 case, a Texas newspaper raised defense in a libel action, saying that although the paper had been distributed, there was no proof that anyone had actually read it, thereby making an allegation only slightly less damaging than the loss of a libel suit. That defense didn't work; the court said that it could be *presumed* that the newspaper had been seen and the article read.

The next consideration is *identification*, and there are several ways in which you can identify someone. You can write the person's name—that'll do it for sure. But you can also provide a description so accurate and so revealing that the person about whom you're writing will be identifiable even though you avoided the mention of any name, or have adopted a pseudonym. For instance:

> Orville Peasley—not his real name—is a young blond dentist that most of Happy Valley knows as the Mercedes-driving resident of Crest Circle—a seemingly happy-go-lucky womanizer and, when he can get away with it, fee-gouger. What his neighbors don't know, however, is that Peasley, through an almost artistic manipulation of cash fees received from his patients, has been able to carve out a $200,000-a-year income for himself—most of it tax-free—enough to send him and his mistresses on 'round-the-world tours and buy him a palatial estate in Boca Loco, Florida.

Needless to say, there are methods of identification that don't require the use of a person's name, and if you'd written the foregoing, you'd have identified your subject in such a way that virtually anybody who knew him could identify him. (Of course, the above paragraph is so loaded with potential lawsuits that no magazine would ever allow it to slide by, and the writer would probably never get another assignment, either, inasmuch as he'd probably strike fear in the heart of any editor—but cases like this are quite common.) By the same token, you have to be careful when you substitute names—a name like Orville Peasley sounds fairly unusual, but if it actually exists it may be hard to prove that you didn't have it in for Mr. Peasley, and hard to convince Mr. Peasley that all the ribbing he's taking from his friends isn't worth some money. The only thing worse than having Orville Peasley suing you would be having Orville Peasley, D.D.S., suing you.

Again, there's a famous case like that. Around the turn of the century, in England, the Manchester Sunday *Chronicle* ran an article about a churchwarden who had a secret life replete with orgies on trips to the continent. The writer of this fiction attempted to select an unlikely name for his hero, and he did so: Artemus Jones. Artemus Jones turned out to be a London barrister who sued and collected despite the *Chronicle's* attempt to soften the blow by running a disclaimer saying that Artemus Jones was not *the* Artemus Jones.

There was a case in Pennsylvania where an article described the 4 a.m. occupant of a parked car as a "buxom brunette of Latin vintage employed by the state to attend to the needs of the indigent," and elsewhere in the piece as a "raven-haired, owl-eyed home-wrecking social worker." Sounds good to me, but she collected.

My policy in using fictitious names is: *One,* check the phone book for the existence of such a name (and you're much safer finding one for which no last name exists, as I did when I once used the name Max Kline in an article; there were no Klines at all in Philadelphia); *two,* since the phone book alone is no guarantee—after all, some people's names are unlisted—pick a name that has some personal significance so that you can prove you made it up and bore no malice in using it (a combination of your middle name and the name of the street you live on, for instance, might be safer than a name taken at random, which in my case would give me a character named Jerald Twentythird); or, if that fails, *three,* you might use a name so common that no one could possibly claim it refers to him alone, such as John Smith. Stupid names tend to sound unbelievable; typical names often sound *too* typical; both cost in credibility. There's nothing like using the real name if you can—but when it's not possible to do that, try to surround your character with enough specifics, even though you've changed all of the details, to end up with some credibility despite the fact that the name is a phony. And the specifics will help you avoid any case of mistaken identity, too, since the chances of anyone meeting all of your descriptive requirements are almost nil. For example:

> Ellie Miller lives in an expensive, tree-lined suburb about 30 miles from New York City with her three children. Her husband is gone— he left the sprawling ranch home two years ago in response, Ellie says, to "slights real and imagined," and since then the attractive 34-year-old brunette has been on her own, a paralegal by day, a law school student by night. Her oldest child, 13-year-old Meg, is very supportive, Ellie says, but it requires a superhuman effort to hold things together.
>
> In fact, it requires some behavior that is condoned by neither church nor state.
>
> Ellie Miller is not her real name . . . .

How about groups? Can you say that the US Army is riddled with drug use? Or that some New York cabbies take "the long way" around? Sure—since both groups are too large for any individual or group of individuals to take such criticism personally or have it reflect upon them personally. In smaller groups, it's best to use the word "some" or "a few"—although that didn't work in one famous case involving Neiman-Marcus and the book *U. S. A. Confidential,* in which the following line appeared: ". . . some Neiman models are call girls—the top babes in town." The court ruled, despite the use of the word "some," that the group was small enough that all nine were included. But in the same case, where a similar reference was made to the salesgirls, the court decided that 385 were too many (only 30 had sued). As a rule of thumb, when the number drops below 100, tread carefully.

The authors could easily have avoided the problem by neglecting to name Neiman-Marcus specifically. They could have disguised *it,* calling it a "large Dallas department store," or better still, "one of Texas's most famous department stores."

Which brings us to *harmful effect.* If a person or group is identified, and if something negative is said about them, it stands to reason that their reputations could be damaged. If that's true, the libel could be complete—but there is no libel unless the effect of the printed reference is to make people think worse of someone—as we said, to damage either a person's reputation, social acceptability or business or profession. The most dangerous kind of published reference would be one that would damage a person in all three areas, such as one that would charge crime or dishonor.

That's fairly clear; everyone knows what it means to accuse someone of having committed a crime, or of having acted dishonorably. However, what is actually libelous under these conditions is not always so clear.

Suppose, for example, you reported—erroneously—that someone had taken the Fifth Amendment seven times before a congressional subcommittee hearing. The person in question, it turns out, *never* took the Fifth. Can he collect?

The answer is no. Despite the fact that most Americans probably feel that lawbreakers "hide" behind the Fifth Amendment when they do not want to give self-incriminating evidence, it is every person's constitutional right to use the Fifth Amendment for that purpose. One cannot be libeled by being accused of doing what he has a perfect right to do. Likewise, if a shopkeeper is accused in print of having shot and killed a 16-year-old boy who was in the act of attempting an armed holdup of the shop—but it was, in fact, a local policeman who shot the boy—the shopkeeper, in all likelihood, cannot sue successfully for libel on the grounds that he was erroneously accused of murder; the fact is that the shopkeeper was accused of nothing more than acting in self-defense, something he had a perfect right to do.

Suppose you erroneously write that a person is deceased. Is that libelous? Not usually—not unless the person can show that there is a harmful effect, as if his wife remarried before learning he was alive.

However, journalists today must be more careful than ever with small details. The country is in a litigious mood—everybody sues these days, and even if there are no real grounds, suits are expensive to defend. Also, the press has occasionally been a target in recent years, and court decisions have gone against it in some notable examples, so the general public is no longer as quick to consider the freedom of the press inviolable.

In libel, the harmful effect requirement is what stops a lot of lawsuits. You learn, and report, that a restaurant has had four cases of food poisoning in the course of six months. This is true, and the restaurant doesn't deny it. Then, in your next issue, you report an additional case—but it is erroneous, the result of a garbled telephone message, and actually took place at another restaurant. The restaurant owner has a case—but, in order to collect, he'll have to prove a harmful effect. Can he parade a series of ex-patrons through the courtroom who will state that they stopped coming to his restaurant because of the fifth reported case of food poisoning? Can he document a loss of income directly attributable to the article? If not, he won't collect.

All of this is subject to variations from state to state, as well as to changes in the public consciousness. In some southern states it was once considered libelous to identify a white man as a black. In the thirties it was permissible to erroneously call a person a Communist without much danger; by the mid-fifties, what with McCarthyism, it was dangerously libelous. Some years ago, to imply that a woman was not chaste would have been considered libelous in every state; it probably still is in some states. On occasion courts have found the identification of rape victims libelous, although that has changed substantially through an enlightened attitude toward rape victims. And then there is the final problem: that considerations of chastity and so on would, in most cases, violate the privacy of the subject unless there was a reason why the information fell into the category of the public's right to know, as we'll see in the next chapter.

Who decides the disposition of a libel suit? Often the attorney involved; many such cases don't even get to court because the outcome is predictable. If the case does get to court, sometimes a judge will decide—unless he can't. In that case, he'll call in a jury.

Of course, the best defense is a good offense, and knowing what libel is enables writers and editors to avoid unnecessary risks. However, this knowledge shouldn't make the journalist skittish. Just what *is* in the public's right to know? Just where does a public life end and a private one begin? What are the defenses against libel suits? What can a writer say without fear?

That's what we'll be talking about next.

Chapter 33

Libel, Part II

You can't spend any appreciable time around journalists without hearing about the famous *New York Times* vs. *Sullivan* case, which culminated in one of the most important decisions regarding press freedom in this century. Oddly enough, the case did not revolve about a news story at all; its concern was an advertisement.

The ad in question appeared in *The New York Times* on March 29, 1960. It was an appeal for funds by the Committee to Defend Martin Luther King and the Struggle for Freedom in the South. As a result of the ad, five libel suits were filed, each of them by Alabama officials, for a total of $3 million.

One of the cases was that of L.B. Sullivan, commissioner of public affairs for Montgomery, Alabama, under whose direction the police department operated. The ad made some fairly strong accusations against the police, many of which were inaccurate, and it was Sullivan's contention that these statements therefore referred to him and everybody knew it. Sullivan was correct—the ad *was* riddled with errors of fact, even though it was contended that these inaccurate statements did not change many people's opinions about the officials in Montgomery, Alabama, very much, something that turned out to be an important consideration. The ad accurately pictured students singing on the steps of the state capitol, but singing the wrong song; it had nine students being expelled by the Board of Education, but for the wrong reasons; and so on. Sullivan pointed out that the *Times* could easily have checked the information contained in the ad, all of which they had in their files. Sullivan used this to support his contention of malice.

Sullivan won his case, to the tune of $500,000. The *Times* appealed, but the Alabama Supreme Court upheld the verdict. However, when the *Times* went to the court of last resort—the US Supreme Court—the decision was reversed. The Court stated:

> The constitutional guarantees require, we think, a Federal rule that

prohibits a public official from recovering damages for a defamatory falsehood relating to his official conduct unless he proves that the statement was made with "actual malice"—that is, with knowledge that it was false or with reckless disregard of whether it was false or not.

This paved the way for a new kind of journalism—a journalism that would conceivably enable anyone to make inaccurate libelous statements about a public official's conduct, so long as he referred to the official's public, and not purely private, conduct, and so long as the statements were not in reckless disregard of the truth.

In June 1967, the US Supreme Court extended the ruling to cover not only public officials but public *figures* as well—that is, those people in whose public conduct society and the press have a "legitimate and substantial interest," as the Court put it. In so doing, they reversed a $500,000 libel judgment awarded to former Maj. Gen. Edwin A. Walker against the Associated Press. The AP had reported that Walker had "assumed command" of rioters and had led a charge of students against federal marshals at the University of Mississippi when James Meredith was admitted as a student there in 1962. Walker had claimed those charges to be untrue, and the courts had upheld him—but the Supreme Court, in holding that he was a public figure, reversed the decisions.

However—and this is particularly important to the magazine writer—the Court made another decision upholding an award to Wallace Butts, former athletic director of the University of Georgia, who was accused in a *Saturday Evening Post* article of giving his team's secrets to an opposing coach. Butts had been recognized as a "public figure," but—because he was not the subject of "hot news," and because the editors of the *Post* should have recognized the need for a thorough investigation, the Court found in his favor, saying that the *Post* had recklessly disregarded the truth.

Note the differences between the two cases: The Walker case was just breaking; there wasn't time, in the interest of reporting the news in a timely manner, to check every conclusion. The Butts case, however, was investigative reporting—a staple of magazine journalism—and *not* "hot" news.

Another case which had an impact on journalism was *Rosenbloom* vs. *Metromedia,* where a former distributor of a nudist magazine brought suit against Philadelphia radio station WIP for comments made in a broadcast about the distributor. The jury awarded in the distributor's favor, but the Supreme Court reversed the judgment, saying that private persons are entitled to no more protection than public persons in matters that involve public interest.

This is, of course, all on a constantly shifting continuum; in 1974, for instance, the Supreme Court upheld a ruling that a prominent

Chicago lawyer, labeled a Communist in a John Birch Society publication, was neither a public figure nor a public official. Later still, Mary Alice Firestone, a socialite in Palm Beach, Florida, successfully sued *Time* for running an account of her divorce on grounds of "extreme cruelty and adultery" (there had been no official finding of adultery). Despite the fact that Firestone was socially prominent, had appeared in the press before and had held press conferences during the divorce proceedings, the Supreme Court said that she was not a public figure in that she held no special role of importance in the affairs of society—certainly not outside of Palm Beach—and had not thrust herself in the forefront of any public controversy.

Almost everything must be seen in the context of *whom*—whom we're writing about. There are a lot of grey areas in libel. Is a public-private person (for instance, a writer like you, who may not be famous but who may have had a few bylines in a few magazines) immune from press criticism? Hardly—in fact, because you help shape the opinions of people, you might be fair game for any media. But just how much depends upon *you*—how widely you're read and how much impact you have on how large a readership. Your reach need not be great; there's a good example in the case of the minister who was accused of seducing a housemaid and whose behavior was described in a newspaper account covering his hearing in front of a private tribunal. The minister sued, saying that the press had no business reporting on a private hearing, but the court said that because ministers are leaders of the people and their influence is great, their behavior is a matter for public concern.

Similarly, the world will probably not long remember the words of Earl Butz, former secretary of agriculture—although it is possible that *Bartlett's* will. Butz was overheard making a negative reference to blacks, was quoted, and lost his job as a result. Butz was in a private conversation, but he had long since given up certain rights as a private person: He was a high-ranking federal official. This doesn't mean that he had no right to privacy—he did—but his comments regarding blacks could not have been held to reflect only on his purely private life; such attitudes would have had to reflect, at least peripherally, on the way he did his job and interacted with people.

As for the purely private lives of public people, check any gossip column. Most of the items where actual names are used are relatively harmless, but where there is something sensitive enough to create an atmosphere for a lawsuit, there is usually an attempt on the columnist's part to defuse it, to disguise the person under discussion: "What well-known (and long-married) Hollywood producer is romantically involved with what bright, fast-rising star?" The item is vague enough to cloak those being discussed with anonymity—not for their protection, but for the columnist's—since the information being imparted would be hard to justify as being in the legitimate public interest. On the other hand, gossip columns being what they are, it's very likely that most people—the average, prudent person, so to speak—would be inclined to take anything that appeared in one with a grain of salt, a consideration which would help defeat a court action. But even in cases where people have, by virtue of their stardom, given up a piece of themselves for public consumption, it does not mean that they have given it all: A couple of years ago, for instance, Robert Wagner and Natalie Wood won a libel suit against a publication which had claimed that their marriage was on the rocks. Although the size of the settlement was not made public, observers said they walked away smiling.

Privilege is a public policy matter in the right of free speech. The idea is that you are granted immunity for liability or defamation that otherwise would be actionable—if what you write is a matter of public or social interest. Privilege is a necessity in creating a climate of free-wheeling, thought-provoking argument. In this category are: judicial, legislative, public and official proceedings. If a legislator calls another legislator a bastard during official proceedings, that's life. The otherwise libelous utterance is privileged; there can be no lawsuit.

However, when the press reports on the same situation, the privilege becomes *qualified* instead of absolute. It all depends upon how the situation is handled journalistically—and a publication can be sued if its reportage of the incident is unfair or inaccurate or intentionally misleading or malicious.

If a person is arrested, the press may report that, since it is part of an official proceeding. However, it is not always clear as to just what is and just what isn't part of an official proceeding, and there is no specific definition that can be applied. For instance, can the comments of a police officer out of court be considered part of an official proceeding? It depends upon the circumstances, upon who's making the statements, upon whether it's in the public interest to consider the comments *news,* upon who's making the judgment.

Again, I emphasize: *When in doubt, check it out.* In some states, certain kinds of court cases—such as divorce proceedings—may *not* be privileged. There was a New York case in which an executive was charged by his wife with infidelity, and a newspaper published the charge. The executive lost his job and sued the newspaper; the newspaper responded that its report was an accurate account of the court proceedings. The court found in favor of the executive because spatting marital partners often make unfounded charges.

Also not normally privileged, or at least in a caution area, are court papers that, by court order or law, are not readily available for public inspection. Statements made on the floors of conventions, as well, even if they are discussing public questions, should not be automatically considered privileged.

Very little that a journalist reports is fact; most often—and this especially true in the case of magazines—it's information obtained secondhand. As one who has dealt with magazine writers and is one himself, I can tell you that it's rare that a writer will be on the scene of an actual occurrence.

There is a notable exception to this, and that is when the journalist or writer becomes the witness—reads a book and then reviews it, goes to a movie or play and then writes about it, goes to a restaurant and passes judgment on it. The writer can condemn everything from architecture to zoos, and is at such times protected by the right to *fair comment*—or opinion. Opinions can almost never be proven, but nobody could write a column or an article without them.

Fair comment is a complete defense—that is, it wholly defeats a recovery on the part of the plaintiff no matter how defamatory or injurious the opinion may be—provided that there is no proof of actual malice. The premise here, as elsewhere in the libel laws, is that it is better for the reputation of one person to suffer, even unjustifiably, than to squelch free expression on matters of public interest. We live in an imperfect world.

There was a funny case recently in Philadelphia. The chef of a local restaurant sued The Philadelphia *Daily News* over a review which described the restaurant's spare ribs thusly: "generous in size but the dull, dry slab on the plate appeared to have been carved from a dinosaur by some Neanderthal chef and left standing all this time." The chef apparently felt that such a review reflected upon him in such a way as to subject him to the odium, scorn and contempt of just about everybody he knew, but Judge Stanley M. Greenberg rejected his claim, stating in part: "In this sophisticated age of restaurant going, the ordinary reader of the Philadelphia *Daily News* could and would not interpret any meaning to the phrase in question other than that the reporter thought the dinner was not good. In no way would anyone believe that it was somehow directed at this chef specifically."

In other words, you're fairly safe as long as you're stating an opinion that deals with a matter of public interest; as long as it is not presented as fact, but clearly as opinion; as long as the facts on which the opinions are based are truly stated; and as long as the opinion is fair and without malice.

Truth of the published matter is an absolute defense in a libel action. It is difficult to attempt to prove, particularly in view of the fact that the writer most often has no real knowledge of the truth, but only what he has learned secondhand. It is not enough to say that you have accurately quoted someone, either; if the utterance is libelous, the responsibility is always placed on the publisher.

Truth doesn't mean that everything that is written has to be absolutely true. It simply means that the substance of the charge must be true. In the *Sullivan* case cited previously, there were several errors of fact—but the court found in favor of the newspaper because the errors did not substantially change the gist of the charges. If a person is accused of the arson of a house on Main Street, whereas he actually burned down one on Broad Street, truth is still the best defense—the defamatory statement, the accusation, has to do with the act, not the location of the act. But if the building was burned down by accident, and the person who burned it was accused of arson by the publication, the truth would be no defense; the reporter cannot prove arson merely by the existence of a building that has been burned down.

You can see the danger in trying to prove the truth of a statement. If there is any foolproof method of doing so, it is to have incontrovertible documentary evidence: Saying a person is a bigamist is one thing, but having copies of two marriage licenses is another. Even at that, one would have to be certain that no divorce decree had been issued in the interim.

Two other common forms of defense against potential libel suits are reply and consent. Reply is just what the word says: If someone attacks you in the press, you have a right to counter the attack. If someone, for instance, were to write an article about you in which it was said that you exploited people in your business, or that you charged more money than your services were worth, or in some other way said something about you that could be considered defamatory (even if what they said fell under fair comment), you could go to a newspaper or magazine and point out that the writer who attacked you had an ax to grind; you might further question his journalistic ability or fairness—in fact, your reply can even libel the person who libeled you, provided that it doesn't over-respond to the situation. That is, if someone throws a tomato at you, you are not entitled to get even by burning the person's house down. So your reply to the person who said that you charged too much for your services can be that a check around town shows that your prices are no higher than anyone else's, and further, that this irresponsible journalist obviously did not bother checking *any* other prices—but you cannot say that he or she is a sex fiend and has been known to be a molester of prepubescent children.

From a writer's point of view, the message should be clear—a magazine under fire, especially one that feels that it may be in the wrong, may be willing to take some flack, even let someone reply in print if that will squelch any further action. Very often, regardless of whether there is a potential for action or not, the editor will publish a letter from the person in question in the letters-to-the-editor column.

Consent is a little different. It closes the barn door *before* the horse leaves. It means getting permission from the person about whom you have written something for its publication. Naturally, this is not done by saying, "Say, I've just written an article about you that's kind of negative; mind if I publish it?"

It's done this way: "My magazine is doing an article about you in which certain statements are made. We thought you would want an opportunity to respond to these statements before we go to press, just to set the record straight. . . ." If the person says "no comment," that's not consent, but at least it shows that the reporter attempted to give the subject an opportunity to reply. If, as sometimes happens, the subject can't be reached, the article should mention that attempts to reach him or her were unsuccessful. In fact, you'll sometimes see a blow-by-blow description of such attempts in particularly sensitive articles.

No magazine *needs* consent to publish material, of course. But it is a useful tactic in forestalling a libel action.

Becoming more and more prevalent is the idea that people have a right to privacy—"the right to be left alone," as Justice Brandeis once put it.

However, when people become part of a news event or part of a situation related to the public interest, they forfeit some of the right to be left alone. For a magazine writer this matter may require thought; one cannot easily dredge up the sordid details of a person's past, publish them, and then claim that they are somehow currently newsworthy. But if there is a rationale by which the public interest may be served by doing just that, the magazine can usually run the previous data, harmful though it may be. In one case, for instance, the Supreme Court ruled against a former child prodigy who had sued *The New Yorker* for invading his privacy. As a child he had been nationally prominent; the article appeared 27 years later. But the Court held that the fulfillment of the child's early promise was a matter of public concern, even though the person had long since slipped from the limelight. On the other hand, when the past of a former prostitute (who had been tried for murder and acquitted) was featured in a film, and she was identified in the film's advertising, the Court ruled that the use of her name and the mention that the story was taken from true incidents in her life violated her right to privacy.

The libel laws exist to protect not only those who might be defamed by the press, but the press itself. Only through the exercise of responsibility can the reliability and credibility of the press remain intact. There are magazines and newspapers in this country that are afraid to publish certain types of stories for fear of libel; however, the libel laws have enough flexibility built into them, and enough regard for the responsible operation of the press, to enable any legitimate journalistic organization to report candidly and without fear of reprisals so long as they report in a responsible and fair manner, without malice and without invading anyone's purely private life, material that is in the public interest.

Chapter 34

The $50 Billion Misunderstanding

After a decade in journalism, I figure I'm entitled to an observation. The observation is that the business community, by and large, does not particularly trust the press, assumes that there is a better-than-even chance that it will be misquoted, and feels that journalists "have it in" for business more often than not. I think the business community is probably justified in feeling that way; happy news regarding business is usually treated as ho-hum stuff; bad news makes headlines. Consequently, over the past few years, businesspeople have become more and more wary of journalists—gun-shy, in fact, is the better word.

Business—and by that we mean Big Business—began building up its own defenses when journalists became more aggressive: It came to realize that the more important function of public relations was becoming the ability to keep a name *out* of a story, not to get it *in* one. Public relations people suddenly had to really earn their keep, but they are, after all, just people. Some of them are so inept and so intent upon keeping the bad news hushed that they play right into the investigative journalist's hands. On the other hand, some PR people are so good that they actually manage to respond to all the issues raised, supply all the information necessary, and generally insulate their top management from annoying questions—while leading reporters to the "proper" conclusions. Sometimes the PR people get away with it. Sometimes they deserve to. Sometimes they actually get favorable press coverage. Sometimes it's a disaster on both sides: The journalist misinterprets and consequently writes something that shows a genuine lack of sympathy for, let alone a shocking lack of knowledge about, the business in question, after which the writer usually hides behind his First Amendment rights and the business tries to shrink into oblivion in terms of the press—which, these days, it can usually do, once it has bled enough—without resolving whether or not the company has been involved in any wrongdoing.

There is—no question about it—an adversary relationship between the press and business, and one sees it at the very root of it: in the magazine office itself. The editorial staff does not like the advertising sales staff, feeling that they would sell their mothers—or at least a little integrity—for a full-page, full-color ad. By the same token, the ad sales staff is likely to consider writers and editors distant, arrogant and snobbish—holier-than-thou types who can afford to have high ideals only because they're never put to the test outside the editorial office. And salespeople know about the editorial knee-jerk attitude toward business: Assume the worst and never give business the benefit of the doubt if it gets in the way of the story.

There's some truth on both sides, of course, and there's probably a subliminal reason for it: Business has always seemed to be the enemy of art. On the surface, at least, business is everything that art is not: It is shirts and ties and three-piece suits; it is large, expensive but not particularly tasteful automobiles; it is meetings in which the individual is reduced to a nonentity; it is loopholes; it is false smiles and false handshakes which conceal life-and-death competition; it is industrial spying and payoffs; it is sublimating principles for the good of the corporation. And when business does attempt to be a friend to art, it is usually attributed to—and no doubt somewhat attributable to—the tax write-off involved.

Art is thought to be the opposite of all that, supposedly free from the constraints of capitalism even though it requires its support.

Journalism, however, is neither art nor business, but a combination of— or at least stuck in a schizophrenic area between—the two. The part of it that is art is often artful, in terms of the writing and analysis and creativity, but then there is the other side: Journalists collect pay checks and Christmas bonuses paid for by advertising dollars, and they may not be particularly consistent in their policies regarding free trips or free samples. They will become outraged, and should, when an official from an American corporation attempts to bribe an official of a foreign power—and that, of course, is *not* nearly the same as accepting a free trip, but it is not altogether that different either.

The point is simple: There is no perfection. And chances are that the press and the world of Big Business will never see eye to eye. But the responsible members of both are trying; more and more business writers are surfacing as business becomes the stuff of which front-page news is made; and there is more room and more need for mutual understanding.

Business is smart enough to know how important this is. If a writer thinks that oil companies are causing massive oil spills on a wholesale basis, or that chemical companies are poisoning us through our foods, one doesn't correct the misconception by writing a Letter to the Editor. That's like closing the barn door after the horse has left; the damage done in a 6000-word article is not neutralized by 100 words in nine-point type. Further, Letters to the Editor always sound like sour grapes—while the journalist, of course, is perceived as some sort of crusader, presumed to have been reasonably objective. So business now sees that it must close the door *before* the horse leaves, and assumes that it *will* leave: that is, it *will* come under attack even if it hasn't *yet*.

The companies, in order to reach the journalists before those 6000-word articles are set in type, have to hit the members of the press where they live—for instance, in the *Columbia Journalism Review,* a national bimonthly published under the auspices of the Graduate School of Journalism of Columbia University that is part watchdog, part educator and part self-flagellator—pretty much what you'd expect.

But reading the *ads* in the CJR is an education in itself. And that's precisely the idea. There are ads which tell how we couldn't survive without chemicals, ads which attempt to explain atomic energy, ads which talk about the differences between trade names and common nouns (like "Xerox"). There are ads that explain the role of trucking in the American economy and ads that attempt to show the positive achievements of electricity. There are ads which seem to have no personal ax to grind at all: They are there just to present a point of view—although the one they present is never unfavorable to them. In a recent issue of the CJR, of little more than 100 pages about one-third were ads dedicated to creating better understanding of, and better public images for, the companies who were advertising.

Many of those companies encourage contact. Allstate says, "If you want to know what's happening in insurance, call us," and supplies the name and number of the person to talk to. So does an ad for Aetna which contains plenty of information, all of which is dedicated to making the journalists more aware of just what is causing the rising insurance rates everyone complains about. State Farm asks, "Did you call State Farm last year for help on a story? 541 other reporters did." The material is heavily one-sided when it takes a point of view; there is no mention of the profits made by the insurance companies, for instance. But these are, don't forget, ads.

There are also opportunities: a half-page ad for the John Hancock 12th Annual Awards for Excellence in Business and Financial Journalism—$2000 each to six winners in as many categories. And some of the ads are obviously trying to gain favor for themselves, like the one for Northrup that contains only a quote by Walter Lippmann, "A free press is not a privilege but an organic necessity in a great society." Well, gosh. Some companies grind their own axes rather noticeably: A Monsanto ad headline points out, "Without chemicals, many more millions would go hungry," a good point which is unfortunately followed by fourth-grade sentences like, "Some people think that anything grown with chemicals is 'bad.' And anything grown naturally is 'good.' Yet nature itself is a chemical process." There's an ad for The Tobacco Institute (that name *kills* me) explaining the fiscal end of the tobacco industry, with a photograph that shows a nice American family, tobacco growers all, standing in a lovely field of green tobacco leaves. I found this ad particularly horrifying, and I'd as soon have seen that family standing in a field of poison ivy—not because of them, but because of the arrogance of the tobacco industry in stonewalling the obvious. There's an ad from Phillips Petroleum about an aritificial kidney made with one of their chemicals, a well-conceived ad which doesn't say, "Hey, look, here's an oil company that isn't just tearing up the earth," but gets right to the point, never adopting a defensive posture: "For thousands of Americans with kidney disease, these are the threads of life." Some of the ads are designed purely for communication and a positive PR response, like the one headlined "Syntex update," which tells how most people think of Syntex as having been involved in the development of the "pill" a long time ago and then goes on to tell what's new with the company, without your hardly giving much thought to the fact that you weren't really wondering.

Well, all in all the CJR is a tour de force in that respect; it's unlikely that there is any publication anywhere which can boast more ads of that kind. And it is a tribute to the copywriters out there that some of the ads are more interesting than some of the editorial matter.

More important than that, they're informational. Forget that they're there to accomplish a particular end. What you should remember is that each ad is sort of an invitation: If a company is going to seem interested in reaching journalists in a magazine ad, it's going to have to treat you right over the phone. And if the company provides the name of the person to contact, well, that simply means that you should be able to call that person directly and get some information. The information you get will be what they want to give you—but if you ask the right questions, if you're really well prepared, and if you know whom to talk to, you'll probably get beneath the veneer of public relations and into the heavy matter.

Perhaps you should remember, too, that the relationship between the press and American business is strange indeed. The press, for its part, would vehemently defend the free enterprise system as one of the cornerstones of America, but "profits"—without which no such system could exist—has become a dirty word. It is strange now that advertising, another cornerstone of the system, is beginning to be used to close the gap between press and business—and may, in fact, be one of the more entertaining and informational aspects of the CJR.

There's something else, too. Not only are the ads informational, if one-sidedly so, but they offer plenty of meat for potential articles.

McDonnell Douglas, for instance, runs an ad telling how you'd expect it to build the world's best fighter aircraft—but did you know (a ploy common among these ads) that it also makes a system to test for and identify microbes, and even to monitor the performance of antibiotics against them? And did you know that they make a computer that can give you, over the phone, sports scores, stock quotes, ski conditions, weather reports, just about anything, in a natural-sounding human voice? And did you know that they can simulate the sea to help designers prepare ocean structures? In any one issue, there must be dozens, even hundreds, of good story ideas—not in the editorial matter, but in the ads.

As journalists become more sophisticated in understanding business, they will learn more and more where to look for chinks in the armor. While this will tend to eliminate dangers of oversimplification and generalization, it will also broaden the scope of the vulnerable areas of American business. So despite any understanding, there is little hope that any journalist will ever write, "There seems to be less and less corruption in Big Business these days." First of all, it's not good copy. Second, given human nature, it's probably not possible.

Chapter 35

Recycled Ideas

They don't make many writers like Thomas Wolfe, which is a good thing, because if there were more than one of him in any given century, I would probably hang up my typewriter and chuck it all. He was responsible for one of my favorite quotations, a line from *Look Homeward, Angel:* "Each of us is all the sums he has not counted: subtract us into nakedness and night again, and you shall see begin in Crete four thousand years ago the love that ended yesterday in Texas." The truth that resides in that quote gives credence to that which we call *human nature,* the never-ending combinations of whatever it is that makes us do whatever we do, and the conclusion of which is the idea that there is nothing new under the sun: not words, not ideas. Each generation may supply its own outstanding, even unique, voices, but they sing hauntingly familiar refrains.

Writers know this or learn it soon enough; those who do not should not be writers. We all have certain things in common. As we grow older, we are, for instance, more aware of our continuity in an historic sense; we wonder about things like our high-school graduating class and believe that it would be fascinating to go back and find those people and write about them. Probably each of us will, at some point, pick up a phone directory and start looking for the names of the little children who were our classmates in elementary school—to see where they live, if they are still in the vicinity. We will look at camp pictures and wonder; we will look at photograph albums and wonder.

I wonder in just this way about one child in the neighborhood where I grew up. He was a tough, not terribly bright little boy who had for a mother the neighborhood floozie. Back then, I could not yet see that his toughness was motivated more by his vulnerability than by his strength, nor that his hostility was a product of his thinking that everybody was talking about him, let alone grant to his mother the understanding that *she* deserved. One day, when push came to shove and he attacked a younger friend of mine, I forgot that he was the neighborhood bully. I pounded him into the sidewalk with my outrage. Not until years later, guilty about the beating that I'd given him, did I look up his name in the phone book—and found him living in a depressed area on the wrong side of the tracks, so to speak—and wonder what had happened to him since that day he went home, bawling, in his oversized, hand-me-down winter coat and bloody nose.

Thereby hangs a tale, which is precisely what writing is all about.

There *is* reason to go back to find the unfinished story, even when it is unfinished only in our minds. And very few magazine articles end with a finality that is the absolute end; the story is only over insofar as it can be *at the time it is written.* That's important. It is the key to everything that follows here.

But let's leave the sentimental side of this, get into the mercenary side of it for a moment (after all, that's why you're here) and advance a theory: *You can find enough stories to keep you busy forever—doing little other than recycling old ones.* In other words, I maintain that you can look in newspaper or magazine back issues of ten years ago and come up with articles that are as fresh—and as interesting—as anything you'll read today. In fact, your own files may be the most logical place to start looking.

To prove this, I started doing just that—poring through my own files.

I found, for starters, an article I wrote years ago about a local women-against-rape organization. The group, working in conjunction with a major hospital, had just gotten off the ground at the time. Today, I know that it's changed—it's gotten bigger, and it's probably more effective, and the public consciousness regarding rape has opened up due to the increased reporting of rapes. There's got to be a good story there even today—with a "revisited" slant.

I wrote a piece about a shopkeeper who was being forced out of his home *and* his business by vandals, shoplifters and other sorts of criminals. The man was trying to sell out on both ends, and he was having a hard time. His family was living through the worst kind of anger, and nobody could blame them. That was several years ago. What happened? I'd like to know, and I figure that maybe readers would, too. That would be a combination of the follow-up and whatever-happened-to types of pieces, and there's a lot to be said for each of them since we have more people lapsing into obscurity than we can keep track of, thanks to the voracious appetite of the media. Just read one five-year-old newspaper or magazine and see for yourself.

Another article I did some years ago was about an exciting new concept called urban homesteading, the turningover of HUD-owned properties to city dwellers *free* on the condition that they bring the homes up to city housing code standards. That was tried in

Wilmington, Delaware—the scene of my story—and now maybe it's time I wondered about the program's success or failure. Are hundreds of people living in wonderful new dwellings that they got for nothing? Or did the whole plan, like so many other urban-development-improvement dreams, turn into a slummish nightmare? And why?

Should I write this? Any of these? The real question is: Are they still interesting? If you can read an article that originally appeared five or ten years ago, and still care and wonder what happened, chances are it's worth looking into.

And there are thousands of ideas like that out there *already in print.*

Easy to say. But just how easily would a freelance writer find ideas in old magazines? Could it be done—or is it just an idea that sounds good on paper?

I decided to put it to the test.

Since I'm lucky enough to have the main branch of the Free Library of Philadelphia just a few blocks from my home, I went there one Saturday afternoon and asked for a year's worth of back issues of *Esquire.* I chose 1970, only because it started the decade, and I chose *Esquire* because it was *Esquire.*

I managed to get up to only April or May in 35 minutes of browsing, but that was enough to convince me. The first thing that caught my eye was a short piece by Kurt Vonnegut, Jr., about his high-school class of 1940, which was contrasted with several short pieces from the "Class of Now," 1969. There's idea number one—maybe it's time, I thought, to do the Class of Now again—what are high-school grads like *today*, considering the differences in turbulence from the late '60s to the late '70s? *Where* are they? Things are quiet out there—but are they worth looking into?

Those issues of *Esquire* were during the early days of Women's Lib, as we all came to call the feminist revolution, and *Esquire,* in its inimitable let's-be-chauvinistic-for-the-hell-of-it manner, ran a picture feature—"Six Jobs in Search of Truly Liberated Women." The jobs were: hockey player, forest ranger, university president, construction worker, ladies' shoe salesman, and locker room attendant. Some of these were meant to be sexist jokes, some were unwittingly so, with *Esquire*'s sexism going right over its own head, and some were slightly serious within the context of the times (although it was hard to take them that way with the scantily clad women being shown in their respective jobs). Interesting—but of what value to us? Well, *are* there jobs that women *can't* get today despite the EEOC and the retroactive awards and fines, etc.? There must be—and what reader wouldn't like to know the jobs where women just don't show up in numbers, whether by choice or by discrimination?

Esquire also had a profile of Helen Gurley Brown, then maturing gracefully. Now she's nine years older. Where is she? And where is *Cosmopolitan?* I'm talking about the woman and the empire in a personal sense, not the kind of thing one learns from TV talk shows. This isn't an easy assignment, and probably difficult to line up, but very likely a most interesting piece for the person who gets it.

There was an article about three Harvard students who traveled the world on practically no dollars a day—one of them, in fact, came back with more than he took. I started wondering: What's the cheapest a student can travel these days? And what ever happened to the three sharpies from Harvard who looked so confident and wordly-wise—did they end up with bills and mortgages and taxes like yours and mine?

There was a section called "California Evil," a neat series of little pieces on the West Coast's sects and sex, its occult and its craziness. *Lots* of story ideas there.

Esquire also did something called "The 100 Most Important People in the World," which opens all kinds of possibilities. It could be done again—or, on a smaller scale, localized for a city or a state. Or how about trying to guess who the most important 100 people will be *two years from now?* Accuracy would be impossible, but nobody takes pop sociology seriously anyway.

There was yet another article about the great jocks, guys like Charles Atlas and Johnny Weissmuller. *Esquire* did its own little bit of revisiting back then to find out what they were doing in 1969. Right about now, though, aren't you getting just a wee bit curious about Mark Spitz?

Well, that's it—not bad for half an hour, I figured. I had plenty of ideas, and I was about to leave, but then something else hit me, something that I'd been looking at all along without really noticing: *the ads.* There was one for a pipe tobacco that jumped off the page with this headline: "If your wife says she doesn't go for the great autumn day aroma of Field & Stream . . . send her home to Mother." Another for some reducing machine called Relax-A-Cizor with a guy standing up, strong and virile, and a woman wrapped around his legs adoringly. You just don't *see* that kind of thing anymore, and there's a terrific article waiting to be done that hardly needs any text at all— the reprints of the ads would speak for themselves and for the changes wrought by the women's movement.

Magazines aren't the only source of magazine articles. In fact, the great newspaper stories of yesterday have a way of becoming terrific magazine articles today. Hardly a year goes by without somebody's writing about the Lindbergh kidnapping or the Rosenberg trial or one or another of countless front-page stories long gone. There are likely to be a few corkers on the local level, too, in your own neighborhood, and it's not uncommon for regional magazines to start digging up 15- to 20-year-old mysteries or to resurrect murder trials which were particularly stimulating. Those that are the most intriguing are, of course, the ones that were never wrapped up—the murders that weren't solved, the unexplained disappearances, the unidentified bodies, the embezzlers who got away—since there's always a chance to come up with a new theory. You can't find those ideas using only your memory—but if you go through the back issues of your local paper, you're likely to be surprised at how many there are.

By now, you have the idea. If you have a good library anywhere near you, or a stack of old magazines in your attic or basement, you probably have enough stories to recycle to keep you busy for a long, long time. And there's one other nice thing about all this: When you're looking at a complete article on the subject, no matter how dated, a lot of the big problems—like where to start, and whom to talk to first—are eliminated. The past is a great road map for your writing future.

Part III

Introduction

I'm devoting this part of the book entirely to one subject—the city magazines. I've decided to handle them separately not because they're somehow more important, but because they offer the best kind of opportunity to a writer looking for a reputation.

That's "best"—not "easiest." The city magazines are nothing *like* the easiest to hit; it is far simpler to sell a trade journal or special-interest magazine than it is to sell most of the better city magazines. Trying to sell them, for one thing, usually will put you in direct competition with some of the best writers in town.

That's understandable, since most reputations are made locally first, and city magazines provide better visibility than both newspapers, where a good piece of writing, no matter the quality, is only around for a day, and national magazines, whose circulations within the metropolitan area will rarely outstrip that of the city magazine there. (For instance, sell an article to *The Saturday Evening Post* and see how many of your friends or colleagues notice it. Or, for that matter, *Fortune* or *Esquire* or *The Atlantic*.)

Besides being less ephemeral and more visible, there's the size of the market to consider. Most city magazines are fairly bottomless; they buy a lot of freelance writing and have a continuous, ongoing and ever-growing (if the magazine intends to stay in business) need for articles, columns, criticism. And your competition, while it's hardly lightweight, isn't as tough as it is in the major national magazine markets.

That's part of my reason for separating this section from the others.

The rest is personal. For ten years—up until the beginning of 1979—I was totally immersed in city magazines, first as an art director, then as a writer, and finally as an editor. I was involved not only on the editorial side, but on the promotional side as well. So I probably know city magazines better than most; I've spent what seems like a lifetime talking about and critiquing them. And I can tell you this: There's no better place to get experience, no place where talent is more likely to be recognized, no better forum for your work, than the city magazine.

Read carefully. This could be your market.

Chapter 36

The City Magazines

Not too many years ago, there weren't very many city magazines, and those that did exist were most often a vehicle for business—spreading the word (and often a bit of puffery) about local merchants and providing a forum for the ads of those merchants. City magazines were sort of incestuous then, more often than not run by chambers of commerce.

Today it's hard to find a city *without* a city magazine, and while they are not oblivious to local business, the publishers and editors of citymags have zeroed in on their real audience: the upwardly mobile residents in and around a metropolitan area. Where it was once thought that newspapers took care of that audience, today's publishers know that a good city magazine can provide a lot more depth, personality and entertainment than lots of newspapers—in a different manner, of course.

Today, that difference has resulted in the existence of hundreds of city magazines in this country. It is, in short, a boom. And if you're a writer, you can cash in on it. But first you have to understand the market.

While I was at *Philadelphia Magazine*, I met one Chicago-based writer who did understand the market. He wanted to do a story for us, and while we weren't often sold by out-of-state writers, his idea was good and we hadn't done it. He got the assignment.

What's surprising in this case is that the writer had already sold pretty much the same article to many citymags all over the country. He had come up with an idea that would work in virtually *any* city magazine; each article may have been different in its details, but the theme was the same, because all cities have certain things in common. My Chicago friend understood this as well as anybody could: There may be vast differences between city magazines, but they are all sisters and brothers between the covers.

Will you be able to sell the citymag market? That depends a lot upon your imagination and your talent. But if you have both, the opportunity is there. In every city, there are people who can write. Many of them *are* writing—are employed doing it full-time, mainly at the city's newspapers and the city's ad agencies.

Then there are the tired, the poor, the huddled masses: the freelancers.

If you are in the latter category, you're in the best position to sell the city magazine. Not because you're the best writer in the city, but because you are *available.* Lots of people who earn their livings in full-time newspaper jobs would *love* to freelance for local magazines, but most newspapers forbid such activities. The *Boston Globe* forbids its writers, for instance, to write for *Boston Magazine;* it did this as soon as the magazine became competition. The Detroit *Free Press* and the Detroit *News* both forbid their writers to write for *Monthly Detroit,* the new magazine there. And so it goes all over the country— because there's no question that citymags, if they're doing any kind of job, are in competition with city newspapers for stories, advertising, readers—and for writers.

But they're *not* in competition with one another; in fact, it's rare that a typical citymag reader will ever see another city magazine—except, perhaps, while traveling. For that reason—and this is worth remembering—in the city magazine business, everybody looks at what everybody else is doing. It's hard to say whether there's as much inadvertent duplication as there is outright copying of ideas—right down to magazine covers. The lightweight and just-starting-out magazines are inclined to be more, um, derivative; the heavyweights tend to originate ideas. Therefore, knowing who and how to copy can be a rather important stepping-stone to citymag success.

I remember that we were copied a lot at *Philadelphia Magazine.* Most of the time it didn't bother us—as long as we kept coming up with ideas worth appropriating, and as long as we were the first to do them. In fact, at one time, when we were trying to get *Boston Magazine* off the ground (both *Boston* and *Philadelphia* are owned by the same corporation), we occasionally copied ourselves, using identical covers in both markets. Now the two magazines are totally independent of one another editorially.

Still, city magazines are similar because cities are similar. They share many of the same problems; they have populations of people who want to be told how to survive and how to have fun in a city. You'd be hardspressed to find a halfway-professional citymag that didn't include, for instance, a restaurant column and a films column. By the same token, you'd be just as hard pressed to find a city large enough to support a profitable magazine—the rule of thumb is about one million residents or more in a total metropolitan area, although I believe it can be done with much fewer if the audience profile is right—that didn't also have a "right" and "wrong" side of the tracks, bad guys and good guys, municipal corruption of one kind or another, singles bars, racial problems, a high divorce rate, welfare problems, crime, drugs, juvenile delinquency, problems with the elderly, and so on, all of which are viable topics for articles. The similarities between American cities are far more palpable than are the differences; people and their institutions are pretty much the same everywhere.

* * *

Just what *is* a city magazine, and what kind of market does it represent for the freelance writer? That's not as easy to define as it sounds; it's not simply a magazine published for a local readership. In fact, in writing this, we had to decide just who was and just who wasn't a "city" magazine, and we ended up with a definition which seemed to encompass an arbitrary conglomeration of magazine titles. But there was a method to our madness. For instance, we decided that a city magazine is not a local "business" magazine or a local special-interest-type magazine devoted to such things as tourism or recreation or natural resources. By the same token, we felt that a city magazine could even be a *state* magazine—like *Texas Monthly*—simply because it seemed to reflect a city-magazine philosophy between its covers, despite its coverage of a much larger geographical area. On the other hand, in some cases, we eliminated state publications because they were interested strictly in performing PR for the state. I guess our final definition really came down to a certain kind of magazine that publishes a certain kind of material for a certain kind of audience, and *Chicago's* editor-in-chief, Allen H. Kelson, said it best when he described what he looks for:

> Analytical pieces on the persons and activities which result in significant local happenings—not "news" so much as why "news" came to be and the effects of "news" on those involved.
> Profiles of significant local figures, celebrated or otherwise.
> Service pieces evaluating or commenting on goods, services and establishments which affect readers' lifestyles.
> Departments coverage of film, classical music, dance, dining, wine, pop music, local history, books, folk music, art, shopping, etc.
> Special sections on travel, skiing, home electronics—all with as much local orientation as possible.
> Studies of lifestyles in particular areas of Chicago, or among certain ethnic, cultural, or other social groups—often whose lifestyles differ from our readers'.
> Newsy short takes about often-overlooked or underestimated happenings.
> Personal journalism relating to aspects of life in the city.

Specialized one-shot columns on peculiarly local aspects of business, law, personal finance, etc.

Lifestyle pieces dealing with fashions, physical well-being, decorating, personal money management, etc.

—all of which seems to cover the subject fairly completely. Naturally, even where not specifically mentioned, the emphasis is on the *local* scene.

Not every city can support a city magazine, and no city magazine would try to attract its area's total population as readers. City magazines normally try to appeal to an "upscale" audience—in other words, readers with money—because no city magazine can exist without delivering to its advertisers the particular readership they want, a readership with enough expendable income to buy the products advertised. If that is a weakness of citymag journalism, it is also its greatest strength: The magazine does not have to write to the lowest common denominator and can therefore expect to reach readers with clout, readers with influence and power, readers who can effect change. But it clearly disenfranchises many lower-income readers, unfortunately, and that's something you have to understand if you're going to sell this market.

Some time ago, in fact, *Washingtonian* (Washington, D.C.) received some criticism from a local newspaper columnist for failing to address itself, or for actively trying *not* to address itself, to Washington's less affluent residents, most of whom are urban blacks; this criticism caused the magazine's editor to go through some considerable soul-searching regarding the entire process and responsibility of city magazines. But it wasn't a problem of his making; the magazine would probably cease to exist if it were seriously to tamper with the demographics of its audience, because its value to advertisers as a business-attracting vehicle would be inversely proportional to the number of lower-income readers it reached. That's worth remembering: Right or wrong, citymags are not meant for everybody; despite the "city magazine" nomenclature, they—like virtually every other magazine—are in business to make a profit, and that profit, unlike the few magazines in this country that can make it on subscription and newsstand sales alone, is inextricably linked to advertising.

What does this mean to a freelance writer who would try to sell a city magazine? Just this: The magazine is far more likely to publish an article that touches the life of the upper-middle-class reader than one that addresses itself to the opposite end of the economic spectrum, and any city magazine that claims otherwise is either lying or going to go broke. City magazines don't want to tell their readers how to make their food stamps go further or how to fight the gas company; they want to tell them how to invest in real estate, show them the new "in" bathing suits, pick for them the town's ten best restaurants. In other words, you're writing for a unique audience here—the more sophisticated city dwellers, a hip readership with the intelligence, supposedly, to appreciate a well-written magazine article—or to write nasty letters about a dumb one. And they have money. As *Philadelphia Magazine* says in its advertising rate card, "When you advertise in *Philadelphia Magazine,* you don't waste money talking to a lot of people who can't afford your product or service." Carol Gage of *Sacramento Magazine* puts it even more bluntly: Asked to describe her magazine's audience on our questionnaire, she wrote simply, "$40,000 + per annum."

But these facts should really be seen in a larger context—since on their own, they would seem less than flattering to many of the better citymags. While the name of the game is entertainment—a point which nobody bothers to dispute anymore—many of the better city magazines clearly manage to put relevance and the public good on a par with having fun and selling copies (not *ahead* of it, because it does no good to run the most important story in the issue on the cover if this means that the magazine won't sell). An editor may, for example, want to publish an article about widespread abuses in local nursing homes, but if he's smart, he'll resist running it as a cover—because far, far fewer people will want to buy the magazine with that story on the cover than would buy a cover about restaurants. In effect, running the restaurant story on the cover ensures that more people will read the article about the nursing homes. (Even at that, the nursing home story will never be addressed to the people it concerns most—those in the nursing homes. It will always be written to an upper-middle-class audience.)

Because magazine covers are what newsstand sales are all about, it's not at all uncommon for magazines to feature attractive females on their covers (almost always sure sellers) regardless of the topic, since females generally sell more magazines than males. And many magazines go even further—and run articles and even covers largely to generate advertising. It's not always blatant—in fact, it's rarely noticeable. But if a magazine runs a Dining Out issue, it's going to tap into a lot of restaurant advertising it wouldn't have gotten otherwise, with new restaurants coming in for the first time and regular customers increasing the size of their ad space.

Is it intentional? When we asked most of America's citymags if they did this, many said *no*—some said *no!*—but lots qualified their negative replies (after all, no advertising sales department is going to ignore a natural and logical tie-in).

Frankly, we thought editor Tim Whitaker's *(Valley Monthly Magazine,* Allentown, Pennsylvania) response as to whether he ever runs articles for the primary purpose of attracting advertising was particularly candid. "Doesn't everyone?" he asked. Probably, and sadly, in one way or another, one does.

Because the citymag must generate advertising, and lots of it, to keep going, some writers have figured out that it might be wise to take a look at the ads in order to see just what kinds of articles to suggest. It won't work in every market, but there's no doubt that it will work in many; at least you'll know who the readers are. For instance, in a magazine with a dozen beauty salon advertisers, it's logical that the readers are people who are interested in their appearance, and it might pay to suggest an article on 1979s new makeups; or if a magazine seems to have a lot of investment-type ads, it might be worthwhile to approach the editor there with an article on, say, retirement plans.

Further, some magazines have their schedules lined up as much as a year in advance—not altogether, since that wouldn't be possible, but in terms of a guaranteed group of dining or travel or how-to or service pieces to enable advertising salespeople to sell, far in advance, specific ads against compatible editorial material. So if you'd be inclined to try to hit the more advertising-oriented of the city magazine markets, it might not be a bad idea to obtain copies of their direct-mail advertising to customers to see just what's on the agenda—after all, why waste time querying if they've already got your article in the works?—and to try to predict what kinds of articles to logically suggest.

Also—and this is something freelance writers never think of—it might not be a bad idea to try to get some demographic information about the readership, which is usually available from the magazine's advertising sales department. After all, that's where you can learn about the average reader in detail: how many plane flights taken, how many cars owned, how many years of college, how many single and how many married and how many divorced, how many bottles of liquor consumed, and so on.

If you're one of the better writers around town, you shouldn't have any trouble breaking into the local citymag market, provided you can slant for that market. Familiarize yourself: Pick up a few copies of the magazine and study it carefully, noting how many people are on the magazine staff and how many freelance articles are used per issue. You can figure this out by looking down the masthead and observing the names—and by examining a few issues, you'll be able to determine which of these people write and which do other jobs. There are no hidden writers except for straight freelancers; citymags list just about everybody in order to look as prominent and successful as possible. Try to determine the size of the freelance group used by the magazine. And take special note of any listing of people described as contributing editors or contributing writers—they're "preferred" freelancers, very often "regulars," and they're your big competition. In fact, that's the list you want *your* name on.

By the time you've done all this, you should have a pretty good idea just how large and how well supplied the market is.

Also, take a good look at who does what kind of article, because it stands to reason that you won't get your name on that list of contributing editors by doing exactly what somebody else is doing, like trying to write a "films" column that's already assigned to a regular— unless you think the columnist presently ensconced in that position is so terrible that the magazine would probably be thrilled to give him or her the ax. Freelance writers for city magazines often have specialties—like being particularly good at criticism, or life-style, or science, or business writing—and you may have to determine yours in order to squeeze in. That's one big reason why citymags find freelancers so useful; most editors seem to agree with James Selk, editor of *Madison* (Wisconsin): "Variety."

On just that note, a lot of people have found that the service article is a good way to get a foot in the door. A service article can be anything from a comparative shopper to a how-to, and citymags are nuts about them. Further, they don't usually get enough from competent writers who are also dependable researchers. And service articles work better in citymags than anywhere else because they're at their best when restricted to a small geographic area in which it's possible to make comparisons. Cities are, for instance, great places in which to choose the Ten Best of anything (several magazines cite "Best and Worst" covers as top-sellers), or to help somebody locate products or services. Even *Esquire,* when it decided a few years ago to present the Best of America, did it city by city. Of course, if the city is too small, this won't work, because the kinds of articles I'm talking about are rather typical of areas in which there's a large choice among merchants; but if the city's large enough to support a magazine, it's probably large enough to support an adequate number of different kinds of products and services about which to make comparisons. The how-to aspect comes in where you not only tell somebody where to find the largest selection of, say, seeds and garden supplies, but also tell the prospective shopper how to then start a vegetable garden on a city roof.

Here's the way a typical idea might grow— and also get you a great assignment.

Say the article you want to write is about pipes. You figure that it should include discussions about what to look for regarding grain, how various manufacturers differ (and what the differences mean to a pipe smoker), how types of pipes differ, a discussion of proper pipe care, etc.—all of which could logically appear in *any* article on pipes. But how do you localize this for a city magazine? Well, you might visit the major tobacconists in your city and create a chart based on their selections, prices, types of tobaccos handled and so on—in other words, rate each store, or at least list its better and lesser points. And perhaps you can do a sidebar, based on local celebs (who might or might not actually smoke pipes), entitled, "Which Pipe Is Right for Whom?" which could serve a double purpose—to localize the article further as well as take care of the discussion regarding which size and shape goes best with which face. Next, everybody knows that academia is supposed to contain more than its fair share of pipe smokers—and you could check out your local universities to find out if that's really true, perhaps ending up with some interesting quotes. Maybe you'll even find some pipe collections in your travels, which are unusual enough to feature photographically. Or maybe there's a "My Favorite Pipe" approach. To *my* knowledge, those particular angles have never been done—but chances are good that somebody, somewhere in this country, has already done each of them. That's how it is in the citymag market.

You can write articles like those on anything from eyeglasses to running shoes to dog obedience schools—if there are enough of them around (*and* if there's either a burgeoning, or constantly widespread, interest in the subject, which would make dog obedience schools the least provocative in terms of citymag sales).

Service articles are great in terms of getting you into the door and providing a showcase for your research talents, imagination and creativity, but you don't want to spend your life doing them because the exertion is usually high and the pay is usually low—probably about half what you'd get for a piece that required less work but appeared in the feature section. So how about a major profile on the mayor of your city? Is that a good idea? Maybe—but probably not for you. That is precisely the kind of idea that would almost never be entrusted to a freelancer, because it's simply too important—it's not just something to read; it's instrumental in defining the magazine's position with regard to the city's politics. Common sense dictates that the magazine would be more comfortable using a staffer, or at least a contributing editor, for that one.

Instead, one of your real strengths will lie in doing articles that only you can do. That may sound presumptuous, but there are articles, believe it or not, that people on magazine staffs just can't write—because they haven't had *your* experience, and there's no way for them to go out and get that experience.

At this point, you're probably wondering if this article is directed toward you at all—maybe you're straining hard to imagine what kind of experiences you could've had that magazine staffers haven't had. If that's the case, here's a list that should be interesting to you—a few articles that I purchased at *Philadelphia Magazine* from freelancers who were in a position to write these articles . . . while our staffers were not. Articles on: Getting lost in the pine barrens of New Jersey; coming of age in an exclusive girl's school; being part of a family in which the mother was stricken by a debilitating disease; entering a pedigree dog in a dog show; canoeing from Princeton, N.J., to Philadelphia; getting an abortion; changing one's name; fighting an insurance company; going to a school for blackjack dealers.

You don't *have* to write about your own experiences, of course. You can write about somebody else's experiences—which become yours only in that you'll live through them with your main characters. You can become a voice for people who are disenfranchised, for people with troubles, for people who don't know how to get help, for people who don't even know how to begin expressing their problems. You can speak for them and find a market that will be interested in exactly that kind of writing.

And keep your eyes open for up-front sections in citymags that go for really short takes—a paragraph or two that'll get you into print. You may get only $15 for the item—or worse, a T-shirt—but it's better than nothing, and it *is* a credit, and a foot in the editorial door to bigger things.

Naturally, any list of articles like the one above could go on and on—you can easily see where most magazines would be grateful to get articles like them, and almost everybody who ends up selling these articles finds them in his own back yard. In each case, the writers wrote about things close to them—things that staff writers couldn't have written about. Likewise, you can probably write a good neighborhood piece, if you think your particular neighborhood (or one that you know as well) is worth profiling for a magazine either because of the neighborhood's changing (or its *un*changing) nature, its problems or its pleasures, its ethnic or racial mix, or, at best, a combination of several of these. Good neighborhood pieces are difficult to write—but often welcome.

And while you're at it, pay some attention to packaging your ideas imaginatively. I was particularly impressed with one article idea submitted to me by a freelance writer whose idea was to find, and write about, the safest and most dangerous suburbs in the Philadelphia area. He wanted to call it "The Ten Most Dangerous Suburbs," as I recall, but we ended up headlining it "The Ten Safest Suburbs," although I believe that the fact that the article contained both polarities and the fact that we wanted to stress safety rather than danger on our cover (it became a cover story) says something about the direction in which citymags are moving: The better life, not the lesser. As for the packaging—that's what sold us on buying and using the piece. Can you imagine how interesting it would have sounded if he'd called it "A Recap of Current Crime Statistics, Neighborhood by Neighborhood?" Yet the impetus for the article *was* taken from the then-just-released crime statistics; anybody could've done the same article with a little imagination. And it's waiting to be done again all over the country, maybe by you. But it's not just a matter of making a list—there are comparisons to be made, interviews and quotes to be obtained from law enforcement officials, and so on.

The newspaper is the variable in most cities. (That last article could've been done by a newspaper with other than a straight news angle.) Find a city with a terrible daily and you'll find a city that's just begging for a hard-hitting, muck-raking young magazine to come in and earn its reputation. Find a city with an excellent paper and you'll find a magazine staff that prides itself on keeping on its toes. Be that as it may, the citymag's survival never depends on being able to beat the newspaper at the "hot news" game, since it can't possibly.

But while a newspaper, good or bad, helps a magazine survive, the converse is not true. A good city magazine can be only an embarrassment to a newspaper; a bad city magazine doesn't affect the newspaper at all. And only a handful of newspapers—the very best in the country, like the *New York Times* (which has recently taken a page or two from *New York* magazine in that it has created daily features that are *very* derivative of the magazine's staple)—can beat the better citymags at *their* own games, because magazines encourage stylists, want opinion, like to develop their writers as personalities and, most important, have the time to do articles in depth—something that's worth doing when you have a vehicle that's going to stay in the reader's home for a month instead of a day. Further, it's possible for a good magazine writer to keep an eye on the newspaper, spot a story that has received only a surface treatment and is worth more—and end up with an excellent piece in a city magazine. You can be certain that most magazine articles would never have seen print if there hadn't been one reference or another to the subject in the local papers; the problem is that the papers either don't know which articles are the ones that might be pursued, or are reluctant to commit their resources to pursuing them. That's simply not their game, in most cases—although when they decide to *make* it their game they can end up, as the *Philadelphia Inquirer* has, with all kinds of national awards. A magazine writer with good solid instincts will pick up on those articles in a flash.

So the writer who is not tied up by other local media connections is in the best position to wind up on the masthead of a city magazine—and even if you never *do* make it to the masthead, "freelancer" sounds nicer than "unemployed."

Let's look at *Monthly Detroit* for a moment (the strange name is due to the fact that one of the newspapers there already owned the name *Detroit*) just to make a point. Here's a new magazine which announced a list of articles they were scheduling for publication. The list is very much like lists that other magazines have created; in fact, if *Monthly Detroit* does nothing more than review other citymags and appropriate some of the ideas (and this is not to say they are doing that, or will), they'll have enough material to last them for 20 years, maybe longer. Here's a part of their list:

> "Governor's Race '78"
> "What's Wrong with Detroit TV News?"
> "Metro Detroit's Most Notorious Slumlords?"
> "In Search of the Perfect Brunch"
> "The Ten Safest Places to Live in Metro Detroit"

All these articles have been done time and again by countless other city magazines, and the last item may sound particularly familiar. But this is not to say that *Monthly Detroit* lifted the idea from *Philadelphia,* nor that it would matter if they did. The point is: There's a story there that is absolutely vital across the country and will work in just about any city magazine you can name. It's a story that's so right for a citymag, it's hard to imagine one that *wouldn't* buy it.

And what if they do buy it? How much money is there in the city magazine market? Not as much as you'd like. Face it, *Podunk Magazine* isn't *Esquire.* It may look like—and be—the biggest game in town, but how much it can pay depends upon how profitable it is, how much the publisher is willing to budget for freelance, and how hungry the talent pool is—and the city magazines that pay ten cents a word to newcomers are few and far between. The bigger the magazine, of course, the more likely it is willing to spend some bucks on a good piece. But it's just as true that the bigger it is, the more you'd like to be in it, and there are more articles around than there is magazine space. So it's a buyer's market, especially if the story's local. Local means it probably isn't going to sell to a major national market—not unless it has a lot of national significance (and if it did, you'd have tried to sell it nationally in the first place). The city magazine is probably one of very few markets for any piece that could conceivably be sold there— the others being local newspapers that buy features from freelancers. If the story you're suggesting is a major feature and it's your first time writing for the particular citymag, you may hear anything from less than $100 up to $500 quoted as the going rate, depending upon the magazine, its size, its management and its budget. For lesser articles and columns, the prices are usually about half. (Most city magazines, by the way, don't pay by the word; they prefer to assign articles at fixed-dollar rates.)

Even if the money won't keep you in TV dinners, my advice is to *take the assignment—any* assignment, as long as it feels right for you— just to break in. If you have to work on speculation, do it; your competition will. The idea is to try to make the magazine aware that you're talented and dependable, get it used to dealing with you, make it dependent, to some degree, upon you. Hang around long enough, do a good job on a continuing basis, and you'll get raises—even if you occasionally have to push. Which you will.

But this doesn't happen through some kind of magic. If citymags like using freelancers because of their "variety of experience and expertise, their different points of view and . . . access to inside information," as Rosalie Muller Wright, executive editor of *New West* says, they also have their problems with freelance help. "Fact checkers," Wright points out, "find many discrepancies" in freelance manuscripts. And Caroline Woyevodsky of *The Washingtonian Magazine,* while lauding freelancers for their ideas and enthusiasm, says that "freelancers take more time to work with, are less dependable." Other common criticisms of freelancers: "They don't understand the nature of deadlines," says editor Beverley Delaney at *Alive and Well* (Ontario), and J. Patrick O'Connor, formerly at *Cincinnati,* agrees: They're "undependable, uneven . . . don't honor deadlines—fall out of touch; don't work hard enough; don't research well; see the assignment as a 'spare time' thing." The same editor waxes enthusiastic, though, on the positive side of freelancers: "variety, new voices, new approach, new experiences, perspective . . . breadth."

The point, then, is that if you're a talented freelancer who behaves professionally, you should be able to make it in spades in the city magazine market.

That market isn't always the same, however. Generally speaking, it's possible to break citymags down into two broad categories—those owned and run by individuals or corporations interested in putting out a good product and making a profit, and those run by chambers of commerce or other local puffers who would also like to make a profit—but whose reason for existence is boosterism of the city or area. The difference is more than just who runs what kind of story. Chamber of commerce publications are notoriously one-sided and contain nothing that reflects negatively upon the area; reading one is like immersing yourself in conversation with a used-car salesman, subjecting yourself to an omnipresent smile and exaggerations. Consequently, the credibility of chamber of commerce publications (and publications that behave as if they're in the chamber's back pocket), on a scale of one to one, is somewhere around zero. And they are just about the most boring publications imaginable, usually featuring covers showing smiling businessmen on telephones or electrical towers or industrial furnaces or flowers in bloom in a local park. C of C publications are the wolves in sheep's clothing among the citymags—pretending to perform a journalistic function while dealing in public relations. Can you sell them an article? Sure—but the pay is going to be minimal, and don't try to get them to publish your exposé on that local bank.

There's an interesting aside to all this. As the independent city magazines become stronger, many mags which used to be owned by chambers of commerce are now in the hands of independents—often due to the chamber's own recognition that the magazine could never be successful—that is, influential—until it had a voice that was free of the civic backslappers.

The independents are, of course, the other category, and there are two major types. There's the high-flying professional journalistic organization that invests a heavy commitment in its product, caring about its content and appearance, balancing it to make sure that there's just enough service, just enough exposé , just enough life-style, etc. This is a freelancer's dream forum: It's hip and savvy and it speaks with a voice that commands attention on a local (and sometimes national) level—and, unlike the local newspapers, it stays around the home for a month instead of a day, which greatly improves a story's chance of being read. Then there's the mom-and-pop operation, the small-time affair that often has several of the publisher's family members populating the masthead and is used by the publisher for the aggrandizement of self, relatives, friends and political allies; the kind of publication that steers clear of controversy, prefers to fence-sit rather than take a stand on anything, thinks the First Amendment is some kind of leftwing manifesto, and is happy as long as the money keeps rolling in—which it will, until a real magazine comes along.

When that happens—and it does every once in a while—there's a horse race, and you get a market that is suddenly expanded: Instead of one magazine buying stories, there are two—and naturally each is going to try to tie up the best talent. These fights to the finish usually take a few months before somebody emerges victorious, and it's not always the predictable product, so when you make your alliances, try to be like Switzerland. Right now I know of one interesting battle for ad dollars and readership—it's *Mpls./St. Paul* vs. *Twin Cities Magazine,* the latter being a newcomer, the former being the result of a recent merger—but for excitement, nothing matched the three-way battle that raged in Boston for a while, where *Philadelphia Magazine* publisher Herb Lipson bought out *Boston* from the chamber of commerce; the old *Boston* editor went out and started *Bostonian;* and then a third group came along and started *Metro Boston.* All this at the same time—three monthly magazines in competition. *Boston* emerged victorious, but it's hard to say whether that was because of its editorial abilities at the time, or its financial staying power.

Needless to say, it's the strong independent operation that freelance writers want to sell; in fact, many have found that by tying themselves to an aggressive, highly visible local vehicle, they've been able to establish their reputations while the magazine established its own, or at least got some high-level experience. There are plenty of examples which make city magazines appear to be the best possible jumping-off points.

Some of those who jump off syndicate themselves—and that's like a dream come true. A couple of the contributing editors at *Philadelphia*, for instance, have managed to sell their columns to other city magazines around the country. Films columnist, Richard Fuller, for instance, is presently selling his work to several markets. Each month, for writing essentially the same column, Fuller collects checks from various citymags. Nice work if you can get it.

Why are city magazines such fertile environments? Because they're not so big that people can get lost in them, but are big enough so that those with talent can really be noticed. If you're just starting out and you can get an article assignment at any hard-hitting independent citymag, take it—even if the pay isn't much. Getting your roots into the proper soil is most important; an oak can't grow in a thimble, and you won't find a better place to get high, fast visibility and a name that can become a household word—locally, anyway—than the citymags. What you do from there on is up to you.

We've already established that magazines sometimes copy one another. It's just as true that, with cities' having so much in common and people's being essentially the same all over, certain ideas are merely ideas whose time has come. There was no way, for instance, for *Washingtonian* and *Boston* to have copied one another's cover on The Return of Romance—since both did just that cover in their February 1978, issue. (No doubt, the proximity of Valentine's Day had something to do with the subject in general—but that *specific* subject?) It's also true that city magazines can start trends at the drop of a hat, or spot trends where they don't really exist, oddly enough, and still manage to get a decent-selling cover out of their inventions.

Newsstand sales are the name of the game, cover-wise, and we asked many of America's citymags to rate various kinds of magazine covers in terms of their anticipated effectiveness on the newsstand. Here's what they came up with:

An overwhelming 50 percent of the magazines responding picked sex as the top-selling cover subject; it was, as it is in real life, very popular. A close second was life-styles (38.5 percent); service pieces also did well in terms of cover preference, finishing third, while the big losers were fashion, cultural and politics (less than 5 percent of the respondents thought any of them good cover subjects; in fact, these three types of subjects dominated the cellar in our poll. In that context, I recently heard Clay Felker, now of *Esquire* but formerly editor of the 52-week-a-year *New York,* say that the "fastest way to torpedo a magazine's circulation is to put Jimmy Carter on the cover.") Neither sports nor restaurants did well as preferred covers either, although they weren't disasters like the bottom three—but the low editorial esteem of restaurants is a surprise to me, since I know how well restaurant covers can do. They always sell well at *Philadelphia,* and in Dallas, *D Magazine* points to a "dirty restaurant" cover story as possibly its highest seller in history. It's hard to imagine a cover's dealing with the subject of dining out *not* doing well, people's being as concerned as they are with their stomachs. In this instance, we'd say that most citymags are missing one heck of a bet.

What does all this have to do with you? Simple: To understand the covers is to understand the market.

In fact, check out the list shown here of June 1978, cover topics from city magazines chosen at random. See any similarities? For instance, would you say that the citymags think that photographic covers are more effective than art covers? How about subject matter? See anything that you might've predicted if you'd thought about it? That's the key: Think about it, and you just might end up selling the city magazine near you.

Name	Cover Photo	Cover Art	Cover Subject
Atlanta	X		Vitamins
Baltimore	X		Summer Getaways
Birmingham	X		City Lifestyles
Boston	X		Summer Getaways
Charlotte	X		Special Summer Issue
Chicago		X	Phyllis Schlafly
Cincinnati	X		Discos, Singles Bars
Cleveland	X		Car Dealers
Connecticut	X		Summer Fun Guide
D (Dallas-Ft. Worth)	X		Why Hockaday School Girls Are Different
Gold Coast (Fla.)	X		Unfancy Florida Vacations
Houston City	X		Percy Foreman (Super Defense Attorney)
Los Angeles	X		Summer Preview Issue/Dolly Parton
Mpls./St. Paul		X	Summer Fun Guide
Monthly Detroit	X		Battle Between Two Detroit Papers
Mountainwest	X		Running
Nashville!	X		Senator Avon Williams
New Jersey	X		The Jersey Shore
Ohio	X		Wayne Hays
Philadelphia	X		Atlantic City & Jersey Shore
Pittsburgh		X	Self-Help Courses
Richmond	X		Hometown Handbook (City Guide)
San Francisco	X		Discos, Dance Spots
St. Louis	X		Getaway Weekends
Valley Monthly (Pa.)	X		Shore vs. Mountain Vacations
Washingtonian	X		Suburban Teens and Their Problems
Westchester (N.Y.)	X		New Rochelle Rises Again

Regional Business Magazines

"We are not interested," a regional magazine editor says, "in where to eat, what to wear, or movie reviews." This is not a *typical* local magazine editor speaking. It's Timothy Clark, editor of *The New Englander,* one of a fast-growing breed of magazines known as regional business magazines. They are, another editor, says, "doing the job of a *Forbes* or *Business Week* or *The Wall Street Journal,* but locally—as if your city or region were one of the hubs of American business. Because for *you,* it *is."*

Although we haven't covered this group of magazines in the accompanying chapter on city magazines, many of them *are* city magazines of a sort—the city magazines of the business world.

And they are on the grow. In Philadelphia, for example, we have one called *Focus.* I can remember when it was 16 pages—just ten years ago. Recently, it ran an issue over 200 pages. *Focus* is published weekly, which means it's fairly current in terms of what's happening in the local business community—bankruptcies, new incorporations, and so on—and contains a lot of magazine-type feature writing. It has, in short, created a substantial audience for itself—and an advertising vehicle for those who want to reach local decision-makers and purchasing agents. And *Focus* isn't the only business magazine in Philly—I can think of at least two others, both of which appear to be growing. The same pattern is repeating itself all around the country.

What is happening here is that an information vacuum is being filled. It's been happening at national publications for years. Circulation at *Forbes, Fortune* and *Business Week* has soared. The emphasis in newspapers on business reporting has intensified dramatically: What used to be called "financial" news and was relegated to six-paragraph pieces in the Business Section (the main function of which was to provide a home for the stock market closings) is now making front-page headlines; business editorial staffs have increased often twofold and threefold in newspapers all over the country.

Why has this happened? Some point to the growth of the multinational corporation, some to the increasing dependence of the American public on foreign goods, some to the shrinking of the American dollar, some to increased sophistication on the part of the American reader. Probably, it's a little of everything—but with particular emphasis on the need to absorb, assimilate and have data available when it's needed in a fast-changing business climate. Being up-to-date is not simply desirable; it's absolutely essential. And business executives are far more likely to be caught with their pants down locally than in the oil fields of some OPEC country.

What does this mean to you? It means that there are a lot of recent entries in the world of local journalism. Most of them use freelancers—some of them heavily. That's the good news. The bad news is the pay—almost always less than the city magazines. This is not surprising; the business mags are dealing with a relatively small segment of the population, and ad rates are based on type and quantity of readership. Further, there are more people than you would expect who want to write for the local business mags—as Fred Russell, editor of California's *Orange County Business,* points out, a lot of the material comes from "local writers from within the business community who contribute the type of articles we want because it benefits their firm, or client, or for ego reasons."

But there *is* room for newcomers, and while the business mag editors often reject authors who come up with articles that would really be more at home in the citymags, the more successful of the business mags are beginning to apply the consumer magazine formula—that is, an article about the growth of a burglar alarm business is doubly desirable because it hits the reader not only as a businessperson but also as a private citizen. A good magazine writer with a lack of experience in business writing (but with good research and interviewing skills) can easily bridge the gap between citymags and those publications; a person with good business comprehension can probably sell the business mags despite some weaknesses in writing—sometimes the information is worth a little work on the editing end. As usual, it's worthwhile to study the magazine before attempting to write for it.

Nine Steps to Selling the Citymags

1. Hit them in advance. Don't wait until two months before the article would best appear to ask for the assignment. Figure six months lead time at a minimum; that gives you time to query, time for them to reply and schedule you in if they want you; time for you to sell the idea elsewhere if they don't.

2. Don't do the predictable; it's already been done. *Washingtonian* doesn't want your article on the White House, thank you.

3. Think in terms of concepts, of new, more interesting ways of looking at things, rather than try to come up with brand-new subject matter (which is always hard to find). For instance, an article on who holds the power in cities can be conceptualized in several ways: *The Ten Most Powerful Men, The Ten Most Powerful Women, Who Really Runs Podunk?* and *The Five Greatest Power Plays of 1978,* to name a few. There's another advantage to packaging things this way, too—it helps you organize your own thoughts and gives you a point of view you might not otherwise have had.

4. Don't think of citymags as being automatically interested in something just because it's in the city. The requirements for a good story are no different from what they would be in any other magazine, city or not. You can do an article, for instance, on one day in the local clothing business—but you'd better be able to write it as interestingly as it would have to be written to sell to a national publication.

5. Don't *strain* for the local connection. Most citymags will want a distinct local tie-in, but an American publisher won't want to run a story about a Parisian designer just because his fashions are sold in local stores. That's not a tie-in; it's simply stupid. On the other hand, if you had a chance to accompany a contingent of fashion buyers from your city to Paris and watch them choose their fall line, that could be a heck of a good story. Also: Sometimes a really terrific article is its own justification even though the local aspect may be token, and sometimes what is predominantly a national article can be used by a citymag because there is a grass roots angle—for example, a Kennedy assassination connection in your town, or a federal program cutback that will eliminate certain features of local schools.

6. Don't be afraid to send an article in on spec; the citymags are the best places to do that because they're not as inundated with manuscripts as are the national markets. To most editors, a bird in the hand is worth two in the bush, and where you might not have gotten an assignment if you queried, an unsolicited manuscript about the same subject just might get you a sale.

7. If you have more than one good idea, include it in the same query. Keep the queries brief and to the point—and make sure they're as well written as your article will be.

8. You don't know whether your idea's ever been done? You can find out. Try the local library; they'll probably have many years of your citymag. If not, you can always call the magazine's back issue department as a last resort and say, "I seem to remember a story about such-and-such; can you tell me when it ran?" Naturally, if it never did run, you'll find out quickly enough, and then you'll know whether it's worthwhile to submit the idea. The library's a better idea though, since it keeps you from becoming a pest. All you have to do is run your finger down the contents pages.

9. Remember that the main gripe city magazines have against freelancers is their lack of professionalism. Don't do anything that will make that image apply to you. If you're going to send clips, make sure they're terrific. If you accept a deadline, get it done in time. If they ask for specific length, don't come in with something that's double that length. Double-check your facts. Change your typewriter ribbon. Everything counts.

Part IV

Chapter 37

A Writer's Bookshelf

One of the world's oldest—and most provocative—conversation starters is this one: "If you were going to spend your life on a desert island, which ten books would you take?" Well, you can spend your life just discussing the question, because your ten books are going to be a matter of taste.

On the other hand: If you were going to spend your life being a nonfiction writer, which ten books would you take? That's different—because there really *are* at least ten books which would qualify for just about every writer's list, give or take a couple for personal quirks.

The problem is, it's not possible to limit the list to ten.

Fortunately, I don't have to. We have all the room we want to list as many as we want. Nevertheless, I'm going to list *my* top ten—and then all the rest. Before we do, a disclaimer: These are my *personal* choices—based on use, not tradition. You may disagree with them—may think I've included a clunker, left out an essential. For instance, I left out both *The Bible* and *Roget's Thesaurus* on purpose, mainly because I've never found a journalistic use for either.

With that out of the way: Here are the top ten on the opinionated nonfiction writer's bookshelf, in order of usefulness, followed by a listing of many other books worth consulting.

1. *The Shorter Oxford English Dictionary.* I'm counting this as one book even though it's in two volumes. (The Oxford English Dictionary, of which this is a, uh, *shorter* version, contains 13 volumes and is expensive. Not to confuse you, that larger edition has been put into a two-volume format which is *not* shorter, but is complete, containing tiny type and a strong magnifying glass. It is also expensive.) *The Shorter OED,* like its daddy, provides spelling, definitions, pronunciation and all the other stuff that ordinary dictionaries do, but it goes much farther. For instance, if I look up the word "magazine" in *The Shorter OED* (which I'm lucky enough to have received as a gift, since

I now consider it indispensable), I get a virtual dissertation on the word, including the word's etymology, earliest recorded uses, dates of those uses, when figurative uses first appeared, a logical continuity of usage that leads to a better understanding of the word (i.e., we start off under "magazine" defined as a storehouse or depository for goods, work our way through a building in which arms and ammunition are stored, find out that the word was then used in the titles of books in the sense that they were "storehouses of information," then finally get to a periodical publication containing articles by various writers . . . a magazine! Wow! So that's how it happened!), plus quotes from the famous in which the word was used: *Here Irish wit is seen! When nothing's left that's worth defence, We build a magazine!—Swift.* And we find that a Magaziner was, in 1758, someone who wrote for magazines.

A reference work like this can be invaluable—especially if you're writing a story, say, about billiards, in which case you can pick up an incredible amount of information just by finding out how the word came about, and how it came to be used in its present form, much of which will be interesting to your readers. And if you just want to curl up with it to relax, the *OED* will provide the most fun you can have with a dictionary—but the two-volume *Shorter OED* is the only one you'd want to take to bed with you, just for ease of handling.

2. *Familiar Quotations.* Terrific stuff even if you never use it for your writing, John Bartlett's famous work contains most of the most memorable statements ever written or spoken, and you can look them up by author, by opening line of the quote, or by period of time in which the author lived. It's handy for an occasional supportive quote, or for shedding some particularly astute light with better (or more powerful) words than you command, or for setting the tone of an article—too handy, perhaps, since many writers overuse this book. At its best, the use of *Bartlett's* should be tempered, like the telling of jokes at a party: One is perfect, two may be acceptable, but tell three jokes and people will begin to think that's all you can do. (And you can quote me.)

3. *Writer's Market.* This isn't nepotism, and I'm not getting paid extra to say this. This book makes the list not so much because it's the *best,* but because it's the *only.* There's no other single place to find out what you need to know about *Reader's Digest* or *Iron Age* or *Road and Track* or *Cosmopolitan*—rates, types of material purchased, taboos and dozens of other tiny details that could easily exhaust your willingness to walk to the newsstand. Plus information in other areas: fiction, poetry, books, etc. It's not the kind of thing you want to curl up with and read for pure enjoyment, like *Bartlett's,* but it is the kind of thing you need before you can sit down and write for a living.

4. *The Yellow Pages.* Surprised? Well, Ma Bell's advice to let your fingers do the walking is some of the most valuable writers have ever received. You can use it to locate prices, major brand names, experts to interview—in fact, you can do stories using little other than this magnificent creation and never run out of things to write about. And the price is right.

5. *The Reverse Dictionary.* A recent entry into the field of words, Theodore Bernstein's work—which I hope will grow even more inclusive in future editions—starts you out where other dictionaries end you up. That is, instead of trying to locate the definition for a word, you locate the word for which you already have a definition. Example: "What's that word, you know, uh, that means a sentence or word that's spelled the same backwards and forwards?" If you owned a *Reverse Dictionary,* you could get the word off the tip of your tongue and into your manuscript by looking up "sentence," then running your finger down to where it says, "sentence or word that's spelled the same backwards and forwards: *palindrome.*" Why didn't somebody think of this before?

6. *The CBS Almanac* or ***The World Almanac and Book of Facts.*** Take your pick; some swear by one, some by the other—but, because of their similarities, you don't need both. Both are published annually; both contain almost everything of importance that has happened through the year prior to publication (as well as a goodly number of other useful facts from former years, plus many other items of interest to observers of the contemporary scene). In short, both books end up being what the older one, *The World Almanac and Book of Facts,* was intended by Joseph Pulitzer, publisher of the *New York World,* when he took the annual over in 1886: "a compendium of universal knowledge."

7. *The Speaker's Treasury.* A delightful book that's full of wisdom, designed not for the writer but for the orator, but every bit as useful to one as to the other; the important thing here is its appreciation of anecdotes that drive points home. And you don't have to use it as a writing tool to love it.

8. *Webster's Biographical Dictionary.* Paragraphs, some short, some long, on every person of importance whose reputation ever survived, from Aagesen to Zwingli: a valuable compendium of names, dates, and fast recaps of people's lives and reasons for their importance to the world. Updated often by G. and C. Merriam Co., Springfield, Mass.; latest issue is 1976.

9. *The Elements of Style,* by William Strunk, Jr., and E. B. White. A truly marvelous little (in size, not scope) book. In fact, if you knew everything that this book knows, you'd hardly be able to keep from being a clear, concise and generally excellent communicator. You can use it as a reference text (when you don't know how to say something, or when you can't figure out why a sentence sounds stilted), or as a builder of taste and style (and forever after avoid using those same old hackneyed ways of saying those same old things), or to check out a usage of which you're uncertain (*Writer's Digest* editor John Brady sent me my copy because I kept saying "hopefully" when I meant, "I hope"), or as a bedside or fireside companion: Taken in small bites, it's delicious.

10. *World Atlas.* Trying to understand the world without knowing what it looks like is like trying to listen to a radio play-by-play of a chess match. Atlases help make plenty of things clear—like how Germany was so well-situated to wage war, and why such a fuss was raised some time ago over two islands called Quemoy and Matsu, and why the war in Vietnam was so interminable and hard to fight. Atlases, good ones, give you information you never need until you need it—population, demographic and geographic facts of particular areas, principal industries, altitudes, water sources and dozens of other bits and pieces of information.

* * *

That's my top ten. Looking back on it, I'm not so sure I wouldn't make a few changes, particularly in view of a similar study that was being made in Des Moines, where the Drake University School of Journalism had begun surveying a goodly number of publishers, editors, etc., in an attempt to compile a list of the books thought to be most valuable to aspiring journalists. One of the editors polled was Alan Halpern at *Philadelphia Magazine* where I then worked; he called me in to see if I wanted to offer any thoughts on the subject; I in turn decided to respond on my own, which in a sense tossed a curve at the study: I became the one person they didn't ask who answered. They handled it rather nicely, I thought, when they described me as an "unsolicited response" instead of as an "unwanted intruder," and since I helped them, and since they mailed me a copy of the survey, I thought I would let you in on the results just in case you're looking for some reading matter which has been recommended by some of the country's literary leaders, not to mention one busybody. Here are the results—at least, the books most frequently named—in categories which indicate how many times they were suggested:

ten times
Magazines in the Twentieth Century, by Theodore Peterson
nine times
The Elements of Style, by William Strunk, Jr., and E. B. White
eight times
Writer's Market
Freelancer and Staff Writer, by William Rivers

seven times

Magazine Editing and Production, by J. W. Click and Russell Baird
Publication Design, by Roy Nelson

six times

The Changing Magazine, by Roland Wolseley
Understanding Magazines, by Roland Wolseley
Magazines for Millions, by James Ford

five times

The American Magazine—A Compact History, by John Tebbel
A History of American Magazines, by Frank Luther Mott

four times

Familiar Quotations, by John Bartlett
The Craft of Interviewing, by John Brady
The New Journalism, by Tom Wolfe and E. W. Johnson

three times

On Writing Well, by William Zinsser
Effective Feature Writing, by Clarence Shoenfeld
Decline and Fall, by Otto Friedrich
Modern Magazine Editing, by Robert Root

two times

The American Heritage Dictionary of the English Language
A Dictionary of Modern English Usage, by Henry Fowler
Roget's Thesaurus
Collected Works of Shakespeare
Smiling Through the Apocalypse, by Harold Hayes
Ulysses, by James Joyce
Crime and Punishment, by Fyodor Dostoevsky
Visual Impact in Print, by Gerald Hurley and Angus McDougall
The Reader's Encyclopedia, by William Rose Benet
The Boys on the Bus, by Tim Crouse
Writing and Selling Non-Fiction, by Hayes Jacobs
Finding Facts, by William Rivers
Magazines in the U. S., by James Wood
Here at the New Yorker, by Brendan Gill
Associated Press Stylebook
The Years with Ross, by James Thurber
Luce and His Empire, by W. A. Swanberg
Magazine Publishing Management, by the editors of Folio
Reporting: The Rolling Stone Style, by Paul Scanlon
Writing in Style, by Laura Rabb
The Encyclopedia Brittanica
The Careful Writer, by Theodore Bernstein
Folio: the Magazine for Magazine Management

There are some inexplicable entries on the list, like *Ulysses* and *Crime and Punishment,* which I included in my response and which I am glad to see that someone else was crazy enough to include. I don't know the other person's reasons, but I imagine that they are somewhat similar to mine—the former because no list of anything that has to do with writing would be complete without it, and the latter because if all writers could write transitions like that, sustain suspense like that and develop character and pacing and mood like that, editors would be unnecessary; and the both of them because lists like this are often too centered on the practical and don't pay enough attention to the aesthetic.

Well, while we're on this, I thought I would pass along some other titles that have come to my attention, all of which are useful for research, or to add to understanding, or to confirm facts, and so on, and a rare few of which are fun at the same time. I think they're all still in print.

Research

Writer's Research Handbook, by Keith M. Cottam and Robert W. Pelton (A. S. Barnes & Co., Inc., Cranbury, N. J.), is a reference book that lists reference books—most of the ones you can think of, by category.

Style/Grammar

A Manual of Style (University of Chicago Press) contains lots of information on books, style, and production and printing. Rather thorough, too.

Words Into Type, by Marjorie E. Skillin (Prentice-Hall, Englewood Cliffs, N. J.), is terrific. It's hard to imagine anything more complete, and I doubt that you could think of anything that isn't covered, from the proper use of an ellipsis to the accepted method of creating a footnote.

Grammar for Journalists, by E. L. Callihan (Chilton Book Co., Radnor, Pa.), tells what's right, what's wrong and what's awkward, with little tests so that you can see how much you've learned.

New York Times Style Book, rev. by Lewis Jordan (McGraw-Hill, New York, N. Y.), may not reflect the style of the particular magazine to which you're trying to sell, but nobody can say you're wrong.

The Practical Stylist, by Sheridan Baker (Thomas Y. Crowell Co., New York, N. Y.), is fun to read and contains lots of exercises guaranteed to sharpen your mind, if not your wits.

6,000 Words (G. & C. Merriam, Springfield, Mass.) is a supplement to Webster's Third New International Dictionary, and its preface says that a dictionary begins to go out of date the moment it's published. Which explains why it's necessary to have a subsequent book containing words like *cutesy, academese, buzz off, campy, para-quat.* Fun even if you never need it, *turkey.*

Harper Dictionary of Contemporary Usage, by William Morris and Mary Morris (Harper & Row, New York, N. Y.). Is "chauvinist" as good as "male chauvinist" when describing a male who is one? Or is it unclear? Rather than answer these and other such thorny questions themselves, the Morrises put them to a panel of experts, a virtual Who's Who of American Letters, and you get their answers—often witty and refreshing, and sometimes not.

Slang

A Dictionary of Slang and Unconventional English, by Eric Partridge (Macmillan Publishing Co., Inc., New York, N. Y.). I don't know how much good this is to a writer, what with words like *fu-fu* and *tear-arse,* but it's absolutely fascinating (and "must" reading) for anybody who loves words and their origins. Even that most famous of all four-letter words has been with us since 1800, proving that there is nothing new between the sheets.

Facts

Guinness Book of World Records, by Norris McWhirter and Ross Mc-Whirter (Sterling Publishing Co., New York, N. Y.), contains all the youngest, oldest, largest, smallest, fastest, slowest, tallest, shortest, you name it, in one book. Must be some kind of record.

Zip Code Directory (Arrow Publishing Co., Inc., Newton Upper Falls, Mass.). Could be a lifesaver when compiling lists, and the book is better than the movie. If you're going to spend your life doing service pieces, you might want one.

Music

Schwann Catalog (W. Schwann, Inc., Boston, Mass.) Very handy for confirming the spellings of names, titles of albums, and so on.

Harper's Dictionary of Music, by Christine Ammer. Terms, histories and biographies, illustrated, from *a* (as in *a cappella*) to *Zwischenspiel.*

Encyclopedia of Pop, Rock and Soul, by Irwin Stambler (St. Martin's Press, New York, N. Y.), contains rather extensive capsule histories of most of the current and not-so-current popular musicians, but not intended to be complete, says the author: no Barry Manilow, for instance. Or maybe he was too current.

The Concise Oxford Dictionary of Music, by Percy A. Scholes (Oxford University Press, London and New York). People and terms, briefly identified but extensively listed.

Medicine

The Stein and Day International Medical Encyclopedia, rev. by A. M. Hastin Bennett (Stein and Day, New York). Just what it says—

Hangover and *Hashimoto's Disease* on one page, that kind of thing, with nice illustrations.

Dorland's Pocket Medical Dictionary (W. B. Saunders Co., Phila.) Compact but impressively thorough—if not in explanation, at least in definition. Very useful if you're about to send your main character into the hospital for a bronchoesophagoscopy—just in time, you'll find out he could've had it done in a doctor's office.

The Book of Health, compiled and edited by Randolph Lee Clark, MD, and Russell W. Cumley, PhD (Litton Educational Publishing, Inc.) Described as a "medical encyclopedia for everyone," that's what it is. And very handy for anyone who'd want to write about any physical process, whether disease or natural biological function. Just technical enough.

Two Centuries of American Medicine, by James Bordley III, M.D., and A. McGehee Harvey, M.D. (W. B. Saunders Co., Phila.), is an overview: the people, hospitals, research, sickies, etc.

Food

Larousse Gastronomique (Crown Publishers, New York). If you don't know what this is, you probably have no use for it. The essential food encyclopedia, intentionally lavish.

Signet Encyclopedia of Wine, by E. Frank Henriques. Great fun if you like wine—and necessary if you like to write about it. Mentions brand names, vineyards, varieties, labels, etc., and keeps you from writing things like *Shattow Noof du Pop.*

Cinema

The Filmgoer's Companion, by Leslie Halliwell (Avon Books, New York). Listings of actors and actresses famous and non, listings of movies, terms, etc. Not complete (understandably) but a good attempt at being relevant.

Once again, I must apologize for being incomplete—but you wouldn't want a complete list anyway. This gives you something to look forward to and me something to update.

After all, why spoil a good meal ticket?

Chapter 38

Stalking the Tape Recorder

A young writer I know wanted to buy a tape recorder. He asked me what kind I used, and I told him: a Sony, several years old, and very good. So he decided he'd go out and buy the same model.

It turned out that the same model wasn't made any longer, but there was one practically identical to it, with little more than a change of model numbers. He bought it.

"How much?" I asked.

"One hundred seventy-five bucks," he said.

That was about a year ago, I guess, and I assumed that inflation had hit the tape recorder market.

Now, a couple of months into 1979, I realize that quite the opposite has happened. Prices have remained surprisingly stable, considering the drop of the dollar on world markets, and considering that most tape recorders aren't made here. I went out just this week to price the Sony that I have, and while I couldn't find the same recorder, I found one that looked fairly comparable—a little less fancy, perhaps, but containing just about all the same functions—selling at $145.86, a discounted price, but one at which I'm sure it is available elsewhere. The recorder, for which a rechargeable battery (at about $25) and an AC adapter (at about $10) are available, is the Sony TC-150A, in case you're interested.

When you go out to shop, check what's around. That's how you learn. And keep in mind that most writers spend between $140 and $250 for their recorders. And don't ask me who comes up with statistics like that.

But first, a word from our nonsponsor: Sony gets a plug here only because I have one that has served me so very well. I once did run into some trouble, but it was no surprise—in other words, it didn't happen in the middle of a critical situation, like an interview—and it was easily fixed. While the Sony was in the shop, I went out and bought myself an auxiliary recorder, figuring that I should have one for occasions like this, and ended up with a Craig 2629. It was almost $100 cheaper than the Sony at the time—it sold for about $70—and it's actually almost as good as the Sony. I don't know if you can still find one, but if you can, buy it.

There are other tape recorders that will give performance just as good, I'm sure, but I can't turn this into *Consumer Reports*. So I'll give you the rules of thumb. Use your own common sense and get ready for some hardnosed shopping, wheeling and dealing. And don't blame me if you don't follow these instructions.

Don't buy a large recorder. In fact, don't even buy a medium-sized recorder. Buy small. Mine is 4x5¾x1¾, which means it's a *minicorder,* and it's the perfect size. It slips into a coat pocket or a briefcase without displacing everything else; it's lightweight; and it doesn't intimidate.

That's the big item: intimidation. To appreciate what I'm talking about, imagine yourself going to tape an interview with someone who is moderately reluctant to talk to you—but has agreed. Now picture yourself lugging in a gigantic reel-to-reel job with all kinds of dials and meters, setting up a mike and ominously asking this person to start talking. Forget it.

I personally don't care for the mid-range size either, the kind that usually comes in a plastic case with a built-in handle. They're bulky. And the quality isn't there.

With a small cassette recorder, the person's words aren't going to be any different. The fidelity will be approximately the same, as on any portable recorder—better than most, in fact, if you're talking about a Sony—and even if it is slightly off, who cares? You're interested only in content; you have no plans to package the interview as an LP. The important thing about a small recorder is that it looks harmless, innocuous. It just lies there and plays innocent. ("Who, me? A recorder? Never.") It's too small to be a threat. It's, ha ha, not to be taken seriously. The psychological aspects are important, and big recorders are worth their weight in problems.

But don't buy too small a unit, either. There are, for instance, plenty of *microcorders* on the market, most of them having less overall volume (I'm talking about size, not sound) than a pack of cigarettes. These are usually attractive little things, very often in silvery cases, whose principal virtue is that they are small. You'll probably love the way they look, and they'll probably make you feel like a real investigative reporter, but here's what you should know about them; while not all these drawbacks apply to all of them, check carefully.

1. Most micros require that you use tapes made by the recorder's manufacturer. You're a captive audience.

2. The longest tape any microcorder takes is thirty minutes per

side. This is fine for most of the uses to which microcorders are put—dictation of letters, for instance, or verbal notes made while out of the office—but it means more fidgeting in interview situations. (Minicorders take up to 60 minutes per side.)

3. Someone might point out that you can tape surreptitiously with a microcorder. The necessity for doing that is, however, probably nil, and in some states it's illegal; but if you're doing it, you can do it with a minicorder and get better fidelity, too, which brings us to this:

4. The fidelity on the microcorder tends to be tinny; I've heard several.

5. Most microcorders are expensive. You pay for miniaturization. And most people don't need the options that some of the more creative companies, like Pearlcorder, offer—AM and FM tuner modules, or voice actuation. Of course, if those are things you *want,* then look for a system that offers them. I saw a fairly inexpensive system from Sankyo that included *two* microcorders, a transcribing machine, a transcriber's foot pedal, an earphone, etc., for $235. The reason for the two microcorders is that while one is being used to transcribe from, the other can be used for recording.

You can buy a cassette tape recorder for less than $40. But don't. The problem isn't fidelity. It's dependability. You can't afford to have your recorder break down, and the less you spend (assuming you're considering spending less than $100), the greater your chances that the company didn't worry much about long life. You get what you pay for—and I suggest you view it as an *investment,* and stick with brands that have proven themselves.

I'd recommend a unit with a built-in condenser mike. Almost all the minicorder units come that way anyway, but you can probably still buy a few that feature a separate free-standing microphone that plugs in with a jack. For my money, that's just another part that can come loose or get knocked around, and is just another reminder to the person that you're actually taping those words that are flying out of his mouth. A built-in microphone is invisible.

Condenser mikes come with one problem, however: They tend to pick up *everything.* Like magic. If you're in a restaurant, you'll get the silverware tinkling, the water gurgling, the coffee pouring, the glasses clinking, the background music, the waitresses, and the conversation at the next table. Plenty of atmosphere, but you'll have a tough time getting any information off the tape. In offices, you'll pick up the typewriter across the room, the Muzak, the love affair behind the file cabinet. In a store recently, a salesperson, anxious to impress me with the capability of a condenser mike, had me stand 20 feet away and talk. Naturally, the recorder picked me up—as well as a couple of guys talking about stereos. Since they were closer to the unit, they were clearer. If you're going to tape, find a quiet spot.

And when you do, place the recorder closer to the person you're interviewing than to yourself—unless the subject has a strong, clear voice—remembering that your questions aren't that important; the answers are. (If you're recording more than one person at a time, hope that their voices are *vastly* different. Otherwise, you may have difficulty afterward deciphering who says what. Therefore, listen *twice* as closely when two or more voices are being recorded—and jot occasional notes when you think one voice may blot out another.)

Make sure your recorder has an adapter capability. Some recorders do, some don't. You don't want to have to run your recorder on batteries constantly; they cost a fortune. An adapter allows you to plug your recorder into any normal electrical outlet. Adapters often cost a few bucks extra, but they'll save you a barrel. That's something else I liked about the Craig. It came with an adapter thrown in. Further, it can be used with nickel-cadmium batteries—rechargeable. (However, if you're using conventional, nonrechargeable batteries with this baby, *take them out* before you use the wall adapter, and avoid a possible fire.) When you're using regular batteries, by the way, don't buy "extra-duty" or "heavy-duty" unless they also say "alkaline." Alkaline batteries are expensive, but you'll make up in price what you'd spend replacing the other less-persistent types. Further, make sure your recorder uses standard penlite-sized batteries, not some off-the-wall fit that has to be ordered from the factory in Taiwan.

You can buy a used cassette recorder. But don't. There's no way to tell how much mileage it has on it—like a car without a speedometer. And don't let the brand-new, imitation-leather case fool you; many people never use them except when they're ready to sell.

Make sure you get a recorder that buzzes or clicks when the tape is finished. Nothing is more infuriating than finding out that the last ten minutes of conversation are lost somewhere because your tape recorder stopped without warning. My recorder clicks, but even that's not really fail-safe. A buzzer is better; a Chinese gong would be ideal.

Try to get a recorder with a tape counter. Most writers don't use them, but many recorders include them. Here's where they're handy: Say you're in the middle of an interview and you've got a talkative interviewee on your hands. You don't want to have to listen to all that chatter *again* just for the two or three points on which you'd like to quote him. So during your interview, you watch the tape counter (which you've put at zero before you started), and whenever he says something significant, you write down the number on a piece of paper. Later, when transcribing, you just run the tape at fast forward until you reach the appropriate numbers.

Make sure your recorder has a battery level indicator. This little device is a must. It will indicate the condition of your batteries, and if it shows them to be borderline, don't take a chance. Replace them. You can't tell battery condition just by listening—batteries that are weak will record slowly and play back just as slowly, so your test will indicate everything's okay. But when your batteries go and you replace them, the new batteries will make your interview sound like a war among chipmunks.

There are other little goodies that you can get on a recorder, like a cue button, which enables you to speed up the tape to monitor it—find the portions you really want to hear—but most of these devices are gravy. Nice to have, but not the meat of the recorder.

* * *

Now, what happens once you have the tapes? Well, you can always tape over them; they're reusable. But don't do that unless (1) there's no chance you'll ever need the tapes, such as when a libel suit comes up regarding one of your stories, heaven forbid, or (2) there's no chance you'll ever want to use the interview as source material for another article. I usually keep my tapes for a while anyway, and sometimes forever, breaking off those two little tabs on the rear of the cassettes which, once gone, prevent rerecording, so that accidental erasures, such as that which apparently plagued Rose Mary Woods, can't occur. On the other hand, if you decide you wished you hadn't removed those tabs from the cassette because you *do* want to retape, you can always use adhesive or cellophane tape to cover the holes where the tabs were. Presto: new cassette.

One last thing: While you're at the store getting all of this great investigative stuff, you might want to pick up a telephone jack—around $2, and great for taping phone conversations. Just affix one end to the phone and the other to your recorder. But watch the law regarding its use—and, for that matter, the use of a tape recorder. In many states, as I said, it's illegal to tape someone without their knowledge, and it's not a law that the government takes lightly. However, when taping with permission, a phone jack is a terrific little tool. Just make sure you know how to use it! One of my least favorite stories concerns a guy who taped a whole phone conversation but, because he had the pickup in the wrong place, got only his own voice on tape.

It was the most one-sided interview ever.

Chapter 39

Taping and Tapping

I once wrote a little something about taping telephone conversations. I told how it could be done inexpensively—with a small device that sells for about a buck, one end attaching to the phone receiver and the other to the recorder. I pointed out that if the person being taped *knew* he or she was being taped, no civil rights were violated; no ethics were flouted.

Well, what a furor. Readers wrote in, most of them not believing a word I said. A women from Marcola, Oregon, mentioned that, as a reporter in 1972, she too had seen nothing wrong with taping a willing subject over the telephone, but "Pacific Northwest Bell saw differently. They say that taping, without their equipment supplying a beep, is illegal. They are more than happy to make your telephone 'legal' with their equipment, if you want to pay the fee. So," she asked, "is taping without their equipment legal?"

I got a phone call from a Midwestern woman who wanted to congratulate me for my candor. She got cut off. She probably still thinks that I hung up on her. I didn't. Maybe the telephone company was listening.

Then there was the letter from a Los Angeles man who thought my remarks on telephone recording were reminiscent: "Who would have known that an age-old lesson—reinforced by a couple of fellas in a Washington, D.C., hotel just a few short years ago—could have been so soon forgotten once more?"

One thing became clear: There were a lot of different opinions and divided sentiments out there regarding telephone conversation recording. It looked like an issue that deserved some attention. It seemed that it would be fairly simple to set the record straight. It wasn't.

That's because there are several areas to be dealt with. There is the federal wiretap law, for one. And the Federal Communications Commission, for another. And then, confusingly, the fact that the federal wiretap law is *not* the same as the FCC tariff requirement. And then there's Ma Bell, who has her own stake in all this.

And then there is the case of the time-honored beep tone, which is apparently about to go down the drain anyway.

First of all, the federal wiretap law states specifically that if at least one of the conversing parties knows about the recording of the conversation, the taping is legal. Since there are usually two parties to every conversation—unless you're crazy—you're legal on the federal level even if one person doesn't know he's being taped. Example: A guy calls me and says he'd like me to hear a conversation between an underworld figure and him. He knows I'm taping; the underworld figure doesn't. The taping is legal. The same would apply if the underworld figure called me directly: I could tape him because *I* am a party to the conversation, and *I* know I'm taping. That's the federal law, and it applies in most states.

The trouble is, all that goes out the window because I live and work in Pennsylvania. Under Pennsylvania law, *all* parties to the conversation must know about the tap. So if I want to tape somebody, I have to tell him so.

In short, the federal law is a minimum requirement, and cannot be made *less* restrictive. It can, however, be made *more* restrictive at the state's discretion, and that's just what Pennsylvania does.

So: Check your *state* laws on telephone recording for possible deviations from federal law. And if you're making an interstate call, check *both* states.

It's not confusing so far, right? Well, here's where we throw the monkey wrench into the works. Since 1948, the FCC has required the use of a beep tone whenever a phone conversation is being recorded, with certain understandable exceptions. But it left it up to the phone companies in each state to warn of the requirement of the beep tone, a requirement which therefore became part and parcel of the phone company's tariff, and one which does not exist in FCC rules or regulations.

We'll come back to this. For the moment, though, let's assume that most writers aren't busy trying to get the goods on bad guys through covert wiretaps; they simply want to have an intact version of a telephone call in order to glean from it information, and accurate, in-context quotes, without missing a beat. Taping is easier than typing. It's a *lot* easier than taking notes longhand. It is, in fact, the only really dependable method of getting your facts straight.

Let's assume that you simply say, "By the way, I'd like to tape this conversation so that I won't have to slow you down by taking notes longhand. Is that okay?" The person agrees; you tape. Are you breaking the law?

No. Taping is not a crime in *any* state as long as it's done with the person's knowledge. That would seem to make sense. If, after all, you were with a person in a restaurant, and you told that person you were going to tape the conversation, that would be okay. Even if you taped that person *covertly* in a restaurant, *that* could be okay, depending upon the state law. The situation—determined by whether a person knows he's being taped—is not changed by the mere fact that you're on a telephone.

The problem is not one of law. It is, as we implied above, a problem of tariff—the fact that your telephone is a device normally made available to you when you comply with phone company tariffs.

The front of your phone book, in fact, contains some instructions on phone recording. These instructions vary depending upon where you live, but they *invariably* say something about a beep tone, the sound that the FCC has been convinced that everybody will recognize as a taping signal.

Take Massachusetts. The Boston telephone directory says of its beep requirement, ". . . This signal is provided for your protection. Use of a recorder without Special Telephone Company equipment containing a tone-warning device is not authorized and is a violation of the Company's tariffs." The wording is important—it doesn't say that such recording is *illegal*. It does say that it violates the Company's tariffs. (**Warning:** If the directory *does* say that recording without a beep is illegal, be sure to check your state law. It just might be.)

I called my local telephone company, Bell of Pennsylvania. In fact, I had a few other people call as well. It turns out that Ma Bell is *very* reluctant to discuss this. The public relations department gets first shot at discouraging you, and it, of course, won't give you any legal opinions about the beep or anything else—although one of my callers got a nifty private opinion:

Question: "Is there any legal action that the phone company can take if someone tapes a conversation without using the beep tone?"

Answer: "No, but we wish there was."

The comment is not particularly revealing. Then again, it could be—depending upon whether you believe that Bell is interested in protecting your privacy, or simply in stemming an epidemic of various recording devices, attachments, etc., many of which are not made by a subsidiary of AT&T.

It may be a little of both.

Nevertheless, because of the reluctance of Bell's lawyers to give straight answers to questions regarding their employer's strengths and weaknesses, all investigations of this nature (sigh) are doomed to end up in Washington at the Public Utility Commission. As we look in, I am talking to a lawyer there:

"I'd like to know something about the regulations regarding tape recording of phone conversations. Tell me—are the phone company's tariffs the same as law?"

"Well, no. That is, not exactly. But you might say they have the force and effect of law. Would you please stop banging that thing in my ear?"

"That's my typewriter."

"I know. Can you write longhand?"

"It's a lot slower. But okay."

And so I wrote. Which is probably the best argument for taping. Unfortunately, I couldn't very well tape the guy before I found out if it was legal, since I knew that he would want to know where the beep tone was if I told him I was taping. Catch-22.

·"You said force and effect," I said. "What does that mean?"

"Well, the tariff has the *weight,* but not the *strength,* of a law." He paused. "It's a nuance that only another lawyer could understand."

In other words, I couldn't. In fact, I wondered where they would find a jury of my peers who could. I said, "Can you be a little more specific?"

"Well, the adoption of a tariff is not quite the same as the passage of a law. But you *could* be taken to court for violating a tariff." He said it in the same way I say I *could* win the Nobel Prize in literature.

"Okay. What would happen if I was taken to court for violating the tariff that says that I have to beep while recording, but there's evidence right there on the tape that I had told the person he was being taped. Would the fact that I didn't beep be a violation of law?"

"No, of a tariff. And I don't know how it would turn out. The court might well say that the person was warned that he was being taped and therefore had waived his rights. It's hard to say."

Well, that's what happens when you ask a question of someone who doesn't know the answer. It's like trying to use a marshmallow as a trampoline.

"Now," I asked the Washington attorney, "suppose I beeped every 15 seconds with that unit that Ma Bell sells, and when the thing comes to court the guy claims he didn't know what the beep tone meant. What about that?"

"Well, my response would be that what kind of person would hear a beep every 15 seconds and not have enough sense to inquire what it was?"

F. Lee Bailey he wasn't.

Anyone reading this might be inclined to say that I'm one of those smart-ass journalists who knows very well why things are the way they are but, because we members of the press like to stick the needle in and pretend that we don't know the answers, etc., I'm trying to make those who attempt to answer sound foolish. That's *not* what I was doing. And, in fact, there's a strong likelihood that the government is going to agree with me (I've been trying to get this point across for years): The FCC's been thinking about discontinuing the requirement for a beep tone for a while now, and has encouraged industry and governmental spokespeople to come forward to give their opinions on the matter. Paraphrasing and quoting from a Notice of Proposed Rule Making (Docket No. 20840) released by the FCC in this matter early last year, the comments filed by the respondents in this docket concluded that while "there is a privacy interest worth protecting in telephone conversation . . . the beep tone requirement is unenforceable . . . and should be eliminated." Further, "Some of the parties believe the unenforceability of the requirement is counterproductive, inducing a false sense of security in a public unaware of the beep tone rule's alleged widespread abuse" (in other words, if the beep tone means you're being recorded, does the absence of it mean you're not?). The FCC concludes that the beep tone requirement should "be eliminated and all restrictions lifted on consensual recording of telephone coversations." However, in terms of enforcement, while "the commenting parties were unanimous in stating their belief of the unenforceability of the beep tone requirement, no new enforcement techniques were proposed."

Put in other words—mine—there is no way to monitor a telephone conversation that will indicate whether it is being taped or not, and people should probably be educated not to say anything on a telephone that they wouldn't want on tape. There seems to be no way around it; the beep tone, as indicated, may be doing more harm than good. Further, as another lawyer told me, "The beep doesn't get you off the hook as far as anti-wiretap statutes are concerned. You must get consent in states where consent is required."

So if a person doesn't know what the beep tone means, he's not protected (and neither are you). The only way the beep tone helps is if somebody knows what it means, and if you're going to have to tell somebody, "The beep tone means you're being recorded," you might just as well say, "You're being recorded," and be done with it. Who needs a beep?

Until the whole matter is resolved, should you violate the phone company tariffs? That's up to you, but I wouldn't publicize your decision. Ma Bell has an investment to protect. She makes all this expensive equipment through her subsidiary, Western Electric, and she wants to rent it. The beep tone is provided as a "service" to you; of course, you pay for it. (Interestingly, AT&T was one of only two respondents who did not suggest the elimination of the beep tone requirement; they took no position on it whatever.) Bell used to prohibit the use of alien equipment with her products, and today one of her tariffs states that you can't use anybody else's equipment unless it and its use complies with her tariffs. But because of all the charges of monopolization and restriction of trade made these days by the interconnect companies—the tiny competitors that are trying to beat Ma Bell at Western Electric's game—Ma Bell isn't inclined to go to court over any of this. Further, if everybody in violation of *that* tariff were taken to court, there wouldn't be enough people left to serve on the juries to try them.

It's interesting that in all my conversations with who-knows-how-many people, I didn't hear of one instance where somebody went to court, or even had his phone disconnected, for taping without a beep after notifying the other person that he was being taped. You can probably check the law books dating back to 1876, when Alexander Graham Bell first placed a call, without finding such a case. The question you have to ask yourself is, "Am I going to be a landmark case because I called up Miller the butcher and taped him on how to pick out a good rib roast for the article I'm writing on meats?"

Then ask yourself:

How will the phone company know I'm taping?

How will they prove it?

They're not going to take me to court for it, so what *will* they do?

Do I have any intention of handing them my tape along with a written confession?

If not, you have nothing to worry about.

Now, what about the issue of rights? A tape recorder actually *protects* a person being interviewed. Take pencil notes and you miss a lot. Transcribe a tape and you get everything that was said. I can't think of a better way to protect an interviewee.

Let's go back to the letter from the guy in Los Angeles who thinks this boils down to another Watergate. It doesn't. Watergate was clearly against the federal wiretap law; taping a phone conversation is *not* against the law: not *ever* when the person being taped knows about it; not *usually* when he doesn't know about it, depending upon the state. At Watergate, *no* party to the conversations knew about the tape recording.

There is a knee-jerk sentiment, particularly after the tumult of the last few years, that a tape recorder in and of itself is a nasty thing, and that when it is used in conjunction with a telephone, it becomes an electronic Mata Hari. That's college journalism for you.

A tape recorder is a tool. It helps you keep your quotes accurate and your facts straight. As far as I'm concerned, the American press can use all of them it can get.

Chapter 40

Smile—You're in a Magazine

I guess I've never been as completely fooled as I was on the day when a freelance photographer walked into my office without his omnipresent camera. At first I was surprised—I'd never seen him without a Nikon or two dangling from his neck, as well as his faithful Leica—but then I noticed that he was carrying a portable radio and looked very much like a guy on his way to a day off. So I didn't comment about the lack of the camera, but asked him where he was going.

After a few seconds of small talk, he told me that he had just taken my picture. In fact, he had taken it twice.

Well, okay, I like a challenge. First I looked for gaps or holes in his clothing, or telltale lenses peeking out from pocket flaps. There were none. I even pushed my index finger into his stomach, of which he has plenty, figuring that the camera might have been concealed there—but the stomach was all his. As it turned out, the guts of something else—his transistor radio—had been removed, and there, inside it, was a camera—not a Minox or any similar small camera, but his full-sized Leica, triggered by a shutter release held in his hand. He was on his way to a rather dangerous undercover assignment with one of our writers.

This may not seem to have much to do with a book about writing nonfiction—and it doesn't—but it does serve as a sneaky way to introduce the fact that most nonfiction writing is illustrated with photographs. And while no writer really *needs* a camera, it can be pretty helpful. Even profitable.

Chances are, even if you've done considerable freelance writing, you haven't bothered to become a photographer of any consequence. Maybe you have a Polaroid or an Instamatic or something more sophisticated—but you don't connect it to your work. Your own recognition of your limited "talent" with a camera has kept you from thinking along those lines, right? No matter. You can use a camera to great advantage. And you're already better than you think.

Let me explain.

Cameras today—that is, sophisticated, professional-level cameras—have removed most of the guesswork from taking photographs. All you have to know is how to operate the camera, and the camera will, in most cases, do the rest. Shooting black and white, for instance, you'll probably find that you can shoot any subject, indoors or out, without flash, if you use Tri-X film and learn how to "push" the film by adjusting the ASA setting on the camera. (While this may sound like Greek, it's actually English, and the procedure takes about four minutes to learn.) A good 35mm single lens reflex (the *only* kind of camera that a writer should consider) with lens-changing capability and a built-in light meter will enable you to shoot at speeds of as little as 1/2000th of a second, control depth of field, tell you when you're in focus, tell you when there is or isn't enough light, and give up to 36 exposures per roll. And the results will be absolutely fine for reproduction; most magazine and newspaper photographers use 35s.

It will take you a few hours, tops, to learn how to use a 35mm SLR, and a few rolls of film for practice. And here's what you get.

• You may become good enough, or lucky enough, to sell your photographs for reproduction. Any time a writer brings me film to illustrate a story, the least I'll do is look at it. Sometimes I'll buy it, assuming it's usable. It rarely happens that the results aren't good enough to publish, since proper operation of the camera practically *guarantees* quality results. No, most often my decision depends on the ability of the journalist to know what constitutes a good photo. You can learn easily enough what sells, just by thumbing through a few magazines. While you're looking, you'll probably find an occasional article by somebody who both wrote the text and shot the photographs.

• If the magazine's editor or art director decides upon an art approach—that is, illustration instead of photography—you still might make a sale. They may need "scrap." It makes a lot more sense for them to buy *your* photographs as a guide for the artist than it does for them to hire a photographer to take the photos—especially since the photographs are simply going to be used as reference anyway.

• A photographic record of the events, people and places about which you're writing will help you to write more accurately. Example: I was writing an article about a federally-funded program in an urban area. When I sat down to my typewriter to describe the homes, I realized that I hadn't made any detailed notes about one of the structures involved. Luckily, I had taken pictures of a main character in the story, standing in front of the home in question. I developed the film, had a few prints made after looking at the contact sheets, and was consequently able to describe the home in detail.

This is more important than it sounds. For instance, say a writer goes to a neighborhood to do an interview, is struck by a certain sordidness there and in the home or institution in which the interview takes place, and then has to come back home and write about it in detail. There's no excuse for doing that from memory—not while there are cameras in the world. With only a few photographs, you can talk specifics about the litter on the sidewalks, the handwriting on the walls, the quality of disrepair of the neighborhood in general, the trash in the streets—and get a more accurate word-*picture* of the area as well. This is particularly true since a writer will often take home *impressions* rather than *facts*: The neighborhood may not be that sordid at all; a few abandoned houses may have created the illusion of squalor. Of course, it's all well and good to remember, and pass along, the emotions you experienced. But it's *essential* to know how things actually *were*.

• Good photographs may actually help you sell an article. Let's face it—sometimes the photographs are more exciting than the story. Every article can't be your best, and somewhere along the way, you know you missed—and wished you could have sent the editor some of the elation or pathos or action that *should* have been in the piece, tied up in a neat little package. Photographs do just that—they can beef up a weak article or even become the most important part of the article. Sometimes, in fact, photographs can stand alone, with nothing more than a caption to identify the action.

Say you've invested in a pretty good camera (it's pointless to invest in anything but—after all, how often do you buy a camera?) and you've used it to shoot photographs to illustrate an article. Do you have to have a darkroom to see the results? No. It's hard to conceive of any major city that doesn't have several professional-level photo processors, and every small city or town is likely to have at least one professional photo finishing firm. Usually you can get your film back in 24 hours or less, and the price for developing is only a couple of dollars.

Just take your film in, request contact sheets (which show you a small print of each negative), then make your selection and order prints (eight-by-ten prints will usually be sufficient). Or you might just take or send the undeveloped roll of film to the publication; chances are that it will cover the cost of processing.

Sound easy? It isn't. You still have to develop plenty of familiarity with the camera, know what it will and won't do, understand how its features and devices affect the finished product. But with a decent camera and a good how-to manual, you can know the technical capabilities of the camera in no time. From there, you can start learning the little secrets that the pros know—partly by reading, partly by looking at photographs and trying to determine how they were shot, partly by experimenting. Then if you're *really* into it, you can take a photography course (many cities offer night courses in the subject) to help you develop the most important areas: your eye, and the technical facility equal to the idea of the moment.

It doesn't happen overnight (if it did, there would be even more photographers than there already are), but you needn't have been raised snapping a shutter, either. And some of it isn't really up to you at all: A boring photo through a normal lens may be much more dramatic through a telephoto or a wide-angle lens.

The field isn't that wide open. But opportunities do exist if you're willing to hang in. What you're up against is the professional photographer who, in most cases, does a combination of newspaper, magazine and advertising photography to make ends meet. However, advertising photography pays more—so it's usually either the excellent journalistic photographer (who makes enough at this craft to specialize) or the promising beginner, who goes after magazine and newspaper work. The competition's tough, but you have an advantage: *You know what's important to your story.*

Check out the way the pros do it. Go through magazines and look at which photographs were chosen to illustrate which articles. If there's a picture of a central character, for instance, don't simply look at the person—study the background, see what the photographer has selected for inclusion *beside* the central character, and see how the subject has been framed by the camera. You can learn plenty just by looking: In action shots, for instance, if you see a *blurred* background, chances are that the photographer panned with his subject at a slow shutter speed. If you see a *soft* background, chances are that the photographer used a wider lens opening, which makes for shallower depth of field. If you see a subject caught in split-second action where also the background is sharp, chances are that the photographer used both a fast shutter speed and a small lens opening. The terms may sound strange, but they're no more than vocabulary with which you have yet to become familiar.

I bought my camera a few years ago, and since then I've photographed my own articles on several occasions. I'm no pro in terms of being someone with a studio, darkroom, and lots of expensive stuff— but I have sold photos. And they do look professional. Isn't that inspiring?

Now you'll probably run out and buy a 35mm camera. But before you do, here are some tips:

1. Why buy a single lens reflex? You ought to know, if you're going to buy one—and the reason is that it lets you see the picture you're taking. You're looking right through the lens. Not all cameras offer this capability.

2. Why buy a 35mm? Why not a $2^1/4 \times 2^1/4$ camera? Because the latter is better for studio use than for carry-along work. The 35mm is easier to handle, usually lighter, takes more abuse and contains more photos on each roll.

3. Don't opt for the cheapest 35mm you can find, figuring that any 35mm is better than none. It's not true. Wait and buy something decent, and buy it at a dependable, trustworthy camera shop. Bargains too often turn out to be less than you bargained for.

4. Don't buy the first camera you look at, no matter what the price. Shop around. Educate yourself. You'll find yourself congratulating yourself that you didn't buy impulsively.

5. Don't buy a used camera from a professional photographer. Can you imagine how much use it's had? Better to buy one from a blind old lady.

6. Make sure that your camera offers lens changeability. That's a big advantage, so if it doesn't have it, don't buy it—not for a journalistic or any other professional purpose.

7. Don't think that just because you're getting 20 percent off list price, you're getting a good deal. In the camera industry, 25 percent off isn't uncommon. Your 20 percent may be more than anybody else is paying for the same camera. Needless to say, if you pay anywhere near list price without checking elsewhere, you're nuts.

Chapter 41

Got the Records

Almost anybody mentioned in a magazine article may sue for libel. The key word is *may*. Most people *won't* sue unless they are seriously offended and think the magazine has overstepped the bounds of good journalism; others will sue—or will threaten to do so—almost as a reflex action. Those that do sue, whether they are motivated by conscience or not, will not necessarily have reasons that will hold up in court, since magazines tend to be careful these days. But it may all be the same to the magazine. If someone sues, the magazine is going to lose money. It is going to lose money whether or not there ever *is* a case.

The reason for that is: lawyers.

Suppose the following harmless quote appears in a magazine: "Jones, who has his two children attending a day-care center while he works, says he has been deeply involved in his business since he and his wife separated." The quote certainly *appears* to be innocuous enough, until Jones decides that his privacy has been violated and he decides to sue.

The information may have been given freely to a reporter; indeed, there's no reason to believe that it wouldn't have been. Jones probably knew he was "on the record." He did not ask that he not be quoted. He was, in fact, a perfectly friendly interviewee. And it would be difficult to imagine a situation in which the published statement would tend to hurt Mr. Jones. But, following publication of the article, he shows up at his lawyer's office and says, "I never said they could print that. I don't see why my private life had to be dragged into it. I don't think that information should have been made public."

Jones is not denying the veracity of the statement. He simply says that he never said it for attribution, and that the magazine has no right to print anything that is not directly pertinent to his business, which he perceives to be the subject of the article.

Any lawyer will tell you that Jones does not have a strong case. But it *will* take a lawyer to tell you that, and that costs money. If the magazine is vindicated, it ends up paying for the privilege. Ultimately, the magazine's lawyers may say, "Look, this guy Jones will settle out of court for $500. If we go to court, we can beat him. But it will cost you a lot more than $500 to win."

Why is Jones threatening to sue? Maybe he doesn't like the way the article turned out and he's looking for a way to get even. Maybe he's the type that sues everybody. Maybe he just needs the money, and every little bit counts. Maybe his brother is a lawyer.

Whatever Jones's reason, the outcome of the case will depend largely on how well the writer has done his work. It must be assumed that every writer has the potential of someday being asked to give a deposition or even appear in court, and at those times the writer's professionalism counts high. Most cases never get that far, partly because out-of-court settlements are common, partly because libel cases are uncommon to begin with: In most situations involving sensitive articles, the magazine's editor and its lawyer will sit down with the writer beforehand and try to eliminate problem areas before the article sees print. And, contrary to the lawyer's advice to settle with Jones, most magazines *will* go to court on a matter of principle—if only to insure that no one gets the idea that a magazine is a pushover for a fast buck.

What can a writer do to arm a magazine in advance in a case like this, assuming that it had some validity?

If the person who wrote the article, for instance, has his interview on tape and transcribed, and it was obviously taped with the interviewee's knowledge, the magazine has a strong defense. If the writer has handwritten notes of the conversation, the defense is also strong, but not as persuasive, since penciled notes are never as accurate as tapes. If the writer has sloppy notes and a word or two written down which could have been a quote, or maybe only an observation, the case becomes tougher. If the writer is unable to find a record of that quote, and simply remembers that Jones said it, the case is still weaker. Forewarned is forearmed.

Here are two real-life stories. In the first one, a writer has just written a damning account about a man who is prominent in his field, but not necessarily somebody that a court would call a "public figure." Because of the potential libel problems, the lawyer meets with the writer and one of the magazine's editors and goes over the manuscript line by line. Each time the lawyer asks the source of a certain piece of information or what led the writer to his conclusion, the writer begins the tedious job of thumbing back through penciled notations, some of them obviously taken in a hurry, trying to find the specific quote. The lawyer finds that often the writer has paraphrased; often he has only parts of a quote; often he has made certain innuendoes and suppositions based on a confusing quote or on a fragment of information.

The lawyer tells the editor that the story can't run; he wouldn't want to have to go into court with that kind of documentation. Of course, that wasn't the only problem; sloppy reportage reflects in many areas. In this case, the piece was unbalanced—there was no semblance of any attempt at fairness—and the writer had not attempted to obtain quotes that would have resulted in putting his subject in a more favorable light. The lawyer felt extremely shaky about having to put this particular writer on the witness stand. (I know an editor who feels that the most educational experience a writer can have is having a lawyer go over his or her manuscript, cross-examining at the same time. I agree. I have seen writers break out in a cold sweat—not in a courtroom, but under a lawyer's scrutiny in the comfortable, familiar surroundings of an editor's office.)

Now for story number two. A writer has just finished writing an investigative piece that's getting a lot of scrutiny, mainly because it's a hot potato. The lawyer reads the manuscript. Again, he calls for a meeting with the writer and an editor. He asks questions; the writer thumbs through a loose-leaf binder that contains typewritten notes, clips, transcriptions of tapes, photocopies of reference material. He is able to say, with complete certainty, when he obtained each of his quotes and under what circumstances, and show them directly to the lawyer. He has lots of backup: newspaper accounts, various public records, and so on. (In this case, when this particular writer was contradicted later by someone mentioned in the story, he was able to respond immediately by giving the time, date, place and actual words spoken in the interview.)

If you were the lawyer, with which writer would you prefer to work? And if you were the editor, which writer would get the next assignment, all other things being equal?

Obviously, there is a good case here for careful record-keeping habits. There's no question that such an effort adds time to every story you'll write—but it will save time and, more important, worry, besides adding substantially to your credibility. If I had my way, every writer who went out to do a sensitive story would use a tape recorder and keep day-by-day, conversation-by-conversation notes. Not that a tape recorder is some kind of catchall—it has its drawbacks, one of which is the tedious job of transcribing, another of which is that it's often useless when more than one person is being interviewed or when there's noise in the background, another of which is that it *can* fail. But it, like nothing else, captures *exactly* what was said. And nobody can deny having said something that appears on tape in his or her own voice.

Say you're about to start on a story. Here are some tips that will make your job easier in the long run, win over editors, and give you a feeling of security you've never had before.

1. Buy a loose-leaf binder to store your information. When the article is completed, leave the binder intact; file it in a large envelope somewhere. Lawsuits can occur considerably later than the appearance of the article.

2. Keep an address and telephone log. List the people to whom you speak or the institutions that you contact in the course of writing your article. This will make it easier to go back for subsequent information; it will also put all your sources in one place for easy reference.

3. Keep a bibliography. List every newspaper or periodical from which you take a clip, including date and page number. List every reference book you use—author, publisher, year of publication, page number. That way, if you have to go back to look anything up, or if you want to credit your source, you'll have it.

4. Keep the phone numbers and bibliography in the front of your binder, since you'll be referring to them often. Keep records and notes of your interviews in order by date of interview. (Telephone interviews, of course, should be noted just as are in-person interviews.)

5. If you have several interviews with one person, mark them accordingly—"first interview," "second interview," etc. This will help when you're trying to locate a particular piece of information.

6. Keep a diary of all your activities while working on the article. Don't leave out anything. Show time arrived, time spent, time departed, whom you were with, what you did.

7. If you get clips from newspapers, mark the date directly on the clip. Often there will be no date, except on wire-service stories and at the top of the newspaper.

8. Before taping any conversation, tape yourself saying something like, "This conversation is being taped at (time) on (date) at (location). I am speaking to (name of interviewee) and taping with his consent." If possible, it's a good idea to have your interviewee agree to the taping right on the tape.*

9. For penciled or typewritten notes, do the same. Put time, date, place of interview, name of interviewee.

10. When dealing with experts, get copies of resumés. That way, you know just what *makes* them experts.

11. List your expenses. When your phone bill arrives, attach a photocopy to your records, particularly if they show long-distance or

---

*It may not be necessary for your interviewee to consent to being taped, depending upon the state in which you're taping. In Pennsylvania, where I live, it's a must. Check the law—including any local laws regarding the taping of telephone conversations. As for the beep tone, in most states it's a violation of the telephone company's tariffs to tape without it, but a tariff isn't the same as a law. (See Chapter 39 on this subject.) Also, if you're taping a phone conversation across state lines, check *both* states.

person-to-person conversations which provided information for your article. Keep all receipts; if they're not dated, date them. These become evidence that you actually went where you said you went, and while they may not be considered "hard" evidence, they can't hurt. Also, most magazines will pick up story-related expenses, and you'll need your receipts for reimbursement.

12. Never throw away anything. Even if you typed up your penciled notes, keep the originals. Someday, you may be asked for these seemingly-insignificant scraps.

* * *

Do you really *need* all that stuff? Probably not. Chances are you'll never run into a problem. But if you do, the care you've taken will pay for itself. Record-keeping is a precautionary measure. So are seat belts.

And clear, complete records are also a good barometer of your professionalism. Editors love them. Lawyers notice them. Usually, so do those with whom you come in contact in the course of writing an article. When you're *that* responsible, potential troublemakers think twice about taking you on.

Once, to demonstrate to one highranking official of a company how his firm had gone out of its way not to cooperate with one of our freelance writers, I pointed out that a certain consultant for that firm, who was supposed to call our writer, never did. The executive, somewhat embarrassed in front of his colleagues, said that I was wrong; the consultant, he said, had spoken to our writer twice. I checked the writer's records; there was no mention of any such contact. I knew that the writer was a good record-keeper, so I called the consultant direct. He denied ever having spoken to our freelancer. It was the only possible answer, and it gave me a little extra ammunition for the article.

Sold? Then don't wait until that big investigative piece comes along to start developing these habits. Start now. That way, when the big story hits, you won't have to try to find this book among the pile you're prepared for the Salvation Army.

Index

Books of Interest From Writer's Digest

The Beginning Writer's Answer Book, edited by Kirk Polking, Jean Chimsky, and Rose Adkins. "What is a query letter?" "If I use a pen name, how can I cash the check?" These are among 567 questions most frequently asked by beginning writers — and expertly answered in this down-to-earth handbook. Cross-indexed. 270 pp. $8.95.

Bylines & Babies, by Elaine Fantle Shimberg. The art of being a successful housewife/writer. 256 pp. $10.95.

The Cartoonist's and Gag Writer's Handbook, by Jack Markow. Longtime cartoonist with thousands of sales, reveals the secrets of successful cartooning — step by step. Richly illustrated. 157 pp. $9.95.

A Complete Guide to Marketing Magazine Articles, by Duane Newcomb. "Anyone who can write a clear sentence can learn to write and sell articles on a consistent basis," says Newcomb (who has published well over 3,000 articles). Here's how. 248 pp. $7.95.

The Confession Writer's Handbook, by Florence K. Palmer. A stylish and informative guide to getting started and getting ahead in the confessions. How to start a confession and carry it through. How to take an insignificant event and make it significant. 171 pp. $7.95.

The Craft of Interviewing, by John Brady. Everything you always wanted to know about asking questions, but were afriad to ask — from an experienced interviewer and editor of *Writer's Digest*. The most comprehensive guide to interviewing on the market. 244 pp. $9.95.

The Creative Writer, edited by Aron Mathieu. This book opens the door to the real world of publishing. Inspiration, techniques, and ideas, plus inside tips from Maugham, Caldwell, Purdy, others. 416 pp. $8.95.

The Greeting Card Writer's Handbook, by H. Joseph Chadwick. A former greeting card editor tells you what editors look for in inspirational verse . . . how to write humor . . . what to write about for conventional, studio and juvenile cards. Extra: a renewable list of greeting card markets. Will be greeted by any freelancer. 268 pp. $8.95.

A Guide to Writing History, by Doris Ricker Marston. How to track down Big Foot — or your family Civil War letters, or your hometown's last century — for publication and profit. A timely handbook for history buffs and writers. 258 pp. $8.50.

Handbook of Short Story Writing, edited by Frank A. Dickson and Sandra Smythe. You provide the pencil, paper, and sweat — and this book will provide the expert guidance. Features include James Hilton on creating a lovable character, R. V. Cassill on plotting a short story. 238 pp. $8.95.

How to Write and Sell Your Personal Experiences, by Lois Duncan. How to write about everything that happens to you. 256 pp. $10.95.

Law and the Writer, edited by Kirk Polking and Leonard S. Meranus. Don't let legal hassles slow down your progress as a writer. Now you can find good counsel on libel, invasion of privacy, fair use, plagiarism, taxes, contracts, social security, and more — all in one volume. 249 pp. $9.95.

Magazine Writing: The Inside Angle, by Art Spikol. Successful editor and writer reveals inside secrets of getting your mss. published. 288 pp. $10.95.

Magazine Writing Today, by Jerome E. Kelley. If you sometimes feel like a mouse in a maze of magazines, with a fat manuscript check at the end of the line, don't fret. Kelley tells you how to get a piece of the action. Covers ideas, research, interviewing, organization, the writing process, and ways to get photos. Plus advice on getting started. 220 pp. $9.95.

Mystery Writer's Handbook, by the Mystery Writers of America. A howtheydunit to the whodunit, newly written and revised by members of the Mystery Writers of America. Includes the four elements essential to the classic mystery. A comprehensive handbook that takes the mystery out of mystery writing. 273 pp. $8.95.

1001 Article Ideas, by Frank A. Dickson. A compendium of ideas plus formulas to generate more of your own! 256 pp. $10.95.

Writing for Regional Publications, by Brian Vachon. How to write for this growing market. 256 pp. $10.95.

One Way to Write Your Novel, by Dick Perry. For Perry, a novel is 200 pages. Or, two pages a day for 100 days. You can start and finish your novel, with the help of this step-by-step guide taking you from blank sheet to polished page. 138 pp. $8.95.

Photographer's Market, edited by Melissa Milar. Contains what you need to know to be a successful freelance photographer. Names, addresses, photo requirements, and payment rates for 3,000 markets. 672 pp. $12.95.

The Poet and the Poem, by Judson Jerome. A rare journey into the night of the poem — the mechanics, the mystery, the craft and sullen art. Written by the most widely read authority on poetry in America, and a major contemporary poet in his own right. 400 pp. $9.95.

Sell Copy, by Webster Kuswa. Tells the secrets of successful business writing. How to write it. How to sell it. How to buy it. 288 pp. $10.95.

Songwriter's Market, edited by William Brohaugh. Lists 1,500 places where you can sell your songs. Included are the people and companies who work daily with songwriters and musicians. Features names and addresses, pay rates and other valuable information you need to sell your work. 480 pp. $10.95.

Stalking the Feature Story, by William Ruehlmann. Besides a nose for news, the newspaper feature writer needs an ear for dialog and an eye for detail. He must also be adept at handling off-the-record remarks, organization, grammar, and the investigative story. Here's the "scoop" on newspaper feature writing. 314 pp. $9.95.

Successful Outdoor Writing, by Jack Samson. Longtime editor of *Field & Stream* covers this market in depth. Illustrated. 288 pp. $11.95.

A Treasury of Tips for Writers, edited by Marvin Weisbord. Everything from Vance Packard's system of organizing notes to tips on how to get research done free, by 86 magazine writers. 174 pp. $7.95.

Writer's Digest. The world's leading magazine for writers. Monthly issues include timely interviews, columns, tips to keep writers informed on where and how to sell their work. One year subscription. $15.

The Writer's Digest Diary. Plan your year in it, note appointments, log manuscript sales, be prepared for the IRS. With advice such as the reminder on March 21 to "plan your Christmas story today." It will become a permanent annual record of writing activity. Durable cloth cover. 144 pp. $8.95.

Writer's Market, edited by William Brohaugh. The freelancer's bible, containing 4,500 places to sell what you write. Includes the name, address and phone number of the buyer, a description of material wanted and rates of payment. 960 pp. $14.95.

The Writer's Resource Guide, edited by William Brohaugh. Over 2,000 research sources for information on anything you write about. 488 pp. $11.95.

Writer's Yearbook, edited by John Brady. This large annual magazine contains how-to articles, interviews and special features, along with analyses of 500 major markets for writers. 128 pp. $2.50.

Writing and Selling Non-Fiction, by Hayes B. Jacobs. Explores with style and know-how the book market, organization and research, finding new markets, interviewing, humor, agents, writer's fatigue and more. 317 pp. $9.95.

Writing and Selling Science Fiction, compiled by the Science Fiction Writers of America. A comprehensive handbook to an exciting but oft-misunderstood genre. Eleven articles by top-flight sf writers on markets, characters, dialog, "crazy" ideas, world-building, alien-building, money and more. 197 pp. $8.95.

Writing for Children and Teen-agers, by Lee Wyndham. Author of over 50 children's books shares her secrets for selling to this large, lucrative market. Features: the 12-point recipe for plotting, and the Ten Commandments for Writers. 253 pp. $9.95.

Writing Popular Fiction, by Dean R. Koontz. How to write mysteries, suspense, thrillers, science fiction, Gothic romances, adult fantasy, Westerns and erotica. Here's an inside guide to lively fiction, by a lively novelist. 232 pp. $8.95.

Writing the Novel: From Plot to Print, by Lawrence Block. Practical advice on how to write any kind of novel. 256 pp. $10.95.

(1-2 books, add $1.00 postage and handling; 3 or more, additional 25¢ each.
Allow 30 days for delivery. Prices subject to change without notice.)

Writer's Digest Books, Dept. B, 9933 Alliance Road, Cincinnati, Ohio 45242